www.samanthameans.com

Book Cover Design by Amy Allen

Samantha Means

Victim to Victorious

Victim to VICTORIOUS

A Journey of Overcoming

by Samantha Means

Also written by Samantha Means:

A Winter Storm

The Fortune Series

Fortune Lost

Fortune Found

Fortune Restored

Find her books on www.samanthameans.com

This book is dedicated to my dear friends, Renae and Colleen.

Unrelenting

Whether riding through the woods,
in worship or on our knees,
hands in cowhide or at work in ministry;
the times lost in our memories,
and the breaths in between.
Woven through like a tapestry
your love was the Savior to me.
Never giving in, unrelenting.
consider this a kind of trophy,
A victory against the enemy.
Love is winning.

Acknowledgments

First and foremost, I must give glory where glory is due and thank Holy Spirit for the 24/7 comfort, care, and conviction He gave while I wrote this book, in the years leading to the book, and every moment of every day since it was finished. Not only would I not be who I am today without Him, but this book would never have come to fruition without His words and influence.

Thank you to Jesus Christ who made union with Him through Holy Spirit possible. Thank you to the Father for sending His Son for me. Without Jesus Christ, my Lord and Savior, I wouldn't be alive much less sharing the gift He's given me to write. I certainly wouldn't have written this book.

Second, I want to thank my ex-husband. No one has taught me more about love than you - truly. Things did not work out or end as either of us planned, but I'm certain I would not have understood how far love can go in Christ without your influence in my life. This book would never be what it was without our marriage and our divorce. I believe it is a true testament to how God can use the most difficult seasons of our lives to create the most amazing, God-glorifying fruit.

I want to also thank the staff, my family, with EMBRACE Equine Ministry. Each of you became a sister, a mother, during the last couple of years in ways I never thought were possible. Your influence in my life gave me the love I needed to get through another day. Your example of hope, grace and bearing with me in one of the darkest seasons of my life gave me a light to continue hoping. Your joy fed mine. I saw Christ in each of you, and it enabled me to keep my eyes on Him, which helped me to write for Him. Thank you for seeing my value and giving me a purpose in the ministry when I felt as though I had nothing to offer.

To Rob and Cambria and your four wonderful girls, thank you for your incredible generosity. Your provision for me to attend the Landmark forum opened my eyes to the importance of *now* and the strength of the story we tell ourselves about what happened in our past. Your example of love for one another, your belief in the potential for each other, and the strength of your family despite hardships, inspired me toward what is possible for myself and my loved ones. That inspiration kept me writing, kept me dreaming, and kept me hoping. Thank you for loving me even without knowing me. Thank you for believing in me when I feared believing in myself.

To my family, ever supportive of my writing, and grace-filled for the process I've needed to heal. Thank you for your persistent love, kindness and patience. Thank you for the forgiveness and grace you've given to each other. Thank you for the Sunday dinners that remind me God answers prayers prayed decades ago.

There were several incredible encounters I had with individuals that felt more like something out of a story than reality, but I feel compelled to thank each of you for speaking truth, sharing your heart, expressing the love of God and helping me hold firmly to the hope set before me. Each of you inspired the continuation of this book: Deborah and Don Lynn; Crystal and Sydney Clark; Bobby Carmody; Raydeane Owens; Kerry Hill; Judy Jeffrey; Kim Meeder; Tiffany Lausen; Katie Jacobsen; Shelbi Micken; John and Buffy Rennie; James Eik; Andrew Terry; Dan Munhall; Stan and Shirlene Perisho; Brooklyn Pelligrini; Zack, Becca, Zariah and Aliyah Ward; Ron, Renae, Daniel and Marina Buck; Chris, Colleen and Cameron Ripatti; Jake and Cassy Davis; Vic and Julie Behnke; Amber Powell; Lindsay Tipton; Heacha Cruz-Masga; Cassandra Nolting.

To God be the glory.

Foreword

I nearly threw this book in the virtual trash a hundred times in the eighteen months it took me to write it. Three words from God stopped me every time: "Just trust me."

Some of the words in this book were poured out in tears. Some came out in a scream. Others leapt from a jaw dropped in silent wonder as revelation of the truth struck me *while I wrote it*.

I believe Holy Spirit helped me write this book, like a co-author in any other manuscript. I understand a little better how the scriptures could be the inspired Word of God. While *Victim to Victorious* is certainly not the holy scriptures, I can say most of the content in this book was written before, or as, I lived it. Revelation would come as I wrote, and it often didn't feel like revelation at all. I questioned everything, often shaking my head at my own words asking God, "How?" Then in the course of days or weeks the Holy Spirit would show me, and I'd walk out what He'd just revealed to me. Often, I simply chose to believe the scriptures, even while my heart

13

grieved and my soul fought and my flesh demanded answers to the unending questions that began with, "Why."

I chose. In a series of choices, I found what I wrote to be true by experience as well as by faith.

This is the most honest book I've ever written. Not only because it falls in the non-fiction category, unlike my novels, but because in order to write about the journey of going from victim to victorious I had to be transparent about my own victim mentality. I had to explain how I got there, and I had to be honest about the weight of sin because it's sin that leads to this way of thinking. Sin I've committed is laid bare. Sin others have committed against me is also exposed, while the identities of those have been kept as private as possible.

To conceal the sin itself would rob God of the glory He deserves for having saved me, and you, from this impossible weight of condemnation by sacrificing His son on the cross. We must see sin for what it is if we're going to accept salvation. We must acknowledge our victim mindsets in order to start walking in victory. I can say that God gave me the grace to forgive and heal because of the truths He revealed to me while writing this book.

If you have trauma in your past, I encourage you to read this book with trusted friends. Alone, the content can feel daunting and will likely bring up things that may have been dormant for a long time. You don't need to read the book from start to finish in any timeline except the one that is most helpful for you. By reading it with a friend or two, or even a trusted group, it offers the opportunity to process the content in a safe environment as well as give and receive prayer.

My accompanying study guide offers expanded perspectives as well as questions and applications that can help with this process.

This isn't a light read, but it's a helpful one.

This book can also offer helpful insight for those who work with people who have been victims of trauma. Those of you who are counselors, social workers, or work in the nonprofit sector helping victims of human trafficking, drug addiction, poverty, refugees, etc. Everyone can benefit from the content in this book.

It is also not the end-all-be-all to walking in victory. Whatever you read I encourage you to study out in scripture for yourself. I could be wrong, and what worked for me could not be helpful for you. Having spent most of my life riding the continuous waves of various degrees of trauma, I did my best to be as sensitive as possible to different types of people and how trauma may impact them.

As always, let love reign above all else. Remove condemnation and shame. Don't compromise a person to apply a theory. Love first and apply what works in the context of love and truth in love.

Thank you for taking the time to read *Victim to Victorious*. I invite you to share your story and how this book has impacted you by sharing on social media #v2v2019 and finding me on Facebook and Instagram @AuthorSamanthaMeans

Victim to Victorious

CHAPTER ONE

THE BIG PICTURE - A CROSS COUNTRY ADVENTURE

The War and the Romance

There's a mysterious romance between Creator and creation.

Whether you're a composer, an architect, writer, painter, sculptor or even a writer of computer codes, when you've created something from nothing there's something that transpires in the making that goes beyond pride.

Thousands of years ago four words erupted from the mouth of an eternal being, and light poured into existence. This was just the beginning to a very long story that had one goal in mind: to create what would eventually and inevitably reject Him, only to have a portion of His most beloved creation come back to Him.

Consider what this beginning looked like. From eternal darkness in the universe we know, words came from the heavenly realms causing particles to collide, mesh and transform creating millions of shades of color from a single sentence. Temperatures surged into space as dirt and stone blasted space apart to make room for planets, suns and moons. Sound bleated where there had never been before as stars surged to life eager to glorify their Creator.

But it wasn't enough.

The radiance of color bled into substances of plants and flowers. Rivers and lakes gushed into the enormous pressure of oceans as creatures swam and crawled and raced into existence; life poured out of the mouth of the One who had always been. And yet even with unblemished mountain ranges cascading a vibrant glacial radiance, billions of glittering diamonds on the surface of untouched lakes and rivers, the yawn of infant creatures perfectly living in harmony with their Creator, the world unvarnished and holy as He always intended it to be, it was still incomplete.

Gathering dust into His hands, the Father, Son and Holy Spirit breathed life into next to nothing, molding and shaping the first man into being. A near-perfect representation of all three of them into one flesh. Still incomplete, however, they put the man into a deep sleep and from his rib they created woman. The trinity rejoiced together at what they made, glorifying in the perfect unity and purity of man and woman. Their children, friends, and the very bride they desired and dreamed of since the beginning of time.

This romance between Creator and creation began with the Creator. Long before we even understood what a relationship meant, He loved us.

He initiated this love before time began and established a world of light and beauty to give the beings He knew would one day lose sight of Him a chance to see Him again. So that no one would have an excuse, He paid such close attention to detail that it would take utter foolishness for His people to deny His existence. From the provision of sparrows that live today and die tomorrow, the intricate cell structure of a single blade of grass that is here and then withers away, to the unmanned ecosystem that functions entirely on its own all over the world. He not only drew up the blueprints of the world we live in, He breathed a heartbeat into every element of it, insisting on being present in the continuation of its existence rather than watch it eventually lose momentum and die.

He ensured that His beloved, the only thing He created that he calls His masterpiece, would see Him. Would know Him. Would desire Him even just a fraction of the degree that He longs and aches for us.

This is the romance that began in the beginning and is still in place today.

What's most beautiful about this romantic story, isn't just that the Creator knew His beloved bride would reject Him and created them anyway, or even that He established a plan for their redemption should they accept it in order to bring them back to Him. The most romantic and beautiful part of this story, the story you and I live in today, is that our Creator loves us enough to give us a choice in participating in relationship with Him.

Even after everything He's done for us, even though He deserves our complete devotion, He lets us choose.

The war began at the fall, when the enemy slithered into the hearts of Adam and Eve and fed a lie that we're still believing today: the One who created us and loves us is holding out on us and we're on our own.

The War for Your Heart

In order to understand how to move from a victim mentality to standing in victory we must first establish that there is a war going on, and I'm not talking about a war fought with man-made weapons. This war isn't only happening between tribes in the Middle East, the slums of Central America or the schools of the United States. This isn't a war on guns, politics or even terrorism.

This is a war not against flesh and blood, but against spiritual forces impossible to see with the naked eye (Ephesians 6:10-12). This is a war for your heart, and just like there is a Creator who loves you and has a plan for your life, there is an enemy determined to thwart that plan and destroy you.

However, destruction doesn't often look the way we think it does. Despite popular belief, destruction doesn't necessarily happen in a prison cell, at the bank after a stock market crash, or at a law office after signing divorce papers. Devastation isn't determined by our circumstances, but by our response to our circumstances. It's not the loss of a loved one that destroys us, but our decision in how to respond that causes us to fall to pieces. An adult child with a loving relationship with her mother will handle the death of that parent a lot differently than the adult child with no relationship with her mother facing the same death. The death isn't the issue - it's how we respond.

Pain and devastation aren't the same thing.

Pain is inevitable. Devastation is a choice (John 16:33; James 1:2-4; 1 Peter 4:12-14).

The war that really matters, the war that impacts our eternity, isn't for our livelihoods, but our hearts. We must guard our heart because from it flows the life we end up living (Proverbs 4:23). The only reason the enemy goes after our bank accounts, our marriages, our careers, homes and families is because he's after the only thing that will affect our eternity. Unfortunately, the great majority of humankind invests their hearts in things we can see, touch and feel; things temporal, rather than in the One who created us to be in perfect relationship with Him.

Jesus is the only source of living water (John 7:37-38) and if we're not drawing from the living water then what we do draw from will eventually dry up.

Additionally, the enemy knows the thing God treasures more than anything else in existence is His people. To cause God the most pain, is to cause His people to reject Him. So, it's important to note, that it's not just our heart the enemy wants to destroy, but our heart toward our Creator. The enemy will feed us with financial success, fame, and security if it means turning us away from the One who longs to give us so much more.

What do I need God for? I have everything I want.

This "everything" will eventually dry up. If not in this life, then at the end of it and there's a whole lot of eternity after our life ends. For those who have a relationship with Jesus, the enemy will attack every possible gift given by the Father in order to cause His faithful children to question His loyalty, love and provision.

Does He really see me? Does He care?

If he can crush our heart, cause us to doubt the love of the One who gave us life, the enemy has won. This is why there are so many scriptures about how God's love never changes, and nothing can separate us from that love. He's determined for us to understand that He is good and He's not going anywhere!

Unfortunately, sometimes the enemy doesn't have to do much more than make a suggestion for us to run with and make a lifestyle based on lies. We decide what we're going to focus on, and what we're going to believe: life with Christ or death apart from Him (Deuteronomy 30:19; John 14:6-7).

We're in a war, and God designed us with the ability to choose which side will win our hearts. He will not force us to choose Him, and He does not give the enemy any power to make us choose death.

It's up to us.

This means we must stop blaming the enemy - he's not that powerful. We must stop blaming our circumstances - we choose how we're going to respond to them. We must stop blaming God - He's made His intentions and love for us crystal clear. We must start taking responsibility for our own decisions.

That will be the most difficult part of this book.

For years the effect trauma had on my life caused me to live in painful mistrust of God. I'd obey His commands to a point, and I'd do the good things I was supposed to do, because I knew I should. However, any sermon or invitation by Him to engage in relationship with Him was not only terrifying but appalling. I believed it was God who had let the horrible things happen to me. God was the one who caused me so much suffering. I did what I was supposed to do because I wanted to go to heaven, and I figured once I got there then all my issues would go away and I could have the great relationship with God I knew I was supposed to have.

Having such a relationship on this earth was impossible. I was too broken.

Living in such lies led to so many wasted years!

Today I'm aware of the war for my heart, and I write this book to make you aware as well. I haven't mastered what I'm about to share with you, but I'm on the same journey. I'm grateful for the grace and mercy of Jesus Christ when I get off course and need help coming back to the main road. I'm grateful that there's nothing left for me to do to earn my place in heaven, or even to earn the Lord's affections. When Jesus said on the cross that it was finished, He meant it. It really is finished. What does this mean for you and me in the aftermath of such devastating trauma?

Abounding life and love at our fingertips.

The Romance Around You

Take a breath.

This book is going to challenge many things about what you believe and it's going to be difficult to read. It's going to challenge what you know from your experiences, your relationships and everything you've been taught. I'm not writing about anything new; it's all in the Bible. I'm simply taking trauma and filtering it through scripture to give you what's left.

I'm thankful, beyond what words could adequately express, that all that remains is victory.

We glanced at what the romance looks like earlier in this chapter, and we looked at the war that's happening for your heart. I want to take some time to really meditate on what God has done and is doing in order to win your heart because when we can grasp the love our Creator has for us, we begin to see the possibility of believing and living in the promises He has for us. They stop sounding stale, even cruel, and instead make us rejoice and respond out of a heart of gratitude. We understand what it means to be free and to live without condemnation.

I'm in a continual state of being renewed in the pattern of my own thinking. I find myself walking this out the way I typically run in nightmares; I'm moving at a tenth of the speed I think I should be going, I stumble more than I walk, and I tend to flail awkwardly, crying out for help rather than managing even a momentary stride of grace. This is isn't a pretty journey because I'm a sinful being prone to stubborn, passionate fits of pride and deep dives into the depths of introspection. With the help of half a dozen women far wiser than I am, I manage the occasional middle ground of simple being still, peaceful before the Lord exactly as He desires me to be.

Even then I'm sure I'm doing it wrong.

So what on earth makes me think I'm fit to write a book about going from being a victim to being victorious? I don't think I am. I'm simply being obedient to what God has called me to do.

That's part of this beautiful romance. The Lord takes those who are not equipped for a task and, by His grace and power, works through them in a way they could never accomplish on their own.

We see it many, many times in scripture. Abram was a wealthy man with everything at his fingertips when God told him to leave everything behind (at the ripe age of seventy-five) and start walking (Genesis 12). It was only after walking quite a few miles with his wife, some family and a portion of his possessions across the barren desert that God told Abram he was going to have more descendants than the stars in the sky, and spoke of the land He was giving him. It was inconceivable in ancient biblical times for a man and woman over the age of seventy to conceive and give birth to a healthy child. Still, Abram - later called Abraham - believed. God did the impossible in response to his faith, and Abraham and Sarah had a son, Isaac.

In a similar time, one of the richest men in the land lost everything he owned and all his children in a single day. He suffered extreme pain, was covered in boils so severe he took broken pieces of pottery to scrape himself while he sat in ashes (Job 1-2). Even after his wife told him to just curse God and die, Job refused. "'Shall we receive good from God, and shall we not receive evil?' In all this Job did not sin with his lips" (Job 2:10). He chose not to curse God. Such a decision, I believe, had to have come supernaturally in response to a faithful heart.

An unschooled man named Stephen was one of the disciples of Jesus after Jesus ascended into heaven. Though he was faced with an angry mob ready to kill him, Stephen still spoke the truth of the gospel in grace and power and did many signs and wonders. He called the people out of their sin and begged them to repent. In response to sharing the truth, Stephen was stoned to death. During his lethal beating, he cried out to God not to hold the sin of murder against the mob that killed him (Acts 7:60).

God loves to do the impossible, the unfathomable. He loves to show Himself in moments of shock and awe, and in subtle shifts of a breeze.

For thousands of years He made himself known to ordinary men and women. He revealed himself in fire, clouds, wind, the shade of a fig tree and even in the mouth of a talking donkey (Numbers 22:22-30). He opened the spiritual eyes of warriors, peasants, armor bearers, sheep herders and royalty to see beyond what the naked eye could see in order to show them that He really was going to take care of them if they'd simply trust and obey Him.

How often do you face overdue bills, an empty fridge, a dying loved one or an overwhelming task at work and wish with all your heart and soul that someone would just take care of you?

For those willing to trust Him, God did it then. For those willing to trust Him today, He still does.

I work with an equine ministry in my community and we currently serve women and teenage girls in recovery. I love working with all of them, but my heart thrives in serving the teenagers. Something about them arrests my heart in a way no one else does. A few days ago, I sat in the grass on a warm May day with one of the girls. At sixteen she professed to be an atheist and had no intention of knowing, much less bowing down to, this Jesus we kept talking about. She just wanted to ride a horse.

As we both lay our heads back to soak up the sun, resting between a craft and her horse session, she let out a little gasp of delight when a tiny grasshopper landed on her jeans. I smiled and told her not to move.

"Look at this little guy," I said. "Think about this a minute. He has a little brain in there. That head that's hardly bigger than the head of a pin holds a brain that is telling him whether he should stay put or jump away in fear. Whether or not he's hungry or whatever. Look at those antennae flickering around. They're sensing stuff. And those legs! Look at how those legs are bent? They're bent that way for a specific purpose of jumping super far."

This teenager, normally resistant to listening, stared at the insect completely hooked.

"You can't tell me that this little grasshopper just happened to exist. There are hundreds, if not thousands of these things just on this property and each has a brain. And God knows exactly where they are, when they're going to jump and how far, and what they need, and He's going to provide them food and anything else they need until their lives are over. Look at this leaf." I plucked a little clover leaf from the ground and held it out to her. "Look at the veins running across it. It's not just green either. Look at the shades of green in this one tiny leaf. God cared enough about that little detail to give a useless leaf multiple colors and to provide it with a healthy stem, until now, to have life for however long it was supposed to have life. You can't tell me my God, who cares about grasshoppers and leaves, doesn't care about you and the details of your life. You know you're the only creation He's ever made that He calls His masterpiece?"

She smiled. A small smile that, for the first time I could ever remember in the six weeks I'd known her, seemed to be drawn directly from her heart. "That's pretty cool." The grasshopper jumped from her jeans to her lip before leaping into the grass. "He just jumped on my mouth!"

"I think God was giving you a little kiss."

She grinned at that and, with a new kind of smile, stood and hurried across the lawn to go love on a horse.

Maybe that girl will forget about the grasshopper. Maybe she'll never look at another grasshopper the same again. She gets to choose, but God provided a little bit of the romance right in front of her.

It's up to us if we're going to accept it or reject it.

Absolute Surrender

Now that we can see the war and the romance a little more clearly, we must decide who we're going to press into and trust. If we decide we're going to lean into our Father and Creator and trust Him, then we must surrender to Him. He's not going to fight with us. He makes it clear what He needs from us in order to help us live in His promises. If we're unwilling to do things His way, He can't help us.

We must surrender.

The only way to surrender is to first be authentic about where you're not surrendered. You can't hand over what you're not willing to admit you're holding onto. You can't let go if you're not willing to admit what you don't want to give up.

Why is it we're so resistant to give in to the romance? For women, even those who have been deeply harmed by men, we're moved by romantic tales of men going to unbelievable lengths to love the woman they desire. I believe those of us who have gone through, or are going through, a season of despising romance stories isn't because we don't like the romance, but because we've been hurt in the hoping and we don't want to be hurt again.

God's romance is an even greater risk, because there is no greater rejection than to be rejected by the One who created us. In all my running and hiding, peeking into the romance and then pushing it away, giving myself over to it for a moment and shutting it off again, I've come to realize that there is One who will never reject or betray us.

He can't, because it's already finished. The story is over, the saving and lengths gone to are already done. What Jesus did can't be undone. It's just a matter of whether we're willing to accept it or not.

So why not?

Why do we struggle so much to believe that what He did on the cross is really what happened? Why is it so incredibly hard for us to grasp our new identity in Christ that's just waiting for us to put on like a brand-new garment? Why do we shy away from sitting in the seat of righteousness with Christ? It's ludicrous to reject it! It's unfathomably foolish to walk away from the greatest love we could ever know. And yet we do it!

Why?

"But I say, walk by the Spirit, and you will not gratify the desires of the flesh. For the desires of the flesh are against the Spirit, and the desires of the Spirit are against the flesh, for these are opposed to each other, to keep you from doing the things you want to do" (Galatians 5:16-17).

We want what we want when we want it. Our flesh is weak, our souls determined, and we're motivated by feelings rather than truth. We're in a constant battle with ourselves. Our flesh and our soul are not at all concerned with the Spirit but with what gratifies us *now*. So, we choose self now, rather than the romance that leads to ultimate and eternal gratification.

We're challenged to be renewed in the pattern of our thinking, to be able to discern the good and perfect will of God (Romans 12:2). Our minds make decisions, and our hearts determine the direction of our thoughts. If our heart is not lined up with the Lord, we'll choose ourselves over Him every time. Unfortunately, we tend to forget that our Creator is for us, not against us, and everything that is ultimately good for us will come from Him and His guidance.

It just doesn't always feel good, which is what quickly diverts our loyalty from Him to ourselves, inadvertently aligning ourselves with the lies of the enemy and, in turn, the enemy himself. We think we're doing ourselves a favor by doing what feels good and following our heart. We forget that our heart is deceitful above all things (Jeremiah 17:9) and that our God sees far beyond us to know what's best for us.

We choose self, and simultaneously reject the Father, because we are sinful, selfish beings.

Absolute surrender means we have to deny self and be willing to walk through whatever God says is necessary for us to walk through in order to be refined into the being He designed us to be from the very beginning, and into the life of victory that's just waiting for us.

It's not about fixing yourself or making yourself better. No one is good but God alone (Luke 18:19) so it's not a matter of fixing or changing ourselves to be better, because even our best falls short! It's about repenting of our pride and acknowledging that our best deeds are filthy rags in comparison to the perfection God the Father requires (Isaiah 64:6). We accept that, on our own, everything God requires of us is impossible (Matthew 19:26). So we reject our way of doing things and we echo Mary when she was told she going to do the impossible, "Behold, I am the servant of the Lord; let it be to me according to your word" (Luke 1:38).

We decide to do whatever God says is necessary that lines up with His word in order to stand in victory and be healed.

This applies to recovering from trauma. No amount of thinking positive, forcing yourself to face the past, attending church or any other litany of religious deeds will be good enough.

Absolute surrender means letting go. Stop trying so hard, and simply rest in what has already been done. It's finished. Stop trying to improve what's already been accomplished and simply receive the gift that's being given. Absolute surrender doesn't mean you have all the answers, it simply means you open your fighting, frightened fists and accept the nail scarred hands that want to hold yours through it all. He'll show you how to take every step as you go.

If you're willing to do this, do it now. Any effort that comes from what you learn in this book, apart from the first step of absolute surrender, will be futile. It won't work, because it will be in your own effort, which will always inevitably fail. Apart from Jesus there is no freedom, no life, and no hope. If you want to stand in victory, you must do so with the One who's already done it. There is no other way (Romans 3:22b-26).

I invite you to surrender right now before you turn the page. And in that place of surrender, allow the Word of God to speak truth into your heart and mind.

Prayer of Surrender:

Father thank you for being a good Father, perfect in every way, and wholly and completely loving. Right now, Lord, I surrender my will for yours. I surrender my desires, my fears, my hopes, my dreams and my passions to you, Jesus. I trust that you will work out all things for the good of those who love you, and today I choose love. Today, I choose you and your will for my life. Forgive me for my sins, for my hardness of heart and rebellion. In your grace and mercy, fill me with your Holy Spirit so I can glorify you as you designed me to from the beginning. In Jesus' name, Amen.

CHAPTER TWO

BEGIN RIGHT WHERE YOU ARE

The Necessity of Pain

I read a book not too long ago by Dr. Paul Brand and Philip Yancey called The Gift of Pain: Why We Hurt and What We Can Do About It. Published in 1997, it centers primarily around the life of Dr. Brand and his research and experience working primarily with leprosy patients. He shares about his childhood in the jungles of India with his missionary parents and how pain was just part of life in the bush. Except for those with leprosy. They couldn't feel pain at all. What causes leprosy patients to become so grotesquely deformed isn't the leprosy itself, but a natural consequence caused by a symptom of the disease.

Leprosy causes a numbing sensation in certain parts of the body where nerves are closest to the surface of the skin, such as the fingertips, ears, toes, nose, soles of the feet, etc. These numbed nerves fail to send a message to the brain when it experiences pain. If your finger doesn't feel pain when you smash it with a hammer, you'll continue to be careless with how you handle a hammer. Even worse, if the said smashed finger doesn't hurt, then a person won't rush to bandage it and ensure it heals.

It doesn't hurt, so why bother? This lack of care leads to infection that results in gangrene and other diseases that eventually lead to the need for amputation.

The fact is, a healthy body depends on pain for survival and restoration.

This concept doesn't just apply in the physical realm, but the emotional as well. Pain is a necessary part of life. How else are we to know if a relationship is toxic if we don't experience pain as a result of harmful actions? How else are we to know if words and actions are beneficial or not if we're unwilling to experience the pain caused by them?

If a child is verbally abused by her parents at a young age and experiences the emotional torment as a result of that abuse, she will have one of two responses. Either she will determine what they say is false and believe the opposite, or she will assume what they say is true and adopt it as part of her identity and live in that cycle of negative self-talk, looking for others to affirm what she already knows to be true.

In order to have healthy relationships, with others, God, and ourselves, we must be willing to experience pain. We must have a choice. We cannot know something is harmful if we're unwilling to experience harm. We cannot know what is healthy if we are unaware of what is unhealthy.

It's the only way we can grow. The truth is, having a verbal warning of the consequences of harmful behavior isn't enough. We must feel the pain in order to be motivated to change our behavior or change the relationship.

This is why absolute surrender mentioned earlier is so necessary. Until we're willing to surrender, pain will be a quick get-out-of-jail-free-card sending us right back to our prior behavior and patterns of self-protection. We must be willing to surrender to God's way, through pain, regardless of how it feels. We have to be willing to feel pain today in order to be free tomorrow.

One of my favorite quotes is by a Washington state native, Jim Rohn. He has a pretty impressive rags to riches kind of story and was a successful entrepreneur and public speaker until he died in 2009. He said, "We must all suffer from one of two pains: the pain of discipline or the pain of regret. The difference is discipline weighs ounces while regret weighs tons."

In the midst of discipline it feels like a ton of weight, but it's only at the end of your days when you feel the true weight of regret that you look back and wish you would have borne the bricks of discipline when you had the chance.

Pick your pain.

Jesus promised we'd have pain, but he also promised that with Him we'd have life to the full. This is what happens when we take the discipline we take from the Father, always from a place of love, and endure it to stand in the righteousness of Christ. The path to fullness goes directly through pain and suffering, because it's only in these that we can be refined of ourselves and made into Christ's likeness (Hebrews 12:11).

A Choice

I lived most of my life a victim while dreaming of being free. I adopted the messages I received as a little girl as truth and they became my identity. It was an identity I didn't need to hold onto, but it would be decades before I would begin to understand this. My prayer is that you discover the truth of who you are today.

In the summers of my pre-teenage years I used to spend hours sitting in my second story bedroom window. I'd read or listen to music, but mostly I just sat there staring at the clouds or listening to the world move around me. I dreamed a lot in that window. I dreamed of getting out of the rough neighborhood I lived in, of walking the beach of some tropical island, or of hiding out in the woods with nothing more than me and some dog I'd have someday. I thought of all the places I'd travel to in Europe or Asia, or anywhere but where I was in that moment. I dreamed of being a writer and publishing even just one book and of someday helping kids like me have a little bit of hope amid their mess.

The hope I wish I had in that moment.

At the time of writing this, I'm twenty-nine years old with four published novels, I've traveled to sixteen countries all over Europe, the Middle East, Caribbean, Central America and Asia, and I've lived abroad twice before settling back in my favorite part of the United States. I have a dog I adore, and she and I have traversed countless mountains together in several countries. I'm part of a ministry that shares the love and hope of Jesus Christ to teenage girls and women in recovery.

I am an adventurer, and God has done immeasurably more in my life to this date than I ever thought was possible fifteen years ago.

If you had told my twelve-year-old self all that she'd have done before the age of thirty I think she probably would have wanted to hear about the adventure, but probably wouldn't have believed it could be possible.

This is because the girl I used to be was stripped of her dignity, her innocence and childhood before she was old enough to understand the meaning of those words. I learned, far too young, to scorn truth and to live in shame. The lie was planted, watered, and grew: I had one purpose and no value. The concept of freedom was foreign to me. For many years, I was a victim. I would still be a victim today if it wasn't for the saving grace of Jesus Christ and the power of the cross.

The truth and the power to live in victory was always there. Jesus pursues me with a reckless love I still don't fully understand, and I came to a point of choosing to embrace it. A simple concept perhaps, and yet more difficult than anything I have ever done in my life.

This book is for those who want freedom. Those who want to help others stuck in a stronghold with no clue as to how to get out. There are plenty of books on deliverance and spiritual warfare. Some of the books are great, and some are not so great. This book is aimed particularly at the victim of sexual trauma, but it can apply to those who have faced any kind of trauma.

Maybe you're like me and endured that pain when you were a child or adult - or both. Maybe you just want more understanding of where God fits in the midst of human suffering. This book is meant to shine a light on the freedom that is in Christ, as the practical steppingstones to walking in that freedom no matter where you are in the world. No matter your political, economic or ethnic status.

In Jesus, there is freedom for all.

I write this book with the hopes that when you curl up on your couch you feel as though I'm beside you talking you through this like a friend. Or if you're shutting out the world in a coffee shop because home isn't the safest place for you, the words in this book feel more like a voice across the table telling you it's going to be okay. My hope is to provide you with compassion as well as practical tools to help you navigate the path of freedom for someone used to being a slave. In most cases, you'll only need the Word and your faith. In every other case you will need nothing more than another person or two who also have the Word and faith in Jesus.

Biblically speaking, it isn't any more complicated than that.

Freedom exists today and is attainable today. The key is balancing both resisting the devil and submitting to God (James 4:7). Freedom is claimed every moment of every day for the rest of your life. This is not a get-delivered-quick book, but rather a guide to deliverance and continual growth in Christ after the fact. In this the journey does get brighter. There is such a thing as living in the light, of living in joy, without denying the suffering or ignoring the pain. It's a simple path. It's not difficult to grasp, but it is challenging to walk because it means denying self.

This journey is about closing your eyes to what you can see and opening your eyes to what you can't in order to walk in victory. This book guides the victim into faith - an assurance of things hoped for and a conviction of things not seen (Hebrews 11:1).

As you begin your own version of this journey, I want you to be encouraged that I will not for an instant pretend to know exactly how you feel or how your journey has been for you. I will, however, tell you that this journey is one to begin, and continue, in sober judgment.

Sober judgment begins in our mind, and so I encourage you - rather, I plead with you - do not take everything you read in this book at face value. Study the scriptures within it yourself. In studying out the concept of miraculous healing, the kind that stumps doctors and makes no sense to scientists (but happens nonetheless), I've found there are some critical truths I had read before but never applied to my walk with Jesus until recently.

The results of the application of the truth, and the faith that went with it, has been life changing. As a survivor of sexual trauma, PTSD, and mental illness, I can say that healing began in my mind. My thoughts. Romans 12:2 says to no longer be conformed to this world but be transformed in the renewal of your mind, and it is in such renewing and transformation that I was able to see my past trauma, present circumstances, and future hope with a spiritual perspective and the ability to claim the authority given to me in Christ and stand in victory.

If you haven't made Jesus Christ Lord of your life yet, this book will hold no meaning for you. You need the power of the Holy Spirit to enable you to do what this book will challenge you to do. It is, truly, impossible without Christ. If you want to make Him Lord, ask Him. Invite Him to take control of your life and speak aloud your allegiance to Him as Lord of your life. This is a beginning to a very long and beautiful journey.

If you have made Jesus Lord, Amen! You are a child of God and equipped for every good work He will ask of you. He has made every provision available to you to be alive and free from the emotional, mental, and spiritual bondage you experience because of your past trauma.

Before you proceed, take time to pray against any Spirits of doubt, fear, witchcraft, control, and pride. All of these will be explained further in this book but praying against them in Jesus name will help open your eyes and ears to receive the information that's to come. I will do my utmost to let scripture speak for itself, but I will use examples in my own life to illustrate how I've seen the power of the gospel at work to change me from being a victim of circumstances to victorious in Christ.

Prayer (speak aloud):

Father God, I thank you that you are the King of kings, and that the name of Jesus is above every name. In this moment I pray against any spirits of doubt, fear, witchcraft, control and pride, in Jesus name. I banish them to the foot of the cross where every knee will bow. As a disciple of the lamb of God I am covered and protected by the blood of Jesus and as the good shepherd He leads me. It is written that his sheep know His voice and I am His. I pray that my spiritual eyes and ears would be open to hear and discern the voice of the Holy Spirit, Lord God and thank you that it is written, I will find you when I seek you with my whole heart. In Jesus name, Amen.

An Example

I have wrestled and warred with how much of my story to share with you. This is not an autobiography, and this book is not about me. I have worked very hard to live in the present, my eyes fixed on Jesus and His redemptive work on the cross, balancing my dreams for the future with wisdom from the past. The enemy tries, incessantly, to pull me back into the shame and pain of what used to be. There's a lot to lose if I give in.

I don't want to share my story in the name of trust and relatability when, truthfully, it's not me you need to believe. You only need to believe Jesus.

It's only in the words of Christ that we find the life we've been looking for. I've been the woman who spends more of her waking hours crying than not, who not only flinches but flies into a flurry of panic and rage at the slightest trigger. I've been a razor blade; unapproachable and untouchable. I've spent time in a mental hospital because I was certain I wouldn't make it another hour if left to my own devices. I've worked seventy-plus hours a week just to push myself past the point of exhaustion so I wouldn't have to think, let alone feel. I've been the one to sneak an extra drink, or two, or three, to reach the point of numbness that allows me to function without feeling. I've been the one to try to do it all on her own and the simple truth is, I CAN'T.

My sexual trauma began, according to documents, before I was three years old. It continued off and on for more than a decade from various boys and men in my family. Divorce, alcoholism, drugs, and violence permeated my childhood like cigarette smoke. When abuse abated, neglect abounded. When I did have attention, it was wrapped in the expectation of perfection and I learned to strive as a means of controlling the approval of people around me. I don't blame my family. I believe they did the best they could and any failures they had will only be used by God for my good, the good of others and His glory in the end. Please know that anything I share is from a place of forgiveness and love.

For most of my life I believed the truth didn't hold any power. The truth meant nothing because when I exposed the truth to those who should have protected me it did nothing but plant a lie from the pit of hell: the truth doesn't matter.

The Lord was gracious in that difficult season. He established teachers in my life at the most crucial moments of my adolescence to give me the one thing I lacked: hope.

Let me tell you right now, if you are a teacher or if you have any influence in a child's life like that of a teacher, you have incredible power and authority that you need to use intentionally and with prayer. Teachers saved my life, multiple times. More than a decade later I still have meet with some of my teachers and I'm involved in the lives of their families. Your influence matters far more than you will ever comprehend, and the ripples of your influence spread farther than you will ever get to see.

Two days after graduating high school I was on a plane for Marine Corps boot camp to become part of something bigger than me, something that could protect me and serve my self-gratifying need to give in order to receive. Unfortunately, it didn't turn out like I hoped. I was raped several times in those four years, spent months in a sexually abusive relationship and, off and on, put myself in situations that only reinforced what I believed: I was a filthy rag, stained and best used to clean up the worst of the mess, gathering more stains in the process.

Desperate for love, but ignorant of truth and twisted in my thinking after the abuse from men in the Marine Corps, I participated in a homosexual relationship. In my mind I claimed it to be pure, manipulating that word, love, to satisfy my sinful desire. I claimed only she could love me, and I justified my behavior based on the pattern of abusive experiences I had with men.

The despair in my soul overshadowed what I knew about God. Authority figures turned a blind eye to my pain and suffering, so I believed God had as well. Man tried to destroy me - perhaps God was behind it. I couldn't see who He really was in the mire of my pain. I certainly couldn't see who I was in His eyes.

I share all of this to let you know, as we move forward in this book, that I'm not here to cast any stones. I've been there, in shame and sin. I'm here to tell you, if you're still breathing, God still has a plan. He hasn't given up on you.

I'm here to offer a hand up out of the pit of sin and shame you're drowning in. I know that hopelessness, and I know that void that seems to expand like a black hole. I share not to compare, but to tell you that you are not alone, and Jesus offers what nothing and no one else in the world can: freedom. I'm walking it out, even now. I have witnesses in the women who have walked this journey with me and can attest to who I was before, and who I am now, all to the glory of God. There is freedom, there is healing, and there is a restorative relationship just waiting for you to grab hold of with both hands.

This is the truth.

I had the hardest time believing the truth and the power that is in the truth. The lies in my head and heart festered like parasites. They grew like mold and the only thing that could get rid of them was the supernatural bleach we call the Word of God mixed with the scrubbing of faith, the splash of deliverance and the sweat of choice. The truth in scripture, the faith we're all commanded to have, obedience and the saving grace and power of Jesus Christ on the cross all culminated into the cure God has for every person in the world.

By the time I was twenty-one years old I finally had nowhere else to go but to my knees. Little did I know it would be another seven years before I would grasp the concept of complete surrender.

I was forced out of the Marine Corps for being unable to meet height and weight standards, and yet managed to keep my honorable discharge and the benefits that went with it after four years of service. I walked out having been baptized into the kingdom of God; more out of desperation than anything else. I was at the end of myself, and I knew I wouldn't make it another year if I didn't give my life to Christ.

I was a very long way from where God wanted me; but I was His.

Let me pause here to say, the enemy has two purposes, and they're very simple. His first and primary goal is to prevent you from ever knowing Jesus Christ as your Lord and savior. If he can distract you with anything else, including money, family, relationships, morality, material belongings, drugs, etc. he will. Anything that replaces Jesus as Lord of your life means the enemy has succeeded. If he fails at this first endeavor, then his secondary purpose is to prevent you from being effective in the Kingdom of God. You may be saved, but he'll do everything he can to hold you back from sharing the truth of the gospel of Jesus to others, and He does this by attacking the very core of your identity in Christ.

How can you share the gospel with others if you don't even know who you are in Christ?

This was my life for seven years! I lived in a place of religion and good deeds and checklists, thinking that it was up to me to prove my worth to God as His daughter, and all the while I was missing it. I missed the fact that I'm already His beloved in Christ and there's nothing I could do to remove that cloak of righteousness, except to simply choose not to believe. I missed the mark so tragically, but praise God I serve a God who is so loving and so gracious and so fiercely and passionately in love with me that He wasn't about to let me stay lost. He wanted me, all of me, and He wants you, too.

The enemy knows it. That's why he does everything in his power to dethrone Jesus in your heart and heap pride, criticism, mockery, cynicism and disdain for the Lord and His Word in your heart and mind and keep you spinning in circles.

Since 2011 God has taken me on a journey of simply drawing closer to Him in relationship; one step at a time.

I don't promise anything but what scripture has already promised. I can't. I've felt the disappointment of false promises. Only the Word of God and person of Jesus Christ has proven true. So, I will do my best to let the Word of God speak for itself, and I share with you my experience putting His word into practice.

I'm no scholar or theologian. Yet God has put it on my heart to tell the truth. To share my story and, ultimately, His story of love and redemption and relationship He wants for the world; especially those who have been devastated by trauma.

Healing and restoration are possible. It's possible.

I'm learning sometimes we need nothing more than a voice on the other side of the Wall of Impossibility saying it's okay to start climbing - in Christ the journey is achievable. Many don't try because they don't know if it's possible to live in joy after extreme suffering. They can't bear another disappointment. I'm writing this to tell you it is possible. More than that, the victory is already had!

The victory I share is to point you to our Savior who offers you the same freedom He's given to me. I share some of the battle to show you how victorious is our Lord, Jesus Christ. The only victory I have is because of Him. It's nothing to do with anything I've done.

Apart from Christ I know exactly where I'd be: six feet underground. If not dead than I'd be far worse off living a life of torment for my sin and shame. But praise Jesus I get to stand in complete freedom and victory over the enemy; not only when the day of salvation comes, but TODAY.

So can you. Let's get started.

Partners: Suffering and Joy

We've already looked at how pain is a necessary part of life, but we'll see here that both suffering and joy are essential partners in this walk.

Some of us see more evidence of the former instead of the latter.

Jesus expresses a sort of paradox when he tells people in Matthew 10 that he came to bring a sword, which in the Greek is the word *machaira*. Used figuratively, as in Matthew 10, it's about bringing about retribution. In Luke 12:51 he says he didn't come to bring peace on earth, but division. And yet in John 10:10 Jesus says he also came to give life (both physical and spiritual) and have it abundantly. When I picture life abundantly, I don't associate suffering and division as part of that process.

Rather than a contradiction, there must be an explanation because scripture doesn't contradict itself in context.

No matter how fully we live, in the life Christ offers in abundance we're going to experience suffering and pain. That's part of living in a fallen world full of sinful people. Paul, one of the most prominent apostles of Jesus, promised suffering would come (Romans 5:3; 8:17-18; 2 Corinthians 1:5). He didn't count himself exempt from suffering either. He never sugarcoated his own suffering (Philippians 4:11-14) and yet somewhere along the line Christians began to believe that to be a Christian somehow makes us impervious to suffering.

That's not the gospel.

In Isaiah 48:10 God the Father is speaking to the prophet Isaiah to tell the people, "Behold, I have refined you, but not as silver; I have tried you in the furnace of affliction." The apostle Peter writes to the churches struggling with all the persecution they were facing several decades after Jesus was crucified and ascended to the Father. Peter writes, "In this you rejoice, though now for a little while, if necessary, you have been grieved by various trials, so that the tested genuineness of your faith - more precious than gold that perishes though it is tested by fire - may be found to result in praise and glory and honor at the revelation of Jesus Christ" (1 Peter 1:6-7).

Suffering is part of the walk with Christ, but we must be careful not to let the suffering be one of regret and laziness and fear, but rather a suffering that results from living a life of self-denial and sacrifice. A life lived in right standing with God through Christ.

The message of pain-free Christianity is rampant, and as a victim of trauma, this can be a very enticing reason to throw on the Jesus jersey and play for the Man Upstairs. Show up on Sunday, pray occasionally, memorize some scripture, quote it at the opportune times, and never change on the inside.

Christianity then becomes this "get out of jail free" card to the pain we have in this life, only to become either sorely disappointed when faced with tragedy, or completely numb in a sort of false reality. We try to convince ourselves what's happening isn't that bad while deep down a part of our soul is crying out for acknowledgment and validation. We know scripture talks about living in freedom and how the joy of the Lord is our strength and yet we agonize in silence and focus on simply trying to be a better Christian in order to make the agony go away. We repeat the scriptures we've memorized, the quotes from famous pastors and evangelists we respect, things that are true, but somehow leave us wanting because we don't have a clue who we really are in Christ Jesus. We don't have any idea what it looks like to be in relationship with the one who died for us, to clothe ourselves in Him and live by His love.

Tragedy is painful. There's no way around this fact. Suffering hurts. That's why they call it suffering. It doesn't make a difference if you're a Christian or not. Being a Christian doesn't minimize the impact of catastrophe. The wreckage of rape and sexual assault will be there whether you're a Christian, Buddhist, atheist or pragmatist. Being a Christian doesn't put this invisible cloak of protection around your heart so when you walk away from years of molestation and rape or sexual assault you can say, "it wasn't that bad." That's a lie from the enemy who is trying to get you to live in an alternate reality that God didn't create you to live in. God wants us to engage our hearts with Him, not shield ourselves from the pain to present ourselves perfect before Him. We aren't called to be perfect and righteous in order to grace the Creator with our perfect selves as if saying, "Look how good I did."

God wants us exactly as we are, in the depth of our pain so He can love us through it in a relationship. That relationship gives us access to the Kingdom, the eternal realm that transcends the pain of this life. It may not make the pain go away, but it will certainly put it in perspective and draw us closer to the Father. He wants us to want Him, not His healing or His blessings, although those are a byproduct of relationship with Him. How heartbreaking would it be to go your entire life swimming in the miraculous and the blessings of the Lord and never know Him?

What a tragedy that would be, to experience the blessings of someone you never got to know.

Relationship with Jesus is what makes the pain bearable and purposeful. We endure unimaginable pain at the hands of another human being, and we crawl to the feet of Jesus, broken, bleeding, blind from our tears and wanting nothing more than to die. He takes our hands and draws us into His lap, weeps for us as He cradles us in his arms because He was with us in our persecution while He bled on the cross. He bore the weight of that shame and pain when He died for you. He knows, intimately, what it felt like for you to be at the mercy of cruelty.

Knowing Jesus, intimately, and knowing who you are to Him enables you to look at the suffering of what happened and say, "But I am my beloved's, and my beloved is mine." You can press your face into the chest of the Father and weep for not only your pain, but the pain of the one who committed the crime!

How depraved and lost must someone be to harm another human being in such a devastating way?

And when you step back far enough to realize your pain isn't all about you, but that it's the product of living in a fallen world, with people who don't know who Jesus is, and who are in desperate need of Him, you are that much more thankful for what He did on the cross.

If Jesus conquered the grave, then your loss and pain is in the realm of what He can work with.

We can't pretend suffering isn't going to happen, nor can we ignore the suffering that has already happened. We also can't wait for this inevitable pain to arrive and just ride the wave expecting it to dump us into a channel of growth. If we don't thoughtfully anticipate how we're going to respond to the harm of living in a fallen world, the pain may simply be pain with no benefit at all. The result will be numbness or destruction, rather than refining and even blessing[1].

The other side of that seesaw is to lean too heavily on a fatalistic approach: whatever will be will be. Suffering is just suffering, and there's nothing to be done about it because "God is sovereign" and if it happened, He must want it to happen. I humbly say this is a poor, and even dangerous, perspective of God's sovereignty. Not to

---

[1] Dr. Dan B. Allender, *The Healing Path* (Colorado Springs, CO: Waterbrook Press, 1999), 5-6.

mention it completely dismisses what he's revealed about his character in other scriptures.

To be sovereign means to exercise authority within a limited sphere[2]. God is all-powerful, but He exercises that authority within the limitations of human freedom. *Can* He do anything and everything He wants? Of course. *Does He* do anything and everything He wants? No. Remember what we discussed in the very first chapter about His loving us enough to give us the choice to choose Him.

He steps back and will not violate that loving boundary He created by giving us the freedom to choose. He is sovereign and exercises His power within the realm of limitations He's put on Himself for us to live in freedom to choose Him. This means you can say "no" and He loves you so much He'll let you.

Consider that for a moment.

Every "no" you said in the past that was ignored, rejected, slapped away or bulldozed over will never happen with God. The God of the Universe, who can strike you dead with the very thought, quicker than the blink of an eye, gives you the option to reject Him. He will not violate the freedom He's given you. He will invite you, encourage you, and give you every reason to accept Him, but He won't force you.

Not ever.

We're given the gift of choosing Him, or not, in the midst and in the aftermath of trauma. We can choose the kind of suffering that manifests in fear, doubt, insecurity, panic and stress. Or we can choose the kind of suffering that is a result of trusting the Father's

---

[2] https://www.merriam-webster.com/dictionary/sovereign

discipline as He leads us into denying self (the person everyone else said we were), to embrace the person we were created to be from before the foundation of the world. We can choose joy, but it comes through the pain, the suffering, of accepting love and walking in obedience to Christ.

Obedience in the realm of forgiveness, loving our enemies, doing good to those who persecute you, honoring our mother and father (who may have been the ones who abused you) and other hard scriptures that are non-negotiable seem to demand the impossible. Yet all things are possible in Christ (Philippians 4:13).

We're made in the image of God, designed to be connected to Him. We're engineered with a specific missing piece that can only be fitted in place after we've surrendered our lives to Jesus. We're engineered for joy and love and life, because that's who Jesus is.

We will forever be ineffectively striving apart from Christ because we are, in and of ourselves, incomplete creations without the final element that only comes when we're connected with our Creator. We're built to be dependent on Him. When we turn away from Him, we reject the piece that makes us whole.

Let that be some consolation in your suffering. The gaping cavern you feel expanding within you is only partially the result of the trauma you've faced. The trauma itself exposed you to the depravity of sin and shame, and the part of you made in the image of God cries out at the injustice and ugliness of it. The hole, however, isn't so much a wound caused by the trauma as it is evidence of your own separation from God himself, whether as a result of someone else's sin, or your response to that sin.

The trauma shined a spotlight on the hole that already existed. This means that the hole can be filled to overflowing by Jesus himself, and it will never fall short of healing any realm of trauma you've endured. He is the well that will never run dry (John 4).

Being connected to our Creator means being open and vulnerable to Him and allowing Him to fill that empty space. Romans 8:23 says we're to "wait eagerly" and that our spirits "groan inwardly" for God during struggle and suffering. We're encouraged to do both, and yet few are willing to dive into the depths of the pain that comes with living in a fallen world and sit with God as we bleed out self and wait in eager expectation for Him to fill us with Himself.

Proverbs says, "a crushed spirit who can bear?" (18:14). We're afraid to even try, so we cling to what we think we understand, or what makes most sense, rejecting the feebleness and fragility of our souls, as well as the greatness of God, in the process. We can't fathom holding onto a God who has the power to do anything - including take our pain away, when the honesty of our own pain washes over us like a tidal wave.

How can a loving God allow such suffering to exist? How can we engage in that pain when we feel we're certain to drown in it? Why can't the process of denying self and being filled with Christ be a seamless experience? Isn't real love the absence of pain?

Any parent can attest to the fact that love sometimes includes pain, but it's never simply pain for the sake of pain. The pain God allows isn't like the pain we feel when victimized. So many of us have made vulnerability synonymous with pain, because in our most vulnerable moments our dignity has been stripped away by our abusers.

It's not in God's character to dehumanize, shame, or hurt us. His aim is, always has been and always will be, to love us (Romans 8:38-39). Where there is love, there is discipline (Hebrews 12:7-11).

There is a bold line between abuse and discipline. One removes dignity and identity at another's expense, while the other removes sin for another's expense.

A common approach for Christians in a response to the confession of one abused is faithful optimism, but this is far too often just a comfort zone designed to distance ourselves from pain. Many Christians swing from one end of the pendulum to another not sure what to believe: life is either decades of suffering we have to endure while we try to convince ourselves that God is good in the midst of it, or it's a life of denial about the reality of pain and suffering. We look at what we can see with our naked eye and figure if prayer, anointing with oil, and an experience of deliverance don't make the hurt disappear, then medical care will do the trick with pills and therapy. If the pain doesn't go away, then we must have done something wrong. There must be a cure that alleviates pain if we're to be "more than conquerors" (Romans 8:37).

While it's in our nature to fall into hopeless cynicism or denial that things aren't as bad as they seem and we need to "just be positive," we can't allow our human perspective to diminish the purpose God has in our suffering. We also can't be so entrenched in the pain and agony of life that we miss out on the divine blessings and joy that comes with having our names written in heaven and in the provision God supplies every day. Pain is a necessary part of life, but it's not the purpose, nor the focus, in life.

Pain can be a blessing, for it reveals our depravity and desperate need for our Savior. Without pain, we would never see our need for Him.

We can't see death, loss, unwanted circumstances or physical hardship as nothing more than something to be resolved as quickly and painlessly as possible. If we do, we miss the potential to grab hold of the true meaning and purpose of the painful event. When faced with this proposition, I struggled to even consider what in the world could the true meaning and purpose of being raped. If my trauma had purpose, then it meant someone initiated it to fulfill their purpose. If God has a purpose in it, did He make those men do what they did?

A sickening molten fire burned in my stomach at the thought.

But God doesn't orchestrate tragedy. He takes tragedy and creates a beautiful symphony with what yields to His loving hand.

Jacob's Example

You might be familiar with the play, *Joseph and the Technicolor Dreamcoat*. It's a play based on the story of Joseph in the book of Genesis. Joseph was the favorite of his father Jacob out of all eleven other sons, and he was sold into slavery by his brothers before they told Jacob his favored son was dead. Joseph spent years in prison, he was falsely accused of rape because he wouldn't engage in sexual affairs with Potiphar's wife, and yet during all of that he kept his integrity and his faith in God.

In Genesis 41 we find Joseph having risen to power, second only to Pharaoh by the age of 30. Over the next few chapters a famine sweeps over the land and his brothers come to Egypt because they hear it's the one place the famine hasn't touched. They don't recognize

Joseph when they see him, and when they discover who Joseph is, they're suddenly terrified. Joseph tests his brothers' character, supplies their need, and by God's grace they reconcile. Finally, in Genesis 50:19-20 Joseph tells his brothers, "'Do not fear, for am I in the place of God? As for you, you meant evil against me, but God meant it for good, to bring it about that many people should be kept alive, as they are today.'"

What you meant for evil, God meant for good.

The enemy has a purpose in initiating harmful thoughts that lead to people choosing harmful actions. The enemy is nothing more than a liar who whispers things into the void and trusts the sinful nature of people to respond in harmful ways. Then he sits back and watches us destroy one another, and our relationship with the Lord, with our words and deeds.

Every good and perfect thing comes from heaven (James 1:17) and the enemy comes to steal, kill and destroy (John 10:10).

While I wouldn't be so bold to assume I know God's every purpose, I do believe one of His purposes in suffering is to bring about healing. Sometimes the deeper our suffering the more willing we are to come running back into the arms of our Creator.

No one is born a Christian, or born close to God, so we all have our own bit of prodigal sonship going on. Our suffering, if we let it, can pave a way to God's heart for us. Sometimes God allows us to suffer, something He hates to see as a loving Father, because He knows it will lead to what He loves: the restoration of our relationship with Him forever.

Suffering can, if we let it, draw us into a more intimate relationship with the One with whom we were created to be in relationship.

Dan B. Allender wrote, "Healing in this life is not the resolution of our past; it is the use of our past to draw us into deeper relationship with God and his purposes for our lives."

This is not to say we spend our lives circling the drain that spins our fecal matter of sin into the sewer. That is not the life God has for us. It does mean, however, that we acknowledge the truth of what happened, the facts, and we respond by pressing into the Father.

Healing also doesn't necessarily mean reconciliation. Reconciliation is possible with healing, but reconciliation depends on the willingness of all those involved. Healing, on its own, is not dependent on others. Your healing is between you and God, and it is possible without the cooperation of others. Thankfully, God is loving and faithful and even if the person who caused you harm, or those who sat idly by, do nothing, you can still be so completely healed that you can love them even if you're not reconciled with them.

It's important to remember that healing isn't about living in or denying your past. Healing is about taking yesterday's trash and, by the grace of Jesus, making compost. The garbage doesn't necessarily disappear, but it's transformed into fertilizer that God will use to grow many others into a deeper relationship with Him. It's transformed. Made new. Gardens that grow from compost are substantially healthier than anything you try to grow from chemicals sprayed on plants trying to grow in trash covered with a fine layer of dirt.

The process of healing is a balance of enduring the pain and allowing God to transform you through it in His time and in His way.

Jesus was a man familiar with suffering (Isaiah 53:3), and He allowed God to transform that suffering, the garbage people threw at him in the form of words and deeds, into compost. It didn't deter Him from His mission or challenge His identity, because He knew exactly who He was to the Father. He knew beyond a shadow of a doubt that He was the beloved Son of God and nothing anybody said or did to Him could change that.

The ugliness others sent His way was transformed and returned in the form of compassion. Those who spoke ill of him may not have been transformed, but the harm itself was transformed through Christ. By seeing it, hearing it and enduring what was in man's heart, it helped Jesus to understand us and led to compassion that motivates Him to constantly intercede on our behalf (Hebrews 7:25). We're all sinners. Jesus became the high priest who can empathize with everything we've ever felt or experienced (Hebrews 4:15), and yet he never fell into cynicism, apathy, despair or callous hope.

Most of my life has been lived with the perspective that there is no alleviation from pain and God simply wants to use immense suffering to "teach me a lesson." Joy was for other people, better people, or would come my way with just enough light to keep me alive until I made it to heaven. Discipline was simply synonymous with suffering. I believed I must have been a pretty bad person, because God disciplined me a lot. I'd been through a lot of suffering.

There are scriptures about discipline, and how God disciplines those He loves (Hebrews 12:6; Proverbs 13:24). My understanding of discipline looked like a Marine drill instructor bent at the waist and screaming at the sweating, tear-stained-face of a recruit in mid-push-up.

My experiences defined the scriptures.

I had to start flipping that around if I was ever going to use the sword of the Spirit the way God intended it to be used (Ephesians 6:17). Scripture needed to define my experiences; not the other way around.

The more I learned about Jesus' character and understood that my perspective of discipline better reflected my abusers than the true God of the Bible, I saw an opportunity for healing. Rather than numbly receiving the blows of abuse, recycling the same thought processes that dug the trenches of bondage deeper in my mind, I turned to Jesus and begged Him to show me that I was wrong. If my thinking and believing is flawed, show me what's true.

The biblical definition of discipline comes from the Greek word *paideía*[3], which means, "instruction that trains someone to reach full development." I saw an image of a father teaching his son how to shave. Or a mother showing her daughter how to put on make-up. Gentle. Patient. Eager. Quick to smile and laugh and praise.

I spent most of my life assuming whatever neglect or abuse I endured was God's way of disciplining me. I kept waiting for the discipline to end and I got frustrated with myself for not getting the lesson I was supposed to be getting. Why was the pain persisting? Hadn't I suffered enough? Done my time? A deep, thick root of despair and anguish took root in my heart. Often, I could cover the root with enough good deeds, declarations of faith and busyness that

---

[3] http://biblehub.com/greek/3809.htm

it was rarely seen. However, interactions with loved ones who had healthy relationships with the Lord reminded me with painful clarity that I was missing something crucial in this whole thing.

Good deeds, memorized scripture, and religious activities weren't enough.

I praise God that he saves us from a life of denial, that He loves you and I too much to let us live a superficial life. He pursues us with the intensity of a lover rescuing His beloved from captivity. I was most certainly in captivity, even after I'd hit my knees in 2011. We've all seen those zoo enclosures where the walls look like the mountains and valleys of the animal's natural habitat. That was me. My heart was trapped in a religious zoo. It may look convincing, but a cage is still a cage no matter how you dress up the bars.

As I prayed for clarity, for help, and for guidance, God had already been at work. I teetered back and forth between simply needing to do more for God in order to wash out my shame and the black vein of unworthiness that twisted its way through my heart and trying to figure out how to simply *be* His daughter. The more I did, the more it felt like trying to use a damp rag to wipe away black mold. All I succeeded in doing was clearing up some of the dirt around the mold, magnifying the very issue I was trying to wipe away!

I knew the truth in my head, but that head knowledge wasn't helping me any. That root of despair remained more resolute than ever.

Knowing - with your mind - isn't enough. Trust me. I tried shutting out the heart for years and there's only so far we can go using that extreme. There are places only the heart can go. We must know Jesus the way God knows us; intimately and experientially. Even more than that, we must know who we are to Him. This means rejecting perpetual despair, and even perpetual happiness. Holding onto God in this process isn't about rejecting our God-given emotions, but rather letting Him lead us into the truth regardless of our emotions. Letting Him teach us to ride the emotional waves with Him, intentionally and with self-control.

By having a firm grasp on who God is, and who you are to Him.

Intentional Lordship

Who you are in Christ is written in His Word, and faith is taking God and his Word seriously.

It's interesting, isn't it? We can have faith in Jesus as the only way to heaven and grab hold with both hands, but the moment we include the concept of love and lordship, we start to slacken our grip. Blessings and curses, demons and angels, and other miraculous things that are woven through scripture are watered down and we start to pick and choose what's convenient to believe, rather than taking God at His Word. There are certainly things difficult to grasp in scripture, but for the most part, the hard stuff is less a matter of comprehension, and more a matter of surrender.

The greatest barrier we face as victims isn't the diagnosis we have, or even the toxic relationships we're still living in. It's our own unbelief that things can and will get better if we simply choose Christ over self.

We like Jesus as our savior. It's easy to believe in Him up to the point of salvation because it requires little from us. Faith, a basic understanding of the gospel, and surrender to Christ lead to salvation. But faith and knowledge of scripture isn't enough if we're looking for life to the full (John 10:10). Even the demons believe in Jesus (James 2:19) and Satan is well-versed in the Bible, certainly far better than you or me (Luke 4). These things aren't what lead to the intimate knowledge and comprehension of the breadth and length and height and depth of the love of Christ and the fullness of God (Ephesians 3:14-19).

Like a garden strewn with garbage, if we just bury the garbage with good deeds and spray a little Miracle Grow on the surface we can act as if the garbage was never there. It looks pretty, but few - if any - people will ever know the toxicity beneath the surface that's choking the growth of our fruit.

We ask Jesus to come into our lives and hearts, rather than responding to Jesus' call to follow Him into the life He's authored for us (Psalm 139:16). He doesn't want to cover up our garbage and sprinkle the soil with good deeds. He wants us to give Him the garbage to turn it into compost, transforming us by the renewing of the pattern of our thinking so that we no longer live a life of sin but a life of sonship.

Jesus doesn't want to *just* be our savior. He wants to be, and is meant to be, our Lord. This means we hand everything over to Him, including our trauma. We need to stop treating Him like a vending machine. Put in the right money, or good deeds, and he pops out what we ask for. This kind of thinking insults the very character of God who sacrificed His only son just to make it possible for us to be in relationship with Him.

The problem is most of us start to get really uncomfortable when we look at Jesus as Lord, and not just savior. We don't use the word "lord" much in modern English. In the original Hebrew it's translated *mare*[4] (maw-ray), and literally means "master." Another, probably more familiar Hebrew word is *Adonay*[5] which is a more personal form and translates into "my lord." It means our life is not our own, and that someone else is in charge. If we don't know who God is, the extent of His character, this can make us feel very uncomfortable.

If we know who we're putting our faith in, if we have a grasp of the true character of Jesus, making Him Lord is less of a concern and more of a relief. The gospel is ripe with insight as to who Jesus is. Don't take the word of your pastor, your friends, or a few history or Christian books to determine who Jesus is - read about the man himself from His word.

Let Jesus tell you who He is.

When our faith is wrapped up in the man of God, rather than the people of God, our healing is no longer contingent on what others say or do, but on what God has already said and done. God doesn't leave anything unfinished. He promises that the work He began in us He will bring it to completion (Philippians 1:6). He doesn't do anything halfway. This means when we decide we're going to be a Christian, we're signing up for more than a Sunday service attendance. This means we're signing up for complete and total transformation, leaving behind the old self to put on the new.

---

[4] http://biblehub.com/str/hebrew/4756.htm
[5] http://biblehub.com/str/hebrew/136.htm

Colossians 3:5-9 addresses this perfectly: "Put to death therefore what is earthly in you: sexual immorality, impurity, passion, evil desire, and covetousness, which is idolatry. On account of these the wrath of God is coming. In these you too once walked, when you were living in them. But now you must put them all away: anger, wrath, malice, slander, and obscene talk from your mouth. Do not lie to one another, seeing that you have put off the old self with its practices and have put on the new self, which is being renewed in knowledge after the image of its creator."

Consider the effects of the trauma you've experienced.

How often have you felt utter rage toward the person who harmed you, or the people who stood by and did nothing to help you? How many times have you spoken obscenely about others, slandering their name because of what they did to you? Have you lied, even slightly, about what happened? Have you lied about how you're doing "fine" even when you feel like you're dying inside? Have you had sexually immoral thoughts that seem to play on repeat in your mind that you just can't turn off, and secretly choose not to think of something different? Have you looked at happily married couples and coveted what they have, knowing your fear and insecurity is cracking the foundation of your marriage? Or perhaps it's already been destroyed with a simple signature on a page?

These sound like reasonable responses to the tragedy of rape and sexual assault. They sound normal, which is part of why it's such a difficult thing to shed because we feel justified in our thoughts and feelings and actions. We take up an offense because our rights have been violated, ignoring the fact that Jesus took the penalty you want others to face when He died on the cross. The hard truth is that this is nothing more than thoughts and actions that come out of an old self living for self, rather than the new self redeemed by Christ in the identity He's given you.

The truth is, when you're secure in who you are in Christ, when you know how much you're loved and adored and precious to the Father, and what lengths He went to in order to save you and bring you into relationship with Him, then the violation of your physical body doesn't affect you the same. What happened to you stops being about you, and it starts being about what Jesus did for you, long before your own pain, and how what He bore on the cross sets you free from the bondage of what happened to you.

It stops being about your pain and starts being about His. When Jesus becomes your Lord, and not just your Savior, you fall in love with him and realize just how loved you are by Him. You realize what He did for you on the cross, bearing the consequences of the sin against you so you wouldn't have to carry that weight. It's in this loving relationship you realize that there are far too many people in the world who have no idea who they are in Christ, like your abuser, and you find yourself no longer hurt by them and simply hurting for them.

This is radical.

This was impossible for my earthly mind to grasp. Yet it's so simple, because it's just a matter of surrender. Choosing to accept Him and what He already did instead of choosing my rights. It in no way means that what my abusers did was okay, nor does it mean they're not going to suffer the consequences of those decisions. Making Jesus Lord simply means He becomes the carrier of my shame. The justifier and the One who purchased my freedom.

Compared to what I did to Christ, my abusers' sin against me pales in comparison.

Is Jesus your savior? Is He your Lord?

As Christians, we're called to follow the Word of God. Before Jesus ascended into heaven, He gave His disciples what we call the great commission: "And Jesus came and said to them, 'All authority in heaven and on earth has been given to me. Go therefore and make disciples of all nations, baptizing them in the name of the Father and of the Son and of the Holy Spirit, teaching them to observe all that I have commanded you. And behold, I am with you always, to the end of the age'" (Matthew 28:18-20).

In Mark 16 the author continues to describe the signs that will accompany those who believe.

The Greek word "observe" in this context is *tereo*[6], which means to keep, guard, and watch over. Observe all that Jesus has commanded you. It's not something to look at, but something to protect. The apostles and the disciples of the first century guarded the teachings of Jesus with their very lives and we see this depicted throughout the New Testament. It was never meant to stay with the first century church but pass on from generation to generation.

We're held to the same standard as the original twelve apostles.

How can we protect what we don't value? How can we guard what we don't know? You have no desire to protect something that has no intrinsic value to you. If you haven't experienced the freedom and the incredible love that Christ promises in Himself through His

---

[6] http://biblehub.com/greek/5083.htm

Word then why would you do anything, much less give your life, to protect it?

The apostles and disciples of the first century church got it!

They weren't motivated to share the gospel and protect it because they feared Jesus would come back with a two-by-four and hit them over the head if they didn't. They understood, deeply and personally, what Jesus did for them individually. It didn't matter what the man or woman next to them did, they knew what they were going to do about the gospel because they knew what Jesus did for them alone in love. Being a Christ-ian is a personal relationship with the Lord that's reflected in every aspect of your life.

Lordship isn't just a corporate decision within four walls. It's very, very personal.

The command, for those who are committed to following Jesus it is a command, comes from a heart inviting us to know Him more intimately, more deeply, than we ever could doing the bare minimum. Scarred hands are held out to us asking us to come with Him, displaying the depth of his sacrifice for us, the pain and death He endured inviting us to die to self, He whispers, "There's more." He doesn't want robotic obedience, but passionate engagement. Until we die, we cannot live. His rescue wasn't from pain, but from the illusion of life without pain, from purposeless pain. He showed us the way to life abundantly and it's in dying to self and making Him Lord.

Intentional faith isn't just about being saved and accepting Christ as your Lord and savior. That's only the beginning. He continues to beckon us deeper into relationship, closer to His heart. He doesn't heap a to-do list onto your lap and lay out a stack of more things you need to work on or do better. He's very aware of how far short we fall from the standard! That's the whole reason He came! He fulfilled the standard in perfect righteousness and offers us the blessing without having to endure the sacrifice. Instead, our sacrifice is the illusion that leads only to death.

His sacrifice meant He endured all condemnation, from sin and shame, on your behalf. There's nothing left for you to do but accept the gift and follow.

His heart is for you to simply draw nearer to Him, dig deeper into relationship with Him and let Him show you how much He loves you.

Your trauma, no matter how severe, does not negate this fact.

For years I thought, "Well, if God hadn't sat idly by while I was being raped maybe I'd have more faith in His willingness to work." I'd look at my suffering in this life as ordained by God, planned and even carried out by Him, and I'd feel disdain toward this god. Why would I ever want to be intimate with someone who allowed such suffering?

What kind of perfect, heavenly Father allows such a thing?

Truthfully, we're missing out on the true character of God if that's the covenant relationship we've entered. We've missed *Him*.

If we're going to intentionally make Him Lord, we need to get to know His character. This means we need to surrender every and all assumptions about His character and be willing to get to know Him for who He is. Not for what we think, but who He says He is. If we're going to go into battle against an ever-present enemy, we need to know we can trust the leader of the side we've chosen. It doesn't mean we need to understand everything about God. We simply need to know his character, and a look into scriptures will tell you the heart of Jesus.

I go back to my original statement about God's sovereignty: God is all-powerful, but He exercises that authority within the limitations of human freedom. There's a big difference between God being sovereign and God being in control. We're fallen humanity, which means Satan is the ruler of this world (2 Corinthians 4:4). God manages to work out all things for the good of those who love Him, but He is not the one behind the atrocities.

He loves us enough to give us the freedom to choose to engage in what the enemy presents to us or choose Him. It's not the enemy we need to watch out for as much as our own selves. "When you are tempted don't ever say, 'God is tempting me,' for God is incapable of being tempted by evil and he is never the sources of temptation. Instead it is each person's own desires and thoughts that drag them into evil and lure them away into darkness. Evil desires give birth to evil actions. And when sin is fully mature it can murder you. So my friends, don't be fooled by your own desires!" (James 1:13-16, TPT).

God loves you. He loves you so much He gave you the free will to reject Him if you so desire. He steps back and will not step over that loving boundary He put in place *for Himself* in order to give you the autonomy to choose Him or yourself. He is sovereign and exercises His power within the realm of limitations He's put on Himself for us to live in freedom to choose Him.

I won't be so bold to say I understand His sovereignty completely, but I can say that scripture is clear enough to say that God's control, in this world, is limited. He's placed the choice in our hands to engage Him and His power. If we choose. It's part of why we pray.

The beauty of His sovereignty is that He'll take every tear and every moment of pain and make it purposeful if we choose Him. It's in our brokenness before Him, our Lord, that He can shine through the cracks and holes and bring restoration and healing. Not only for you, but for those around you.

Jesus can't just be our savior if we want to live in the fullness of what it means to be a Christ-ian. We have to intentionally make Him our Lord. This means engaging with Him, dying to self *daily*. I lost count of the number of hours I've spent weeping on the floor asking God why. Even later, asking Him what He was possibly going to do with my pain. In that wrestling my prayers became spontaneous and from the heart rather than repetitive. I'd read and beg God to show me that what I was reading was not only true, but true for me.

My pain was so great after speaking my hurt, the time I spent in tears unable to speak gave room for Him to respond.

My child... I love you so much.

The shell I'd put around my heart, one I thought was made of rock, tore like tissue paper and I crumbled. "God, it hurts."

I know. I'm here. I will never leave you or forsake you.

And I'd be still and weep, struggling to trust Him, without any more strength to push Him away, and I'd see myself being drawn into His arms.

Intentional faith is about deliberately seeking His Word, so you know when it's His voice, and not the enemy's. Take the leap of faith to trust Him and put His Word to the test.

We can't keep living a life of mediocre Christianity and expect to see miraculous results. We can't go through the motions, checking the boxes, keeping God at arm's length and expect Him to prove His faithfulness to us.

He already has, and He did it on the cross over 2,000 years ago. He gave us everything on that dark day. Why would He withhold anything else (Romans 8:32)?

The cross has to be the very bedrock to which everything else about our faith is established. God has already proved Himself to us. It's up to us to accept it as truth and respond by making Him Lord. If we're going to engage in spiritual warfare, go from being a victim of our circumstances and our relationships, a product of our past sin and shame, to victorious in Christ no matter what the enemy or this fallen world throws at us, we have to be in relationship with Him every day. We must pursue Him and his heart for us with such abandon that we can have the heart of Paul and say let God be true, and everyone else a liar (Romans 3:4).

How My Adventure Began

I had a mountain top experience on April 28th, 2017 that changed my life. It was a moment I decided to believe, and it took four other women who had more faith than I did, who showed me how to fight the battle.

We sat beneath a cross made from the stripped trunks of a tree, overlooking a valley in the high desert of Oregon. As the sun set, these women of God prayed with and for me, digging around the root that was limiting my growth in Christ. They pointed at it for what it was: a lie that needed the power of Christ, generated only through faith and words expressing that faith, in order to rip it out of the soil of my heart. They went to war for me.

I thought the root was Trauma. Sexual, emotional, mental, physical....

Spurred on by the Holy Spirit to get time with me, one woman gently encouraged me to share whatever I felt like sharing. Bundled in coats and blankets, huddled together on a bench overlooking a frozen valley, I began to shake uncontrollably. I clenched my hands in my lap to keep myself as still as possible as I opened my heart. My fears, my pain and my desires tumbled out in halting sentences - the stars above seemed to swallow my words. A short few minutes later we began to pray.

On that mountain top, in the trenches of spiritual warfare, I saw myself as a little girl no older than six, standing in a dark, gray valley full of bones. The chains used to keep ships docked were piled on and around my small ankles. I stood in the vast wasteland, alone and defenseless in little more than a nightgown.

Where's Jesus?

I couldn't see Him.

Turn around. Where is He?

Behind me, turning as I turn to keep Himself hidden.

Prayers against the enemy in Jesus name ensued. Then, *Where's Jesus?*

In my vision I turned around, chains pinning me in place, and there He was. I don't know that I'll ever forget the expression I saw on His face. There was such grief in His eyes, a desire I didn't understand mixed with what looked like disappointment. I felt ashamed. Ashamed to be found in the dark valley, chained in place with no ability to remove the chains on my own. Ashamed of my weakness, my passiveness, and my failure to do what needed to be done.

It's my fault.

Ask Him to take the chains off.

I shook my head... I'd done that before. He wouldn't.

Ask Him.

I began to cry, the involuntary shaking worsening as we prayed. He won't set me free. He won't help. He never has...

Ask Him.

I don't remember how many times she told me to do it. I don't remember how long it was between her instruction, prayers against the enemy, for me, and my answers. I just remember her voice encouraging me to speak, a message of urgency in her tone that translated into the eyes of the man I saw in my vision telling me to trust Him. I never felt like I could, not even when I opened my mouth and the words tumbled out, "Jesus, please. Please save me. Take the chains off, please."

What was left of my resolve crumbled with a sob. I buried my face in my lap, undone as I waited for Him to turn away. I hoped, desperately, He wouldn't.

To my utter amazement, He moved toward me. He knelt and reached out His hands. His fingers hardly brushed the iron twisted around my ankles when those that held me down suddenly vanished. He stood, slid His strong hands around me and pulled me up into His arms, wrapping me in a fortress of his strength and love. My legs dangled around his waist, my arms clung to his neck as I stared in shock at the pile of chains and the valley of bones that slowly disappeared behind us as Jesus carried me away.

I buried my face in His neck, clung to Him like a lifeline and just said, "Oh, Jesus. Don't let go. Don't let go, please, please, don't let go. Thank you, thank you, thank you..."

My prayer warrior women rejoiced.

Who is Jesus to you? Is He your Lord and Savior?

Resolutely, I said, "Jesus IS my Lord and Savior."

My shaking ceased and there was a peace inside I couldn't explain. An emptiness and a fullness at the same time. Using a bottle of frankincense, she anointed my head, lips, hands and feet and said a prayer setting me apart to share the gospel, the healing redemptive power of Jesus Christ.

How are you feeling?

The weight of what had been left behind needed something. I needed a rock.

A large rock was placed in my hand and I felt four sets of eyes staring at me wondering what was going to happen next. I stared at the stone, twilight falling around us like a velvet blanket pierced with holes for the light of stars to shine through. My breath coming out in a plume of fog, I put every sin, shame, fear and burden that's clung to me into the rock. I stood, my legs weak beneath me as I approached the edge of the hillside.

I reeled back and threw the rock as hard and as far as I could and screamed: I'M YOURS!

I dropped to my knees in the dirt and held out my hands. I worshiped Him. I begged Him to take my life. I surrendered it all to

Him and told Him I trusted Him to do with me what He willed. The women got on the ground in the dirt beside me, on their knees, praising Jesus.

Then, my hands went numb. They tingled from the inside out. There was no pain, no sensation of falling asleep or having the circulation cut off... they were simply numb. I couldn't move anything from my wrist to my fingertips.

I didn't know at the time what any of this meant. I was told such an experience is often a sign of an anointing of the Holy Spirit.

For what?

Healing. You've been healed by Jesus Christ. Your story can lead the way to Christ's healing redemption. God has such big plans for your life and ministry. Wow, Jesus... I can't wait to see what God will do with you.

The root we dug up wasn't trauma.

It was Unbelief.

CHAPTER THREE
THERE'S AN ENEMY TO FIGHT

See What Few Others See

It's hard to believe what you can't see - I'll admit. But that's called faith (Hebrews 11:1). It's the assurance, the conviction, of what isn't there.

I've gained most of my physical attributes from my mother. Put us side-by-side and, to her utter delight, we could pass as sisters. To some degree this is an incredible blessing; my mother is a beautiful woman. Unfortunately, I've also inherited her failing eyesight. She wears contacts that, thirty years ago, would have been coke-bottle glasses. She's practically half-blind, and at half her age I'm slowly inching in that direction.

I've needed glasses since I was in high school and while it's never been a huge problem, it's always been just enough of one that corrective eyewear is necessary. I spend most days behind a computer rejecting bad eyesight in Jesus' name before I begin writing. Someday soon I'm going to need glasses. My eyes are constantly at war with one another as to who is right.

Our walk through this world is similar. We're all in need of spiritual glasses, and without them we're blind to the reality of what's going on around us. We can't see it. We're in pain and our circumstances should be enough of an explanation for it, but far too often they're not. Something always seems off, worse than the consequences of our circumstances, or just not fully explained by what our five senses can comprehend. This is usually where the enemy gives himself away.

As a Christian, and a victim of trauma, we're told that we should simply be able to pray our pain away. We should be able to simply believe hard enough that we're okay and things will be okay. When we can't, or we don't, we think we've failed.

Satan doesn't just give up without a fight because we said a prayer. We must persist, pray continually, because the enemy has a whole lot more stamina than we do. Our prayers are powerful and effective, but they are only as effective as we believe them to be.

It's God's grace and Jesus praying continually on our behalf that keeps the enemy at bay even when we're not praying. We can't be on our knees engaged with the Lord 24/7. This is why Jesus, our advocate, is continually pleading on our behalf and why we have a great cloud of witnesses battling for us in the spiritual realm.

Truthfully, nothing makes sense without a spiritual mindset. Not everything can be explained, and not everything can be understood - certainly not in the timeline that we want to understand it. However, there is much wisdom to be had if we seek to see things through the eyes of God. From His perspective, a kingdom perspective, rather than our own.

We can function in this world well enough without spiritual glasses, and we can even convince ourselves that pain is just a necessary part of life. The hurt is too much, the task of gaining wisdom too hard, and the likelihood of disappointment or repeated trauma too great. It's better to shut off desire completely, or at least partially, and exist safely in spiritual mediocrity.

But we'll never be satisfied.

That distance from God is just enough to be living outside of the way He created us to live. We were made in the image of God, which means we were made to desire. If we shut that off, we're rejecting the reality of our own creation.

We can do that, or we can decide to live from a kingdom perspective. This perspective changes how we behave, which makes us stand out in our community. It's different. Weird, even. But when we decide to do whatever it takes to learn how to live from that perspective, our world shifts and changes, and leads to victory.

If you're like me, you'll take the criticism and contempt from others, the pain of suffering and disappointment, even the risk of being traumatized again if freedom is attainable.

It's more important to see, to desire, to *know* your purpose, to be victorious, and to not go out of this life without a fight.

Choose a Kingdom Perspective

Spiritual glasses aren't just about seeing right. Having a kingdom perspective enables us to receive the grace given by Christ through the Holy spirit to walk in the identity we already have, which is what enables us to live victoriously.

For some of us, our pain is so great, and the negativity is so entrenched in our thinking that the world seems more like a hopeless mess with no positive outcome. Even a compliment aimed perfectly well can feel like acid in our souls. Grasping the idea that there is a spiritual realm fighting on your behalf sounds great, until you take another hit and find yourself on your knees in the dark again. Reeling from the blow of disappointment we wonder, where was that spiritual realm at again?

Beloved, though our world is drenched in the ugliness of sin, war-torn by an enemy who wants to destroy you, there always is and always has been a King just waiting for you to cry out to Him. You must first be willing to open the eyes of your heart to this fact. You must allow hope in.

How you view the world isn't just about looking with your earthly eyes; it's about knowing (experiencing) and acting based on our knowing. James 2:17 says that faith without works is dead. Intentional faith is one thing, but often for that faith to be more than a nice idea we need to walk it out in order to perceive it. It's in the steps of faith, not the thoughts, that we see God at work. It's in the steps that our knowing becomes perceiving.

First, we know by faith, then we act, then we see.

Having a saving faith is only the beginning!

To live victoriously we must have a surrendered faith. A faith that lays down our life, our moment-to-moment existence, for His glory. This surrendered faith says, "I choose your kingdom, rather than my own. I choose to exist in this world for the sake of bringing your kingdom into it, which unleashes the overwhelming tidal wave of love and purpose into my life as well as the lives of every person I touch."

I choose *you*, Jesus.

If we're going to walk the narrow path that leads to the narrow gate that flows into the Kingdom of heaven, we need to understand that we need to cast off our worldly perspectives and see what Jesus sees. We can't have both a worldly mindset and a spiritual mindset. They work in opposition to one another. This means we must make an active choice throughout our day, not just once, but many times in a day, to see things beyond what we can take in with our five senses. Our sixth sense is our faith.

What does this look like?

In 2013 my mother and I were, by the grace of God, reconciled to one another. There are still times of difficulty where my soul cries out because of pain caused in the past, and in those moments, I turn to the cross and remember the forgiveness and grace God extended to me there. This "remembering" is actually a two-part word that involves re-membering the pieces broken by sin; re-membering the brokenness on the cross made whole for me in Jesus' resurrection, and therefore making me whole again; dying to self in the moment of remembering. This usually happens in tears, acknowledging the brokenness of Christ on the cross, the brokenness of my sin and others' sin against me, Christ's overcoming that sin and death in His resurrection, and therefore the overcoming I have in Him having been made new and clothed in Christ. It's allowing the brokenness to exist, the reality of sin to have its full effect, so the greater triumph of Jesus' victory can fill the broken places.

He fills my broken heart with Himself. But He can't do that if I won't acknowledge the full effect of that sin in my life and on my heart.

He's already finished the work on the cross, the justice that needs to be paid, and the healing that needs to be done has been done in the resurrection. *It really is finished.*

I take my pile of rotten tomatoes that is my hurt, and I give it to God to work out, in His time. Such remembering isn't passive, and it's certainly not just a matter of saying some magic words to make the pain go away. Thankfully, and miraculously, my mother and I have a pretty wonderful friendship today. We both love Jesus and we get to share an amazing sisterhood while still being mother and daughter. How is that even possible?

Daughters of the world who have felt the betrayal of a mother would say I'm completely justified in punishing her for the rest of her life. Mothers who have felt the sting of rejection and rebellion from their daughters could say the same thing to my mother about me. There's a lot of garbage in our past, but to hold onto it like a trophy rejects God's power and willingness to transform it into something purposeful.

It rejects His sacrifice and His victory.

Too often I believe we take the cross for granted and water down the excruciating truth of what it was that our Creator and Lord did up there. He didn't just die. He bore every judgment, every ounce of shame, every drop of emotional torment shed in tears for all of humanity in those hours he struggled to breathe until his final breath came. He poured out His blood to cover the injustice, the betrayal, the pride and the gut-wrenching, soul-searing trauma that turns us inside out; He covers us with His blood to literally wash all of it away - if we'll just choose Him.

To not accept this incalculable gift is to walk around like a dressed-up corpse, reeking of decay.

If we're looking only at the physical, earthly realm, the betrayal between my mother and I deserve punishment, and letting each other off the hook is simply unjust. I should be punished for all I did to my mother, and she should be punished for everything she did to me.

And yet neither of us live according to those standards. When Jesus died on the cross, He took on the punishment for all my sins, and my mother's. We're both forgiven because of what He did, and if we're going to accept His forgiveness then we have no place withholding forgiveness from one another. The only way to really accept such a gift from God is if we have the humility to accept and acknowledge our role in putting our Lord on the cross.

No matter what suffering we've endured, no matter how atrocious, it pales in comparison to what Jesus went through on the cross for us. The trauma we've survived is not to be taken lightly, and every emotion we feel is justified. It still pales in comparison to what Jesus endured on the cross for our sake. For your sake. For mine. He not only endured the physical abuse; he bore the weight of separation from His heavenly Father. He bore the weight of darkness and isolation that threatens to consume you in your grief - He already carried it. He chose to carry it so you wouldn't have to.

This is the most difficult thing to grasp, is that it is because of you, of your need of Him to do it, that He was willing to up there in the first place.

We must stop looking at what we see in each other, in this world, and look at what happened on the cross and what that resulted in in the spiritual realm. We must magnify Jesus. Our very existence, and our embracing of sin, caused Jesus to die. Apart from His redemptive work, we're incapable of living in freedom, victoriously.

This is God's honest truth: We. Are. *Trapped.* In our sin, in our shame, apart from Jesus.

This is why His perspective matters. This is why kingdom awareness is imperative. Without it, without Jesus, we're lost.

Ephesians 6:12 tells us our battle is not against flesh and blood (people of this world, including self). I know that I rarely go through a day where I don't feel like I'm battling people. I get cut off on my drive to work, a sound triggers the memory of rape, someone who looks just like my abuser stands in line next to me at the bank and I'm suddenly paralyzed with fear, a friend's odd behavior reminded me of something someone toxic from my past used to do all the time. The battle isn't against the people, but according to scripture it is "against the cosmic powers over this present darkness, against the spiritual forces of evil in the heavenly places" (v. 12, ESV).

The enemy knows what will set you off. When we decide we're going to start doing things Jesus' way, living for Him instead of ourselves, the enemy throws it your past in your face, as often as he can, just to watch you lean on your own strength and flounder.

Friend - turn to Jesus!

Sometimes this battle is in the subtleties of life when I try to pray, and my mind is running a million miles an hour. Or when I try to read my Bible and I can't get a thought in order to comprehend what I've just read. There have been other times I've felt the weight of a boulder on my chest, or the pressure of an unseen hand on my throat when I try to sleep. The idea of living this way for the rest of my life while I wait for Jesus to come is just unacceptable. The torment of these things, and much worse, is far too heavy for me to carry. I needed more than faith in God's goodness - I needed to experience the person of Jesus and all that He promises!

While the rest of humanity is battling race wars, targeting their neighbor for autumn leaves that blow onto their grass, and using freedom of speech to abuse people in leadership, Satan is prowling around the earth like a roaring lion looking for people to devour (1 Peter 5:8). Who better than those already doing his work for him, unaware of his schemes, unsuspecting of his attacks and who will not identify him as the culprit when he strikes? We have to be aware, and this awareness isn't just helpful; it'll change your entire life and how you view yourself and relate to other people if you let it.

Who is this Enemy?

This isn't a book about spiritual warfare as much as it's about turning from a victim mindset to being victorious in Christ. I'm not about to spend a lot of time explaining the details of who this enemy is because, frankly, he's just not that important in comparison to Jesus. He needs to be acknowledged, because ignoring the reality of his existence is as detrimental as dwelling on him.

I wrestled with how much I should venture into this topic. I believe our eyes should be focused on the cross and far too often the enemy likes to distract us with himself and boast of his own power to intimidate. Let me just roll my eyes right now. The enemy has power, but his power is nothing compared to Jesus. Bill Johnson said it well in one of his Sunday sermons: "It's not Satan versus God. Satan is a pawn on God's chessboard. It's Satan versus the archangel Michael." Our authority in Christ therefore elevates us above Satan's schemes - provided we walk in step with Christ.

That being said, we are not called to dance or war with the devil. We're not to argue with him, plead our case before him, or entertain him or his firework show in any fashion. We're called to operate out of our sonship as children of the Most High God, and when the enemy starts to attack we're called to stand and do what Jesus did: resist the enemy with the truth and stand firm on our identity in Christ (Luke 4). Period.

In my personal experience with trauma, as well as my experience helping others walk out their freedom journey, I can attest to the fact that the enemy uses trauma as a doorway into our soul. He sinks his teeth in like little fishhooks and does not like to let go. When the trauma passes, he stews the pot of bitterness to maintain a foothold. Bitterness is simply murder in its infancy.

We can be battling triggers, nightmares, flashbacks, severe depression and anxiety and not understand why we simply cannot get out from under this oppression. A little education can be helpful to know how to move forward when simply repeating "greater is He who is in me than he who is in the world," doesn't seem to be making much of a difference.

There is an array of evil spirits. Just like there is a variety of angels. We cannot be so obtuse as to think one dimensionally, or to even think we can understand the spiritual realm by comparing it to the world we see with our naked eye. We must have a kingdom perspective in order to understand what we cannot see. We also need to humbly admit that there is much about the spiritual that we will never understand, and therefore complete understanding is not necessary for us to operate in obedience and trust.

Let me first put out a word of caution: many will leap to the extremely charismatic end of the pendulum and claim that everything is caused by an evil spirit and we have zero control and there is no free will. Many churches claim that there is no responsibility of the individual and we're at the whim of either evil spirits or angels. This is directly contradictory to scripture and should be recognized for what it is: a lie. The truth is, we have free will and the ability to get ourselves in plenty of trouble without the help of a demon. James says it quite simply, "Temptation comes from our own desires, which entice us and drag us away" (James 1:14, NLT). However, we must also not leap to the other side of the scale and say that evil spirits are dormant, or inactive, or nonexistent. This is equally dangerous as its opposite because it is just as un-biblical.

The truth is we fall somewhere in the middle. We have free will and a responsibility for the choices we make, but we are influenced by a spiritual realm. If we stay blind to it, it will carry us like a plastic bag on a breeze. If we make ourselves aware of it, we then are no longer powerless and can live out the life God designed us to live: in submission to Him, resisting the devil, denying self, anchored in the Word, and therefore destroying the devil's works.

Like most kingdoms, Satan's kingdom is highly organized, but he's not creative. He doesn't deserve any credit for the organization of his kingdom because he merely copied what God had already created in heaven. Satan, who was previously an angel in heaven named

Lucifer (Isaiah 14:12-15, KJV), was cast down into another realm because he rebelled against God, guilty of pride in his desire to be greater than God. He took a third of the angels in heaven down with him, and they now roam the earth with Satan doing his dirty work.

Many people are under the misconception that demons were active when Christ walked the earth, but stopped working as much, if not completely, when Jesus died and was resurrected. This theory makes several passages in scripture (notably Ephesians 6) void for today's time. Since the word of God is living and active (Hebrews 4:12), scripture then is valid for every era and this theory is proved false. Why else would Paul make such an effort to tell us to put on our armor and Peter tell us to keep an eye out for the roaring lion looking for people to devour?

Others claim that demonic activity back then is now simply understood as mental illness. We've "progressed" in our understanding. Unfortunately, any mental diagnoses based on observed or client revealed symptoms, with no physical or psychological cause found, provides no explanation for the cause and are merely labels classifying symptoms, such as schizophrenia, paranoia, psychosis and so on[7]. There's also the belief that some problems are divided psychologically and spiritually. This theory assumes there's a division between human soul and spirit, as though each has its own compartment in the human body. There is not a single moment in time when your emotions are not engaged with your mind, or your will is disengaged from your emotions. They are all interconnected.

---

[7] Anderson, N. T. (2006). *The Bondage Breaker.* Eugene, OR: Harvest House.

We need to stop engaging the enemy's schemes to think the spiritual realm is disconnected from all other aspects of life and acknowledge that medical, psychosocial and spiritual are all part of the makeup of the human condition. Satan masquerades as an angel of light, and since you are the light of the world, far too often the enemy is masquerading as YOU. If he can keep your focus off him and blame someone or something else for the trouble in your life, he wins.

We must approach every aspect of our life holistically and respect the incredibly complex and advanced body, soul and spirit God has given us by treating them all with care, discipline and humility.

Satan's kingdom isn't reserved for the worst sinners or extremely violent circumstances. It's not just the rapists and murderers locked behind bars or loose on the street that are engaged in the enemy's schemes. There's a reason Satan is called the father of lies (John 8:44) and disguises himself as an angel of light (2 Corinthians 11:14). Deception is his favorite strategy and he has the soccer mom down the street, or the accountant in the next cubical, just as deceived as those doing his most atrocious handiwork. When we operate willfully in sin, it swings open a door to the enemy inviting him in to take up residence. The Bible puts the sins of jealousy and argumentative behavior right next to drunkenness and debauchery (Romans 13:13) so while the effects of certain sins cause more damage, in the eyes of God sin is sin, and in the eyes of the enemy, every willful act of sin is an invitation for him to come hang out.

Living a victorious life is not about having the most power. It's about standing in our God-given authority.

In Christ you stand on the authority of One who's name will one day make every knee bow. There is power in the name of Jesus, but only if you're in Christ, submitted to and surrendered to His will, His truth, and not your own.

Satan has power, but no more authority than we give him. No matter how big his kingdom is or how many demons he has at his disposal, he can do nothing about your position in Christ. Think of him as a linebacker with the New England Patriots. He gets pulled over on the highway. A 90-pound female cop puts him in jail for drunk driving. His physical power is no match for her authority.

You are the cop. You are a representative of Christ, holding the badge of the ultimate Judge on your behalf. This badge is only as effective as your obedience to it yourself. In Christ there is nothing that can stand against you and win. It doesn't matter if you're on your face, weeping in tears, on the verge of swallowing that bottle of pills - if you choose Christ, any and all efforts to take you out fail. Choose Christ, choose life, and the enemy doesn't have a chance.

But you have to choose Him. By not choosing Jesus, you choose the enemy because he owns the fence you're sitting on.

If you still don't believe in the existence of an enemy or demons, I encourage you to throw your Bible in the trash, because scripture doesn't give us the option of accepting or denying the existence of demons. They exist. Your belief doesn't dictate their existence. It simply determines how much control you're giving the enemy over your life.

So how do we recognize the two different kingdoms?

From the very beginning God's Word declares heaven as plural: "In the beginning God (Elohim) created [by forming from nothing] the *heavens* and the earth" (Genesis 1:1, AMP, *emphasis mine*). Thousands of years later Paul writes to the church in Corinth, "I know a man in Christ who fourteen years ago was caught up to the third heaven. Whether it was in the body or out of the body I do not know - God knows. And I know that this man was caught up into paradise - whether in the body or out of the body I do not know, God knows - and he heard things that cannot be told, which man may not utter" (2 Corinthians 12:2-4, ESV).

I like logic. Typically, if there's a "third" of something, there is a first and second as well. Since Paul also mentions Paradise and hearing the voice of God, it stands to reason that this third heaven is God's dwelling place. While we don't know exactly how many heavens there are, we do know that there is a kingdom somewhere between God's kingdom and the earth that is hostile.

"One day the angels came to present themselves before the Lord, and Satan also came with them. The Lord said to Satan, 'Where have you come from?' Satan answered the Lord, 'From roaming throughout the earth, going back and forth on it'" (Job 1:6-7).

The presence of Satan and his demons is undeniably present on this earth. Just like the presence of angels is also apparent. "Do not forget to show hospitality to strangers, for so doing some people have shown hospitality to angels without knowing it" (Hebrews 13:2).

How do we tell the difference between the influence of Satan's kingdom and God's? It's a lot easier than you think.

Satan seeks to dominate, and his kingdom is one of darkness. Therefore, anything that is hidden, desired to be kept hidden, and seeks to dominate belongs to Satan. Anything that seeks to steal, kill or destroy is from the enemy and those at work in his kingdom (John 10:10).

That incessant urge to keep your trauma hidden is not from God. Let me reiterate that: anything that is desired to be kept hidden, and anything that seeks to dominate, is from Satan. God is a ruler, but He never dominates His people. He is the light of the world, and light doesn't hide otherwise it ceases to be light. It is for freedom Christ set us free (Galatians 5:1).

How do you see the enemy? Look for what dominates, hides, sneaks around, is wrapped in fear and the only outcome is destruction, whether that be relationships, quality of life, work ethic, character development, finances or any other area of life.

Possessed or Oppressed?

There are movies out there like *the Conjuring* that address demon possession and oppression in Hollywood fashion, but it really isn't too far from the truth.

Possession and oppression are real.

In Mark 1:32-34 the author tells a story of how many who were possessed with demons were brought to Jesus. Remember that the Bible was not originally written in English. The Old Testament was written primarily in Hebrew, and the New Testament was written in Greek. The Greek word for "possessed" in this passage is: "daimon-izomai", which means "under the power of a demon"[8].

---

[8] biblehub.com/str/greek/1139.htm

A Christian, one who is a faithful follower of Jesus Christ and has been baptized in the Spirit and has received the Holy Spirit cannot be demon-possessed. This is because possession implies ownership, and once a person has the Holy Spirit taking up residence in that individual they are eternally owned by God unless the one with the Holy Spirit willingly, deliberately and consistently rejects the Holy Spirit. No demon can take over what God already owns.

A person who is not saved and does not have the Holy Spirit can be possessed by a demon.

However, a disciple of Jesus who does have the Holy Spirit can, in fact, be *under the power* of a demon. This is not the same as being possessed. I look at oppression like a leech. A habitual sin in my life has given the enemy access and permission to latch on and wreak havoc in my soul. Until I repent of that sin and come under the authority of Christ and operate in the identity He has given me as the daughter of a King, it doesn't matter how many good deeds I do, or perfect attendance records I have at church. That demon will continue to suck the life out of me.

We see this example in Luke 13:11-16. Jesus was in the synagogue preaching on the Sabbath. He was at church.

"And behold, there was a woman who had had a disabling spirit for eighteen years. She was bent over and could not fully straighten herself. When Jesus saw her, he called her over and said to her, 'Woman, you are freed from your disability.' And he laid his hands on her, and immediately she was made straight, and she glorified God. But the ruler of the synagogue, indignant because Jesus had healed on the Sabbath, said to the people, 'There are six days in which work ought to be done. Come on those days and be healed, and not on the Sabbath day.' Then the Lord answered him, 'You hypocrites! Does not each of you on the Sabbath untie his ox or his donkey from the manger and lead it away to water it? And ought not this woman, a daughter of Abraham whom Satan bound for eighteen years, be loosed from this bond on the Sabbath day?'"

The woman was in the temple of God, was a devout follower of God, and was under the power of a disabling spirit for eighteen years. Only Satan comes to steal, kill, and destroy so the disabling spirit was of the Enemy. Jesus loosed her from the bond. He freed her from the spirit and only after she was free from the spirit was she healed of her physical ailment.

I wish healing was as black and white as scripture sometimes makes it seem. What I have learned in my experience, and in witnessing healing in others, is that our God is a wild God, and His purposes trump our best and most honorable intentions.

It's always a good thing for someone to experience healing. That's one of God's desires and intentions - to heal the sick (James 5:14-15; Isaiah 53:4-5; Psalm 147:3).

The when is the part that has often baffled me. Why not now? Why doesn't every person I pray for to be healed get healed when I pray for it like it happens in scripture? There are dozens of potential factors, but one thing I know for certain, is that when we think God is doing one thing, He's often doing a thousand things.

I was recently in a car accident that resulted in a broken elbow. Let me add that you never know just how many things are connected to your elbow until you have a fractured radial head. Five hours after the accident I was out of the hospital and at a church service with my arm in a sling. A gentleman came over and asked if he could pray for healing for my arm. Any time someone asks if they can pray for you, beloved, take it!

He laid hands on me, prayed for me to be healed, for there to not be a need for surgery, and while I felt a cooling, tingling sensation in my entire arm, I was still in pain and the elbow was still broken. Two weeks later I went in for a follow up appointment, and while the x-rays looked better, the elbow was definitely still broken.

In those two weeks I realized I had a habitual sin in my heart that had given the enemy a foothold on my life. I'd found a leech, and it was sucking the life out of my relationships. It was a leech from which God wanted to set me free.

I believed a lie with every fiber of my being: I am a burden. I believed that I was one favor away from being "too much" for the people in my life so I made every effort to be as easygoing a friend and family member as I could. I rarely ask for help, and if I do it's a task that doesn't take more than a few seconds for the other person to accomplish, (i.e.: can you hand me a cup from the top shelf?)

I don't typically have "favorites" of anything unless I'm the only one involved in making a decision. I learned at an early age having favorites can quickly lead to disappointment or division in relationships.

Where do I want to get a burger? If I'm alone, I have my opinion. If I'm with a group, I really don't care. I enjoy being around people who are enjoying what's in front of them. My taste buds are secondary to the happiness of those around me.

What show do I want to watch? When I'm alone, I have a few "go to" shows. When I'm with people I love, I couldn't care less what's on the television. Seeing people I love laugh and being with them as they enjoy their favorite show, if it's not something detrimental to my walk/relationship with God, is more important than watching mine.

While this is most often the truth, there was a seed of a lie woven in all of it that whispered, "If you tell them what you really like, what you really want, who you really are, they're going to reject you."

The sin in my heart that gave the Enemy a hole in which to wiggle through and latch on, was that I believed the lie. He fed it day in and day out, his voice sounding an awful lot like my own, or the voices of people in my past who had laughed at me, said I was "weird" or stopped spending time with me. I believed my heart and all it desired was inconsequential (at best) and disgusting (at worst) to those I cared about. "If they really knew me..." the possibilities of rejection, hurt and disappointment were endless, and the Enemy enjoyed fueling that fire.

My broken elbow revealed the brokenness in my heart I was trying to hide with selflessness and serving. Suddenly I couldn't even wash my own dishes or tie back my own hair. Basic tasks and chores were, for the first week, impossible. I had to ask for help, and I flew into a panic. The enemy loves to create chaos and disorder. He's out to steal your joy, kill your hope, and destroy your heart.

My heart broke at the idea of asking for help. I couldn't do it. I would say all the things I couldn't do, but I couldn't actually ask someone to help me do them, much less do them for me. Someone would respond by asking, "What do you need?" I knew what I needed... I just couldn't say it.

Over the phone a friend boldly asked, "Do you need me to do your dishes?"

I nodded because I couldn't speak past the lump in my throat. "Well... I mean..."

"How about this..." and she told me what time she was coming over to do whatever it was I needed to be done.

I burst into tears when my friend showed up with a pile of home cooked and microwave ready foods, fluffy blanket, chocolate, a fall-smelling candle and rolled up the sleeves on her nice sweater and got to work scrubbing my plates and mugs. I didn't own a dishwasher.

I'd just moved so my house was a mess. The car accident happened on the day I planned to clean house since I was mostly moved in. That didn't happen. My friend helped me finish putting clean sheets on my bed, folded my laundry and offered to clean my floors that were badly in need of a broom and mop.

Then we sat on the couch and had a cup of tea and talked.

The thing is, she didn't just clean my house.

In the days that followed her serving me our friendship remained mostly the same as it was before. I hate to admit it, but part of me believed the lie and I watched and waited for the shift. I waited for her to distance herself, to become resentful or even more irritable toward me.

She didn't.

"Just wait," the voice cautioned. Meanwhile, others stepped up and offered to do the little things I took for granted being able to do in the past. I have six trees in my yard and live in a community that required the leaves to be raked by a certain day. I had no rake and no ability to properly use a rake to get the job done. Upon hearing of my need, another friend's husband came over one day while I was at work and did it for me.

Living alone can be difficult for me - especially in the evening. Another friend and her entire family treat me like a member of the family and have an open-door policy at their home for me. I can come over anytime. Admittedly, even after more than a year I found myself counting the days of the week I've used that policy as though it's a punch card I can only punch so many times before it expires.

I know that I am the daughter of a King, a new creation, a precious child to the One who paid the highest price for me to be saved from a life of torment and in perfect joy and peace with Him. I know this - and I'm still learning how to get that knowing in my brain the eighteen inches into my heart. God has been revealing ways I've let the enemy in and make a mess of my life. His oppression is always happening because of some foothold I've given him. That foothold looks like sin. Or a lie. And God is not about to leave a single stone unturned while He transforms.

I have to take a good look at who I'm surrounding myself with, what environments I'm putting myself in, what messages I'm believing, what behaviors I'm expressing and activities I'm engaging in, that could be swinging open a Vacancy sign to the enemy to latch on and create havoc.

Only in Christ, completely and wholly in Christ, am I free from being a victim and free to live victoriously.

Pick a Side

Truth is liberating and, for me, freedom came when I began to learn, to know and to actively choose truth over the enemies lies. That truth, in Christ, is what gives us the authority to defeat the enemy. When we engage the lie and believe it, we hand over our authority to him and he goes to town stealing, killing, and destroying our joy.

Have you noticed that one of the biggest lies, and most easily believed lies, is that you don't matter? You're insignificant. You're a waste of time. You're stained, tarnished, worthless... why else would God "let" you be so horribly violated?

Beloved, the fact is you were abused, the lie is that you don't matter. The *truth* is we live in a fallen world that God died to redeem that trauma and use it for your good and His glory. You *do* matter. Why would the enemy work so hard to get you to believe the opposite? God paid the highest price that could have been paid to purchase you from this world. When you realize that you are precious and beloved by the Most High King who cast Satan out of heaven for all eternity, the power at your disposal makes the enemy look like an ant on a picnic table.

Yes, Jesus died on the cross to save you from your sins, but that's only part of it. The more you pay for something the higher it's value - correct? How much more could be paid for *you* than the Creator of all things dying in your place?

Satan will do whatever it takes to crush you because he knows you are the thing God treasures most of all. Satan doesn't care one whit about you or me. He hates us, only because God loves us. He cares about causing God the most possible pain, and what better way to do that than go after those whom God loves the most?

Both Satan and God's kingdoms are at war with one another for one purpose: taking hold of you. We are always on one side or the other in this battle. If you're a Christian, you're on Team Jesus. If you're not, you're on the enemy's side. It's that simple. We play for one side or the other, and every time we believe a lie the enemy tells us we give the enemy more ground to destroy us.

There is no Switzerland, or neutral sides, to this battle. Not choosing is, in effect, choosing the enemy's side because, as Edmond Burke once said, "all that is necessary for the triumph of evil is that good men do nothing."

Satan owns the fence you're sitting on. So, get off.

In Matthew 12:24-28 Jesus exposes the spiritual realm for what it is.

He had just finished healing a demon-oppressed man who was blind and mute when the Pharisees mutter under their breath, "It is only by Beelzebul, the prince of demons, that his man casts out demons," (v.24). Scripture illustrates what happens next:

"Knowing their thoughts, (Jesus) said to them, 'Every kingdom divided against itself is laid waste, and no city or house divided against itself will stand. And if Satan casts out Satan, he is divided against himself. How then will his kingdom stand? And if I cast out demons by Beelzebul, by whom do your sons cast them out? Therefore, they will be your judges. But if it is by the Spirit of God that I cast out demons, then the kingdom of God has come upon you," - Matthew 12:25-28, ESV

When I've had a bad day and decide to pour a large glass of wine to take the edge off of my pain, and a friend calls and asks what I'm doing, my desire to lie is influenced by my sinful nature and the enemy's kingdom of hiding. I'm afraid, and since there is no fear in love (1 John 4:18) I'm living apart from the love of God.

There's nothing wrong with a glass of wine.

There is something wrong with using it as a means from hiding from the reality of life God calls me to live in rather than bringing the pain of that reality to Him in relationship.

The shame we feel for the trauma we've endured, the self-harm we induce to punish our bodies for desiring, or simply existing, the suicidal thoughts and the need to delete our browsers history on our computer in case someone sees, all stems from the influence of the enemy. He's got a foothold because we refuse to believe the truth of what God says about who we are.

We need to take responsibility for what we're believing. We don't get the luxury of sitting back and shifting blame for everything that happens in our life as though we're removed from it.

We have free will, so we choose what we will entertain and what we will not. Sometimes the choice feels almost impossible - but the choice is still in our hands.

We tend to see pain, and anything associated with pain, as bad. It's something to avoid. Pain is also evidence of growth, which is good. No Olympic athlete achieves excellence without making his body feel the pain of growth to reach that standard.

Are you experiencing pain from regret and suffering, or pain from growth and change?

If we can wrap our minds around the differences between God's intentions and the enemies, we can see a lot clearer to where each is at work in our circumstances.

The death of a child is never easy and will never be something to rejoice in. Such a devastating loss is never something God *causes* to glorify Himself. However, in the midst of the loss as a grieving mother draws near to God with her shattered heart in her palms, crying out to her Creator, *"Why?"* God is honored because His child is drawing near to Him in relationship.

The *enemy* comes to steal, kill and destroy. Jesus came to give life, and life to the full (John 10:10). Christ is our peace (Ephesians 2:14). Not what Christ provides, but Christ *Himself* is our peace. In relationship with Him, we are wrapped in that peace.

The enemy's kingdom and God's kingdom are not the same. One gives life, the other takes it away. *Both are at war for your heart and soul.*

Pain derived from living in the dark, from hiding, from rebellion against God is, indeed, harmful and comes from the enemy. Unfortunately, because we live in a fallen world of sinners who have free will, we can be on the receiving end of someone else's rebellion even though we live an upright and righteous life. We see it all the time. A drunk driver kills a valedictorian and youth group leader, yet the drunk walks away unscathed. A twenty-two-year-old missionary dies in a plane crash on her way to the mission field. A mother of three who leads a simple, but valuable, life has an aneurysm and is left a vegetable.

The enemy comes to steal, kill, and destroy.

As I write this, I'm acutely aware of a time when I heard the same words spoken over and over again, and the pain of my past screamed above it like a storm outside drowning out the gentleness of a crackling fire.

This is where it came down to a choice. I needed to decide whether the Bible was true, or it wasn't. I was either going to believe in all of it, or none of it. I can't say it's the Word of God and deny bits and pieces because I didn't like what they had to say, or because it didn't make sense. If it was true, I needed to believe it as true and give myself the grace and God the time to wrestle with me through the parts I didn't understand.

How does your heart respond to the statements separating God's kingdom from Satan's? How does this contradict what your experience has taught you, or what your own heart has believed, or others have told you? What will you decide to believe?

Stand firm on the fact that in Christ you have authority that trumps every bit of the enemy's power. In Christ you have the Holy Spirit residing in you, who sees the spiritual realm perfectly, and because He is a counselor and guide, He will guide you into all truth. He will help you see, and He will never leave you or forsake you.

The enemy belongs in hell, and when you stand firm on your identity in Christ as a son or daughter, and when you hold fast to the promises of our King, our Father, who loves you and whose word never returns void, you crush Satan. He'll try to convince you otherwise - that's part of his game. He'll whisper, taunt, yell, and do all sorts of things that will make the hair on the back of your neck stand up. He'll put up a fight.

But you hold the badge that puts him behind bars. Let the Lord deal with him, and you stand firm in victory in Christ.

Practical Identification

We can't fight what we can't see. We can't see the enemy with our naked eye, so we must put on those spiritual glasses I mentioned earlier and recognize areas where demons like to manifest (or make themselves clearly known). When you have the Holy Spirit in you, He sends off all sorts of warning bells when you drift toward sin. He convicts you of your righteousness. You are right with God, don't go near that! You're right with God, don't violate your right standing with that thing you're drawn to!

When we're new to the voice of our shepherd it can be difficult to distinguish Him from the enemy, or even from our own desires. The following is a general guideline taken from a collection of sermons done by Derick Prince that will help to identify the snake in the grass so you can stomp on his head. It's also important to recognize these when you find them in people you work with, your family or even your closest friends. It's a way to identify when they're behaving in a manner not in line with who God created them to be and love them through it.

How do you recognize characteristics of the enemy and his demons?

1. Entice - They tempt. Anything with a voice is a person, but a demon can most certainly speak a temptation into the ear of another person who then speaks it aloud to you. If it is enticing you to do, speak, or even think anything that is not within the Word or will of God, it's influenced by the enemy. The choice to engage it is human.

2. Harass - They study and know your weaknesses. Do you struggle with anger? There will be all sorts of people, or even just one person,

who continue to get on your last nerve. While God can use such harassments to help you to grow in character, the source is not from God.

3. Torment - There are various kinds of torment and they include:

(1) physical - such as abdominal pain. Even in writing this book I have felt wave after wave of intense abdominal pain that has felt like a knife carving out my insides. I rebuke the enemy's attempts to stop me from writing in Jesus' name (out loud) and it fades. A little while later it happens again, and I repeat the same process.

(2) mental - such as a fear of going insane. In the worst of the aftermath of my trauma as I was going through EMDR counseling, I struggled with this for months. I'm immensely grateful for the counseling I received, but I was not spiritually prepared for what it would do to my mind. I was certain I was losing it, and when I began taking sleep medication because I couldn't get more than a couple of hours of shuteye a night (and that was with horrific nightmares), I ended up in a locked down mental health hospital.

(3) spiritual - an accusation burning in your heart and mind that you've committed some unforgivable sin. I was a victim of some pretty horrible sins. Unfortunately, that led me to believe some pretty horrible lies, which led to committing my own list of horrible sins against others. Adam and Eve's argument with God in the garden continues today - "I only did it because of *this* person's actions!" There is a grain of truth in that, but we must own our own sin. I took it a step too far and saw my sins as unforgivable, even though scripture says otherwise.

4. Compel - Compulsive behaviors are liable to be demonic. Such compulsions include eating, smoking, drugs and alcohol, exercise, working, etc. I'm guilty of all of these. Jesus himself called Peter "Satan" simply because his mind was fixed on the things of man, and not God. This is radical, but truth. What things are you fixated on that are not of God, but of man? Even good things can be demonic things if they're not submitted to Christ.

5. Enslave - Demons can create a rut in the heart of an individual that acts like an intense drive to repeat a sin you've already repented of, such as any form of addiction. This ties in with compulsions and can leave you feeling as if you have no control, no way of saving yourself, and freedom is a myth.

6. Defile - They love to smear your heart and mind with the lie that you are dirty and unclean. Have you ever walked into church, or known you were about to spend time worshiping God, and felt this unmistakable shame about the uncleanliness of your heart and mind and how you shouldn't even go near the building much less inside? I lived in this perpetual state for years. As a child I never felt like I belonged in Sunday school because no one would want me if they knew that I was ruined. When I became an adult, I took matters into my own hands and figured since I was already permanently stained then I would be in control of who spread the stain. A knew I needed God, but the uncleanliness of my soul kept me at arm's length. It takes a lot of truth to fight the lies. It takes knowing who you are in Christ.

7. Deceive - They are masters at deception, and our own pride swings open the door and invites demons inside. Obadiah 1:3 says, "The pride of your heart has deceived you, you who live in the clefts of the rock, in your lofty dwelling, who say in your heart, 'Who will bring me down to the ground?'" Pride is what separated Satan and his demons from God in the first place. If you tend to think you're immovable, that nothing will knock you sideways, watch out.

8. Weaken, make sick or tired, Kill - People who are under the influence of a demon are often on the verge, or frequently fighting such things. The enemy comes to steal, kill and destroy (John 10:10). To live in a continual state of weakness, feeling as though you're at the end of your rope, you're sick all the time or just plain tired with no logical explanation... you can be sure you're under attack. Most certainly thoughts of suicide are from the enemy.

This list is not exhaustive, nor is it definitive. I encourage you to study this out for yourself and examine your own life. Where do you see these showing up in your daily activities? Whatever you find as demonic is simply an area of your life that's not in submission to Christ. It's not something to fear, but something to address. It's not something to condemn, but something to repent of and make obedient to Jesus.

CHAPTER FOUR

THIS JOURNEY CAN'T BE DONE ALONE

You're as Guilty as Your Enemy

Humanity is the only thing God created that He calls His work of art (Ephesians 2:10). The King James Version says we are his 'workmanship' and the New International Version says 'handiwork', but the Amplified version says 'work of art.' We are the only thing in all of creation that is made in the very image of God. Yes, even you, regardless of your past, are a work of art to the Creator of heaven and earth.

There's no debate over this matter.

How beautiful is that?

What's so miraculous, even preposterous, about this, is we are also the only thing God created that can reject or accept our Creator. We were created to be in union with him, but we can choose not to be. Everything else that exists fulfills the purpose that God created it to fulfill. You never find a horse trying to be a cat, or an apple tree trying to produce oranges. Nothing resists the Creator and what He intended for it to do except the very beings God longs for most. He pursues us with unmatched tenacity. He grieves for, rejoices with, and delights in us in a way He does with nothing else, and yet we live in a state of perpetual rejection of Him. Yet even then, Jesus pursues us with unyielding hope and tenacity.

Even as you actively choose the lie, choose to believe in what the world and the enemy says about you instead of what God says is true, He still hopes for and pursues you. Passionately.

But we must choose Him in return.

When we sin, we voluntarily engage in an act that violates God's plan and design. The Grand Canyon of sin is dug deeper and wider throughout the course of our lives. Hurting people hurt people, and when we're sinned against it creates a wound that leads us to sin against others. The cycle, apart from Christ, is truly never ending this side of heaven. Even if we do our best to simply be kind to others, it won't be enough to stop the cycle because it is in our nature to sin. Our hearts will never be in a condition of having achieved sinlessness, thereby bridging that canyon that separates us from our Creator.

Even doing something with the best intentions can be a wrong thing done well.

Isaiah 64:6 says all our righteous deeds are like filthy rags in comparison to the Creator. Even when we're doing the best things for God, if we're not living aligned with him, in his love, we are separated from Him. Every righteous deed is like trying to leap across this canyon. So how is it even possible to be in relationship with someone so far beyond us and so impossible to reach?

"With man this is impossible, but not with God; all things are possible with God," (Mark 10:27). Yet while we are fallen, the Grand Canyon between us and our Creator, we're not without hope. In order to grasp this hope, we must see that we're not just victims in need of a savior. We're perpetrators in need of a redeemer.

Jesus Christ is the savior, the redeemer, and the bridge across the canyon, because he is infinite love. God's demonstrated love is our glorious victory over everything (Romans 8:37). His demonstrated love is Christ Jesus. He is our perfect mediator and we need nothing and no one else in order to be reunited with our Creator in perfect unity and victory (John 14:6) We all sin and fall short of the glory of God (Romans 3:23), and this means every last person who takes in a breath of this beautiful earth's air is in need of Jesus to take them from a life swarming in sin and pain, to the Healer and Redeemer.

Belief is the first step. To make it a lifestyle rather than a dogma we must rewire our thinking processes.

There's a big difference between a believer and a follower of Jesus. It's an excellent step to believe, but even demons believe in Jesus, and they shudder (James 2:19). Faith without deeds is dead (James 2:17), which means acceptance and belief in Christ as your savior is merely the beginning. You need Him first and always. Yet the Father desires so much more for you, and this includes healing those places in your heart you believe are forever wounded by people.

Sometimes we can put people in a place they were never meant to be. Instead of being helpers, we make them saviors. "We befriend the world when we demand that others be what only God has promised to be: faithful and sure. If we don't know His deep care and protection then we will insist another human being provide what we lack[9]." This is why we need Christ before we grab onto people.

Being born into a world full of broken people doesn't mean God wants us to stay there! He came to heal the brokenhearted (Psalm 147:3), to seek and save the lost (Luke 19:10) and bring your life to the full (John 10:10). These are all promises for those who believe if they will take the next step and do what Jesus called every believer to do:

"Follow me" (Matthew 16:24).

If you've been terribly wounded by people in the past, God is going to use people today and, in the future, to help heal those wounds. Not perfect people - broken ones. It will be His perfection that will bridge the gap and fill the cracks in relationship. He's in the business of restoring and redeeming that which was lost, and He does this in so many creative ways. By following Jesus in relationship in every moment of every day, He makes the impossible possible.

Relationship with Jesus means He'll draw us into the desert to a point where all we have is Him so He can do the work in our hearts He intended to do in the very beginning before the harm took place.

He is your rock, your fortress, your helper and healer, but in order to follow him we must join his body, and to be a member of Christ's body we must be attached to other parts of the body. We have to be involved with people, we must love people and allow ourselves to be loved by people, if we're going to follow Christ.

---

[9] Allender, Dan B., *The Healing Path: How the Hurts in Your Past Can Lead You to a More Abundant Life* (Colorado Springs, CO: WaterBrook Multnomah, 1999), 52.

Truthfully, we must become love as God is love (1 John 4:18). When Christ, who is love, resides in us in the Holy Spirit, we then become love as He is love.

Jesus was not, and is not, a hoarder of His love, but He gave it away generously. He engaged with people everywhere He went, loving and receiving the love others gave. His demonstrated love is our glorious victory. Victory cannot be experienced in a vacuum.

We must love and allow ourselves to be loved if we're going to step outside of the victim-mindset and walk in victory.

There is a deeply seeded fear in every person who has ever faced harm: we'll be hurt again. For those who have endured trauma, this fear can seem like a permanent brand on our souls. Such fear seems to be part of who we are, and there's no escape.

But this isn't true!

By living in fear and avoiding hurt, we'll never love again. If love is the essential element to following Jesus, who is love in the flesh (1 John 4:18; John 1:1), then self-protection is the antidote to love because self-protection is what we do in place of love to prevent from facing harm, which is an inevitable part of entering into love. The difference between your past harm and your future harm in Christ, is that His love transcends every other failed attempt at love, so you never have to be devastated by the harm caused by others again.

Pain is inevitable, but in Christ you can rise above it and even love deeper because of it.

His perfect love transcends the failures of others. When you're drawing from the well of love that never runs dry, Jesus Christ, then the love others lack cannot take love away from you.

Following Christ, receiving and walking out the victory He gives, means taking your journey with people. Love doesn't exist apart from people. I needed people in my life who knew how to love better than I did, who drew from the well of Jesus' love and had the patience and perseverance to love through hardship, to show me what God's love looked like.

I needed the imperfect love of those same people to learn to run to the well of love that never came up empty.

We need the body of Christ in order to learn how to give and receive love. Without love, you will not make it on this journey. Victory is only possible because of love - the love demonstrated through Christ on the cross. People, in all their beautiful flaws, make up the hands and feet and heart of Christ. We need the body for this journey.

Purpose of the Body

There is a lie floating around churches today and has been around for thousands of years before today, that a relationship with God can be done alone. As long as I have my faith, I've received all I need for eternity and being right with God. This is an incomplete depiction of being a Christian.

Being a Christian means being part of a group of other broken believers who know they need Holy Spirit, and each other, in order to follow Christ. The Word of God is abundantly clear that it is not good for man to be alone (Genesis 2:18), the body of Christ is meant to operate together (Romans 12:5; 1 Corinthians 12:12) for the sake of encouraging and building one another up (Ephesians 4:12; 1 Thessalonians 5:11).

We *can't* do this journey alone. Whether you've had extensive trauma from birth or whether you simply tend to fall into a victim mindset, the solution is never isolation.

If we're going to be transformed from a victim to being victorious in Christ, we need the body of Christ. We're made to co-exist with other people.

There's a reason Jesus sent his disciples out two by two (Luke 10:1) in order to proclaim the gospel, and that it's considered wise to have many advisers for the plans of a man to prosper (Proverbs 15:22).

The body of Christ is meant to function like a human body. The human body responds to the workings of the brain, which is directed by the mind, both of which reside in the head. The head of the body of Christ is Jesus Christ himself (Ephesians 5:23), which means that when the body is functioning properly, they all respond to the instructions of Jesus, which are clearly laid out in His Word and in the leading of the Holy Spirit. Now, we're a sinful race who seem to spend more time misinterpreting the instructions of our Creator than we do actually getting them right, and yet somehow, He manages to make our fumbling efforts work out for our good and His glory.

Praise God!

Any harm we have from Christian's isn't because of Jesus, but the people who make up the body of believers who fail to see who they are in Christ. When you know who you are in Christ there's never a need or desire to hurt people, and any unintentional harm is quickly fixed because there's no pride that prevents one from admitting they may have accidentally messed up! When you don't know who you are in Christ, you live a religious, task-oriented faith serving a God you think is keeping score.

People fall short and sin all the time. Imperfection is not a valid reason to stop doing life with each other. Everyone is imperfect and demonstrating the love of Christ all the time - you and I included.

Mahatma Gandhi once said, "I like your Christ. I do not like your Christians. Your Christians are so unlike your Christ." Most Christians today claim to be Christians and yet how many follow Christ? We pick and choose what parts of the Bible we like and think we can manage, and then substitute what's more convenient for the difficult truths we don't want to address in our life.

Sometimes Christians treat the body of Christ more like a sports team.

Many of us are happy to cheer for our favorite football team in football season. We sit on our couches and wear the jersey and hoot and holler when our team scores and lose heart when they fumble a pass. Some of us are even willing to invest in buying tickets to attend a championship game. Most of us would rather sit in the stands than risk trying out for the team.

Doing the work of playing the game is an entirely different level of commitment. The concept of getting up early every day to exercise, practice and then dream and center our entire lives around making and living life on the team is far too much work. We like the game, but we don't love it. If we do love it, it's not enough to do anything about it. We're content to wear the jersey while we pretend, for a short couple of hours, we belong.

How many of us treat our faith with the same heart?

The body of believers is, to use a sports analogy, Team Jesus. We are meant to work together in order to win the game, and our Sunday morning services are merely a time of getting in the huddle before the next play.

Service hours aren't the game; they're the time-out in the game!

The actual game is what we do in the day-to-day in our workplace, our homes, our classrooms or even when we're in front of a computer alone. Christianity isn't something that you attend or take part in once or twice a week; it's a lifestyle that is lived out every second of every day. Team Jesus wins the championship when Christ returns, but it's only in operating with the body of believers that we have a shot at winning more games than losing on our way to the championship.

In order to stand in victory, to live in joy and fulfillment regardless of our circumstances, we need the body of Christ. We need help to get off the couch and get onto the field. Everyone must play in order to participate in the after party. There's no way around this.

So, who can you trust? God provides the right people. We must be willing to use discernment and let them in. Often, they don't look like you. Some of my most amazing "teammates" on this journey have been at least ten years older than me, have had some character trait that acted like iron sharpening iron and may have been painful at the time but was always for both of our benefit. My teammates don't let me stay in my comfortable bubble - they have all helped me grow, whether they were intending to or not.

It's not likely you'll find this group of people in a bar or at a club. It's also not likely you'll find it at a coffee shop with your headphones on, or even on a walk in a park. Your best chance at meeting people of God willing to do life are in a Jesus glorifying, Bible-based, Holy Spirit filled church.

Many churches claim to be the "right" church, but how do you know if what they're teaching is truly from God?

True Church: Jesus, the Word, the Spirit

When in doubt - ask God. Pray about it. Seek His guidance, and if you're listening, He'll guide you. Here are some other guidelines to consider if listening to the shepherd's voice is still a little new to you.

The true church of Jesus Christ holds to the words of Jesus Christ, and the words breathed out by the Holy Spirit (1 Timothy 3:16-17). Period.

In the book of Revelation, the very last book of the Bible, in the very last chapter, the apostle John writes: "I warn everyone who hears the words of the prophecy of this book: if anyone adds to them, God will add to him the plagues described in this book, and if anyone takes away from the words of the book of this prophecy, God will take away his share in the tree of life and in the holy city, which are described in this book" (Revelation 22:18-19, ESV).

"In the beginning was the Word, and the Word was with God, and the Word was God. He was in the beginning with God. All things were made through him, and without him was not any thing made that was made. In him was life, and the life was the light of men. The light shines in the darkness, and the darkness has not overcome it" (John

1:1-5). The Word is Jesus, and Jesus shines a light on all things because he is the light of the world (John 8:12).

While there is no such thing as a perfect church, there are three indicators a church is a church representing the God of the Bible, Yahweh, His Son, Jesus Christ (Yeshua), and the Holy Spirit.

Jesus Christ is Lord

"Jesus said to him, 'I am the way, and the truth, and the life. No one comes to the Father except through me" (John 14:6). Jesus is the only way to God the Father, the only way to eternal life (Romans 6:23), and the only one "who gives us the victory" (1 Corinthians 15:57). If anyone is proclaimed as Lord other than Jesus Christ, it is not a true church. Run. Keeping in mind the enemy likes to masquerade as an angel of light (2 Corinthians 11:14), it's important to consider the "good" areas a church might magnify above Jesus without abolishing Jesus.

These might include, but are not limited to:

1. Church tradition - this is the way we've always done it, so even though scripture tells us to do it differently we're going to keep doing it the way we've always done it.
2. Church doctrine - what we say about God and the Bible is more important than what the Bible says about God and His Word.
3. Service - doing things for God, or one another, to earn points with God, rather than surrendering to Jesus who's already done everything there is to do and we serve from a place of gratitude rather than greed.

4. Status - Being the biggest, most wealthy, most giving, most prominent, etc. church in the community is a greater focus than following Jesus.

Having church tradition and doctrine, as well as serving and being well-known in the community are not bad things. Let me make myself clear. It's when these elements - or any other - are elevated above Jesus Christ that it becomes a people serving self, rather than Christ.

The Word is the Ultimate Authority

Above popular vote, above church leadership, above government leadership and even opinion. The Word of God, both written in the scriptures and spoken by the Holy Spirit, determines their course of action. Leadership memorizes scripture and encourages others to do the same, they use the Word of God like the weapon it is (Ephesians 6:17) and live under its authority as it is "piercing to the division of soul and of spirit, of joints and of marrow, and discerning the thoughts and intentions of the heart" (Hebrews 4:12). They let the Word have full reign in their personal lives as well as in their positions of authority in the body of believers understanding that it is "breathed out by God and profitable for teaching, for reproof, for correction, and for training in righteousness" (2 Timothy 3:16). In addition, they hold others accountable to the Word of God.

The Holy Spirit is as Essential as Jesus

Many churches today acknowledge the Holy Spirit as part of the trinity, but reject His power, authority and position in the personal life of every disciple. He's often pushed to the back of the pile of priorities somewhere behind service, performance, faith and salvation. The true church not only acknowledges the Holy Spirit's position in the trinity but gives Him the glory and authority due in personal relationship and congregational worship. The Holy Spirit guides their lessons, community involvement, interpersonal relationships, and implementation of scripture in every aspect of their inner workings.

The church will never be perfect, because it's made up of imperfect people. Those three elements, however, must be non-negotiable in order to be pursuing the true God of the Bible with a body of believers. Is every person going to do this perfectly? No. Is leadership going to demonstrate this perfectly? No. But if leadership, as well as the congregants, approach the Bible, Jesus and Holy Spirit with humility and submission to the Father, it's a good place to begin.

Don't look for perfection - look for humble worship and obedience from a place of relationship. Ask God to reveal to you where that church is located and how to have the spiritual discernment to see it when you do find it.

The same goes for personal relationships. It may be in one or two friendships, rather than a large organized body, that you find this church. Just as Christianity isn't a hobby, but a lifestyle, church isn't a building but a people. We "do church" when we love one another the way Christ loves us. Sometimes that's between two people, and sometimes it's in a larger group. However, church always involves at least one other person and church is a necessary part of walking out healing in Christ.

This book may find its way into your hands when you're the only Christian you know. There was a season of my life I lived on a tiny island in the South China sea for three years. I knew only a small handful of Christians at that time, but that was my church. Those were my people because they loved Jesus and they did the best they could to follow the Word of God.

We need the body to hold us together when we're falling apart. We need the body to remind us why we're following Christ when the going gets rough. We need the body to show us Jesus. We need the body to speak life and truth to us when the lies run rampant.

We need the body for us to be Jesus *to* as well.

As mentioned earlier, this is not a concrete set of rules but rather a helpful guideline. The support needed to step out of a victim mentality and walk in victory is one that recognizes where victory takes place - in Christ, and Christ alone. The true church, or *ecclesia* in the original Greek text, is a group of people following Christ. The only way to walk in victory is to be following Christ, transformed from the inside out, and held accountable and loved by those who are doing the same.

Any support outside of Christ seeks to do what's best for you, with you and you alone in mind. Support in Christ seeks to do what's best for you according to God's will, who is your Creator and knows exactly what you need and who He created you to be. Support from the position of love in Christ looks at who and what you were originally designed and created to be and guides you toward that.

We often think that what's best is what's less painful, but as any athlete knows, physical therapy after an injury can be excruciating but it is necessary for a full recovery. Sometimes what's best is pain, and sometimes it takes a loving coach, or a helpful teammate, to help us in that journey.

Support must come from those who know Christ Jesus personally, seek Him in His Word and follow the guide of the Holy Spirit who was given to empower us in grace to do what cannot be done outside of Him. That's not to say Christians won't fail you - they will.

When they do, your faith and trust will have been built on Christ and His provision, not on the people you surround yourself with.

When Self-Protection is Self-Sabotage

I mentioned earlier that self-protection is the antidote to love.

One of the most difficult parts of letting a body of believers into our hearts and lives is the fear of what will happen to our heart when we get rejected. Not if, but when. Apart from one hundred percent obedience to Christ people can be sinful, harmful, often destructive beings. You can't get close to someone without feeling the sting of pain.

Even in Christ, people have a way of causing harm without meaning to, and unintentional hurt still hurts.

We often feel our hearts have already endured so much suffering we need to enclose it in bubble wrap if we're going to go out in the real world. In fact, a suit of armor would be better.

It's called control, and it must go.

I have lived much of my life reinforcing the walls of self-protection to control what I allow access to my heart. I spent years choosing what I'll allow in that could make it hurt, want, cringe, sigh and weep. I have ignored the quiet plea for things that my mind says is unacceptable, or too dangerous. I have shut off the spontaneous pain that occurs when I have faced rejection, and I've told it to buck up.

That hurt, my heart whispers on the verge of tears.

No, it didn't, my mind quickly reasons. *You're fine.*

This resulted in years of training my heart to never speak unless spoken to, and that is not what God wants for His children. I even used scripture to back this up! Jeremiah 17:9 says the heart is deceitful above all things. I interpreted that to mean the heart and its desires was evil.

I took that scripture completely out of context. God convicted the Jews of idolatry and was condemning them to captivity for it. They followed their hearts and rejected the law God had laid out for them, claiming that they were doing what they felt was right rather than doing what *God told them* was right.

God never wanted us to squash the desires of our hearts. Quite the contrary, he says he will give us the desires of our hearts if we will submit ourselves to Him first (Psalm 37:4).

And therein lies our predicament: submit to God?

As we've discussed already, part of being in line with Christ means allowing ourselves to open up to a body of believers who will, inevitably, hurt us. Jesus was aware of this fact. "But Jesus, for His part, did not entrust Himself to them, because He knew all people [and understood the superficiality and fickleness of human nature]," (John 2:24, AMP). He entrusted himself to One being alone, and that was the Father. He loved people more than we will ever be able to grasp or even begin to comprehend, but Jesus didn't entrust himself to those He loved. He expected nothing and He was well acquainted with the evil and petty natures of mankind. He didn't put His hope in people to fulfill Him - He had that perfectly complete in His relationship with His Father.

He just loved people without any expectations.

This is a very delicate and difficult balance. Loving someone without entrusting our hearts to them doesn't mean we won't ever feel the pain of betrayal or deception. It simply means the pain will not leave us in a state of personal devastation when it comes. By submitting to God, we follow in Christ's footsteps of how He loved people but did not entrust Himself to them.

As we walk in our identity in Christ, standing on the victory He alone has given us because of the grace of the Father, by the power of the Holy Spirit in us, people turn into supports.

Like climbing a rock wall, our lifeline is Jesus, our harness the Holy Spirit, our anchor the Father. But the grips that we reach for to keep us climbing instead of dangling in space are the people in our life. Sometimes the only handle we have is a tiny ledge, but it gets us to the next foothold. Our harness, line and anchor never change. The handles we reach for in every step change shape and position, but what we need is there when we need it.

Paul wrote, "We are afflicted in every way, but not crushed; perplexed but not driven to despair; persecuted, but not forsaken; struck down, but not destroyed;" (2 Corinthians 4:8-10). In order to be in such a place, we must entrust our hearts to one who will never disappoint. We must let go of control, the control we use like a shield to protect ourselves. Our own histories are evidence enough that we cannot adequately protect our own hearts. We therefore must hand over our hearts to our Creator if we genuinely want to be at peace.

Not peace that the world offers, but peace Jesus alone gives (John 14:27).

This is not an easy task. When those of us who have faced trauma think of how we've been so horrifically harmed, it appears impossible.

The alternative, however, is a far greater loss than the risk of being hurt amid giving up control. When we try to protect ourselves, we essentially give the Enemy the freedom to do as he sees fit with our heart. We believe a lie that sets up a stronghold enabling him to set up camp and wreak havoc on our hearts and minds. We are inadequate protectors of our hearts because any protection we think we're creating is simply a stronger fortress for the Enemy.

As we've seen thus far, it is the Enemy who comes to steal, kill and destroy - not God. The sin of fallen man, the spiritual warfare at work in the invisible realm, and our own sinful nature orchestrated our suffering and pain - not God.

Our desire for control feels like a safety net, but what it ends up being is a Venus flytrap. A place of death masquerading as a place of refuge.

When we think of control, we tend to understand it differently than the Bible intended. Scripture refers to control as witchcraft (Galatians 5:19-20). We hear 'witchcraft' and we think of pointy black hats, cauldron's and wart-ridden noses, but this isn't the Bible's definition - it's western culture.

Biblically, witchcraft is the attempt to control someone, or self, and make him or her do whatever you desire using any spirit that isn't the Holy Spirit. Rather than living in the state we were designed for, submission to the Creator, we live in a type of antagonism seizing control of others, our environment, ourselves, and God.

There is a direct connection between rebellion against God, and witchcraft. Witchcraft comes from the Greek word *pharmakeia*[10], which means magic, sorcery or enchantment. Typically, when you find the word sorcery and witchcraft in the Bible the words are used interchangeably. Why would someone want to use magic or enchantment?

To control an otherwise out of control person, environment or situation.

Why do we rebel against God? We don't trust His way of doing things, His sovereignty, so we take matters into our own hands. We want to be in control of our own lives.

Rebellion, as it were, is the root of witchcraft (1 Samuel 15:22-23). Rebellion rejects God's authority. Unfortunately, we can't exist in this world without authority. If we reject God's, then we turn to an illegitimate authority supported by an illegitimate power.

Often, that authority is self.

---

[10] http://biblehub.com/str/greek/5331.htm

In Galatians 5:19-20 we read about the works of the flesh - or selfishness: "Sexual immorality, impurity, sensuality, idolatry, sorcery, enmity, strife, jealousy, fits of anger, rivalries, dissensions, divisions," to name a few. We use these methods to get people to do what we want. This is the most basic level of control and we do it *all the time.* We are so desperate to protect ourselves from the remotest experience of pain we do whatever it takes to manipulate every person and every situation to our benefit.

Now picture every person you meet, every day, doing this exact same thing. It's no wonder there's so much conflict, and it's no wonder we're all so exhausted!

How do you know if this is something you're battling?

Three red flags: manipulation, intimidation, and domination. Typically, though certainly not always, women will manipulate, and men will intimidate. Both are ways of attempting to control another person. It's in this type of thinking and living that we cannot co-exist with others in any form of love. Control and love are opposites. Control is about fear, and there is no fear in love. Healthy, loving relationships exist outside of control and gives the other person the freedom to harm us. We don't condone it, and we certainly don't like it or approve of it, but love extends the freedom for the possibility of it and promises to remain.

Once again, if you're drawing love from the well of Christ that never runs dry, no harm can take away from your well. There's nothing to fear because no one can take from you what they didn't give to you, and what can never run out.

No one gives more freedom than God does. No one gives as much as He does and demand nothing in return. His only request, His only desire, is our love and life.

Self-protection is a means of control, it is witchcraft, which is of the flesh (Galatians 5:19-20). We desire to be safe, not realizing that the safest place is being laid completely bare before the Father, protected by Him.

The Role of Counselors & Psychiatrists

We need Jesus and we need people if we're going to walk this journey of transformation from a victim mentality to victorious in Christ. There is no victory apart from Christ, and we need the body of believers to fully experience the victory as God designed it to be.

I spent about seven years thinking this was all I "should" need in order to "get better." If I had enough faith, I'd be getting better. If I could just do better at what my support system was telling me I needed to do, I'd be getting better.

My personal trauma was so deeply ingrained in the very fiber of my identity it felt like a black thread woven through an enormous colorful canvas. At first glance the black looked as if it belonged as part of the design. A closer look at the canvas, however, revealed the black was a flaw in the pattern... and the flaw was everywhere.

I spent seven years pulling at that thread watching it break off in tiny pieces, seeing this wall-to-wall canvas growing with each passing year, the black fibers expanding with it, feeling utterly hopeless that I would ever be free from the consequences of the trauma I endured. I got my degree in human development and suddenly the black thread became even more ominous as I saw it weave its way through the most formative years of my life. How could I possibly undo what had been done? How could my "praying it away" ever be enough? How could memorizing the Bible undo what had been done to me? How could my church ever help when the simple act of sharing what had happened to me left them embarrassed, uncomfortable and hurting for me with no idea of how to help me?

I needed more help, so I started going to people who understood the brain and scripture far better than I did. For about ten years I went to secular counselors and psychiatrists. In 2017 I began seeing a Christian counselor who knew scripture, the human body and brain far better than most people I'd ever met. I learned something in that relationship:

The church is not limited to those who attend your congregation on a Sunday morning.

It is far bigger than that. A specific body of believers you meet with regularly is essential, but what that looks like can be different for many people – as long as Christ is the focus.

Sometimes our pain can go so deep, our trauma can leave such a scar on our flesh, soul and spirit, we need help from someone who knows the body, soul and spirit better than we do. Whether a counselor or therapist, even a psychiatrist, it is my personal belief that in order to walk out victory in Christ, it's pointless to get help from someone who does not recognize Christ as Lord. To accept medication from a psychiatrist who believes medication is the cure, misses the Cure.

This is different than the psychiatrist whose goal is to balance the chemicals in your brain in order to give you the opportunity to do the work you need to do to renew your mind, be One with Christ. Whether you need to stay on the medication is a decision you must make within your relationship with Holy Spirit and your support system.

A counselor who doesn't know Christ might tell you to do what's best for you. Let's be honest - when we're vulnerable and in pain we don't have the slightest clue what's best for ourselves in the long-term. A counselor who knows Christ will be able to tell you what IS best for you based on the message from the One who created you - not her opinion, and not what's based on your unbalanced emotions.

Once again, such a person is a guide and a support, not the solution.

I believe these careers are a noble and admirable profession to embark in. I also believe that there is a time and place for people to benefit from these careers as patients. I have been in an out of counselor's and psychiatrist offices for more than fifteen years and can attest to their success in helping me obtain very helpful knowledge and personal insight.

I have dear friends who are counselors who have done incredible work, powerful work, in the physical, emotional and the spiritual realm on behalf of those they serve.

This being said, no counselor, psychiatrist, or therapist can *cure you* of the pain and suffering you've experienced. No amount of cognitive behavioral therapy, EMDR, dialectical behavioral therapy or any other kind of psychotherapy will do the work apart from that work Christ has already done on the cross.

It's not possible.

There is a time for everything, including a time to cry and a time to laugh, a time to mourn and a time to dance, a time to speak and a time to be quiet (Ecclesiastes 3:4, 7). Introspection can be a good thing. We can't repent and move forward if we're unaware of where we've been and where we are. The key is looking inwardly through the lens of Christ. Apart from Him all we can see is our sin, but when we look at ourselves through the lens of sonship, of being a daughter to the King, where we are no longer looks like a black hole, but rather a foundation of unimaginable grace where anything is possible.

A Christian counselor will point you to your true identity in Christ and reminds you who you are in Him, guiding you to live from that place - not toward it. He or she doesn't cater to who you are not. A Christian counselor focused on Christ will allow you to be where you are, while speaking to and believing in who you are in Christ. He or she will lead you to a victorious life, not a victim mentality.

Always through the lens of the truth.

Too much introspection takes your eyes off Jesus and onto yourself, which leads to nothing but spinning your wheels in the mud of your own soul. Paul tells us exactly what we're to think about in his letter to the Philippian church: think about whatever is true, honorable, just, pure, lovely, commendable and anything of excellence and worthy of praise (4:8). Think on Christ.

We're to be transformed in the renewal of our mind, taking every thought captive and making it obedient to Christ (Romans 12:2; 2 Corinthians 10:5).

It's hard to know where you're headed if you don't know from where you're starting. Those in the psychotherapy profession can help provide clarity in this area. They provide assistance to individuals going through struggling circumstances of varying degrees. They provide psychotherapy, assessment, diagnosis and crisis management. They make no promise to heal their clients, but to help their clients achieve a more advantageous mental health.

There is one Healer, however, and His name is Jesus Christ.

Anyone in the mental health field can provide excellent education, resources, and practical guidelines toward a healthier lifestyle. Their input needs to be viewed through the lens of an assistance toward healing, not healing itself.

This assistance needs to be chosen wisely and with much prayer. Digging into a wounded heart and mind is a delicate matter and the guide for this endeavor needs to be chosen with great care. Any approach to healing must be done on a holistic approach - mental, physical, emotional and spiritual. Without even one of these addressed you're not getting complete support. This is why this often takes a team of people.

Such a team is one that must be chosen carefully. Just because someone has a few letters after their name and a couple of degrees hanging on a wall doesn't make them a good fit for you.

This is an investment of time and money and will either help or harm the one seeking assistance. The benefit of choosing someone who has a relationship with the Lord is that he or she will be able to give you the greatest perspective of all - the perspective of the One who created you.

CHAPTER FIVE

A HOLISTIC APPROACH TO TRAUMA - BEING FULLY PREPARED FOR THE JOURNEY

Science and Scripture

As I mentioned in the beginning of this book, if we're going to truly heal, we can't have a one-sided approach to healing. If we're to only address the spiritual we'd be neglecting the very real physical, emotional, social and intellectual aspects of our selves that God has created in His image. Prayer is as essential as a good night's sleep and healthy eating habits on the road to recovery. A spiritually minded support system is just as valuable as recognizing your emotional triggers and just how drastically your trauma effected the workings of your brain.

If we neglect the physical or emotional, we're limiting the spiritual, and if we're only focused on the physical or emotional, we're walking into the situation with only part of the story.

As research continues to expand, scientists are proving that the relationship between your beliefs, hopes, dreams and thoughts has a huge impact on how your brain operates. For years scientists believed the brain dictated the workings of the mind, but over the last several decades research has proved the opposite is true: your mind determines the function of your brain.

This means our DNA can and does change shape according to our thoughts.

This is crucial to those who have experienced trauma. This means, contrary to what we've been told and have been telling ourselves, we are not a product of our circumstances or our biology. We can choose the thoughts that will dictate the construct of our DNA that changes the architecture of our physical brains. Using this, as well as other tools at our disposal, we can choose, with the help and power of Jesus Christ, to heal.

Or we can choose not to.

As I write this book, I'm nearly two years into a process that, a few years ago, I would have said is idealistic - even impossible.

In theory, it seems too good to be true. Such an idea must come from people in lab coats isolated from suffering by numbers and figures, padded from the reality of pain with theories and charts. *They don't know what it's like. They don't understand.*

In her bestselling book *Switch on Your Brain*, neuroscientist Dr. Caroline Leaf writes, "Research shows that 75 to 98 percent of mental, physical, and behavioral illness comes from one's thought life." Having been made in the image of God (Genesis 1:26) we are therefore designed for love, both giving and receiving it (1 John 4:8). Science is catching up to scripture, showing that people are wired for love and optimism[11], which means when we think negatively or make negative choices the quality of our thinking suffers. The results of scientific research are finally showing what the Bible has been telling us for millennia: negative thinking is not the norm - it's not a state the human mind and body were designed to operate in.

You and I know there is a whole lot of ugliness in the world. To overcome this with love and positivity is in direct contrast to our flesh. When we're faced with something harmful, our five senses activate an emotional and physical response almost immediately. If we don't take the time to process those responses, the unprocessed emotion will run rampant in our brains[12]. Like a child let loose in a candy store with no adult supervision, that emotion will wreak havoc. Whatever you feed grows, whatever you starve dies. Whatever you think about, you feed. Therefore, whatever you focus on will grow. The more a dominate emotion drives our thinking in a circular pattern, the stronger it becomes.

Without the "adult supervision" of our minds, trauma can turn our emotions into a frightening resemblance of Dr. Jekyll and Mr. Hyde. We don't know what side is going to be exposed or when. The very process of thinking and choosing is one of the most powerful things God has given us, and it is an amazing gift that we can use as a tool for our good and growth, or as a self-destructive weapon. It is our mind, and only our mind, that determines whether we will grow

[11] Leaf, C.(2009). *The Gift in You: Discover New Life through Gifts Hidden in Your Mind.* Nashville, TN: Thomas Nelson
[12] Leaf, C. (2015). *Switch on your brain: the key to peak happiness, thinking, and health.* Grand Rapids, MI: Baker Books.

and heal from our experiences and move forward, or whether we'll keep flinging mud and digging ourselves into a grave.

It comes down to choice.

This is a difficult truth to accept, but science as well as scripture have given ample evidence that "as he thinks in his heart, so is he" (Proverbs 23:7).

Or, to put it in more scientific terms, the very substance of quantum physics is free will, a choice that results in focused attention, and the effects and consequences of these choices. Your brain then becomes what you focus on, and your body carries out the will of the spirit and soul. Finally, what your brain has become produces what you say and do and how you feel physically and mentally. This is the fruit of scientific research, and there are scriptures that have been telling us the exact same thing for centuries.

Proverbs 4:20-27 is an excellent example. If we direct our attention to the Word of God, we will align our thinking and subsequent choices with God, and the outcome will be healing and health[13]. How else do you fix what's broken except to go to the one who created it for the solution as to how to repair it?

There is no denying the depth of pain and suffering you have endured and the impact it has had on your heart and mind. Denying this does nothing to move toward healing. Only accepting the facts of where you are enables you to address what needs to change in your thought processes to enable you to move forward into the truth of who you already are.

---

[13] Leaf, C. (2015). *Switch on your brain: the key to peak happiness, thinking, and health*. Grand Rapids, MI: Baker Books.

Where you are, and what you've been through, has no impact on *who* you already are.

The good news, really the *great news*, is that it's a matter of renewing your mind to make this transition. You're not what happened to you. You're not your symptoms. You're not your pain. There is healing within your reach because you're simply grasping what's already been done and changing your mind to accept who you already are because of what's already been finished.

The enemy would love nothing more than to convince you otherwise. As a disciple of Jesus, you already have several advantages against him he doesn't want you to know about:

You are Hardwired for Love

The Enemy is like a virus on your computer. Originally everything was designed to work flawlessly, lovely and perfectly. The enemy comes to steal, kill and destroy and messes everything up so you not only end up running slowly, you also end up doing things you were never designed to do. A reset of your system (your mind), by the Holy Spirit, and you'll be functioning properly again. You need to simply reset your mind to the way it was originally intended to work and stop engaging in the thought and behavior patterns that perpetuated the damage. This reset, like any other, can take time, and there will always be viruses to fend off, but with the right security in place (the Holy Spirit and the armor of God as described in Ephesians 6) and frequent "system checks," you'll be able to fight them off before they get out of control like they feel now.

You know when you're about to do a reset or an update on your computer and the disclaimer comes up and says something like, "Do not shut off your computer during this process. It may take a while..." The same advice applies here. Don't let the waiting get to you so much you end up shutting off halfway through the process. It may take a while, but the waiting and work is worth it. Most of it can't be seen on the surface, it looks like a spinning color wheel, but enormous work is being done behind the screen. Trust it.

You Have the Almighty Creator Fighting on Your Behalf

The Enemy wants you to believe you're on your own in this and it's too big to even attempt to tackle. It's impossible. It's daunting and overwhelming and just not worth the effort. Things aren't that bad after all, right? When those doubts, questions and statements come into your mind tell the Enemy to SHUT UP in JESUS' NAME. That's part of taking captive every thought and making it obedient to Christ (2 Corinthians 10:5) and nothing is impossible where Jesus is concerned (Luke 1:37). You are His concern, because He loves you and you were designed to be in relationship with Him (Luke 19:10). You have the Almighty on your side working things out in the spiritual realm as you do your part in the physical. Hebrews says Jesus is our advocate and that we have a great cloud of witnesses fighting on our behalf (Hebrews 12:1).

You Are as Successful as You Make Up Your Mind to Be

We can't control the events or circumstances of our lives, but we can control our reactions. Controlling those reactions and choosing to have the mind of Christ in those circumstances, is the difference between a healthy mind and body and a sick mind and body. It feels impossible, but your mind gets to decide whether it is impossible. Henry Ford once said, "Whether you think you can or think you can't, you're right." The same goes for your desire to be free from the bondage that enslaves you. The power is at your disposal, and it's entirely up to you whether you're going to make it happen. It really doesn't matter what happens in your life - your mind gets to decide what to do with those happenings.

I know much of what I tackle in this book is going to wreak havoc and stir up offense. My aim in this book isn't to cause harm, but to share my experience walking out scripture in the realm of healing from trauma. There are many psychosomatic disorders that I do not understand and have not experienced, but I do believe that the Bible is not particular when it comes to what Jesus did on the cross for all. All means all. Jesus was not limited in healing and miracles. What He did on the cross was for everyone, regardless of their state of mind and body.

The Bible is either true, or it isn't. There isn't room for middle ground, so the choice is yours. I invite you to choose truth.

We can't move forward until we know where we are, and we can't repent of self-destructive behaviors and thought patterns until we know what those behaviors and patterns are. As we step into the evidence of trauma and the mental and emotional defenses we create in order to survive, I caution you to not take on what isn't yours. If you have to wonder if you've ever experienced certain symptoms I believe it's safe to say you haven't. Don't adopt a symptom that was never yours to carry. This isn't about making sure you have the most traumatic history, but rather a chance for you to understand what exactly is trauma, whether or not it applies to your circumstances, and take yourself to the shop and see what kind of repairs need to be done.

As the old saying goes, if it ain't broke, don't fix it.

Physiological Impact on the Brain

The brain is, by far, the most complex organ of the human body. We marvel at the superior speeds of computers to process information while our brain is moving... well, a lot faster. We're made in God's image, so the most intelligent, emotionally sound mind is a mere shadow of God's. Like all things He created, He created it to function a certain way. When sin entered the world, it corrupted everything - including, if not especially, our minds.

This is why there are scriptures about the need for us to be transformed in the renewing of our mind (Romans 12:2) and that we need to take captive every thought and make it obedient to Christ (2 Corinthians 10:5).

When we experience trauma, our brain shifts into self-preservation, even survival, mode. While this is helpful in the midst of trauma, if we allow our brain to maintain control after the trauma is over, it will operate in a way contrary to God's design with self-preservation as its primary aim.

According to the fifth edition of the Diagnostic and Statistical Manual of Mental Disorders (DSM-5), written by the American Psychiatric Association, the definition of trauma requires "actual or threatened death, serious injury, or sexual violence." It is a legitimate experience and it has specific boundaries in it's application. For the sake of this chapter, this is the definition I'm using when I refer to trauma and the physiological impact it has on the brain. Everyone faces trials, but trials do not trigger the same reaction in the physical brain as trauma.

In scripture, the word "trauma" shows up only once in the Amplified Bible in 1 Corinthians 15:7-9 when Paul is referring to his birth; other translations say he was born premature. The word surfaces again in the Passion translation in Psalm 116:10-11, which reads, "Even when it seems I'm surrounded by many liars and my own fears, and though I'm hurting in my suffering and trauma, I still stay faithful to God and speak words of faith." David's trauma could be anything involved in the years he spent in the wilderness fleeing for his life from Saul, or in the wars he participated in as king, or a dozen other experiences.

Scripture uses the word "trial" multiple times, notably in James 1:2: "Consider it nothing but joy, my brothers and sisters, whenever you fall into various trials." The Greek word for trials here is *peirasmos,* which is also used in Jesus' teaching the disciples how to pray - "do not lead us into temptation (or *peirasmos)*" (Matthew 6:13). It's defined as an experiment, a trial, a temptation or testing.

Trials are an expected part of life that, I believe it's safe to say, everyone must face.

Trauma, on the other hand, is far more severe. Many people spend their whole lives without ever being touched by trauma. There is a distinction between trial and trauma, and for the sake of this chapter the difference must be made well known. The effect of trauma on the brain is drastic, even devastating, and without intentional remedial therapy focused on the Word of God, it can destroy a life. But it doesn't have to be this way. Complete and total victory is possible in Christ.

While scripture doesn't spend much time dwelling on what is and is not traumatic, there are dozens upon dozens of biblical examples of traumatic events.

Paul confessed to murdering Christians. The twelve disciples were in storms so big they nearly lost their lives to drowning had Jesus not shown up. There are multiple records of rape in the Old Testament (Genesis 34:2; Judges 20:5). Paul was beaten, almost to death, whipped and lashed and thought to be dead, multiple times, as were many other disciples of Jesus.

The age in which we experience a traumatic event influences how the trauma impacts our brain. It's important to understand that while most brain development happens in utero, the brain continues to develop after birth. There is never a point in a person's lifetime the brain becomes a stagnant organ, immune to change or growth. Quite the contrary; our brain is always growing and changing.

The *direction* of the growth of our brain is a matter of choice. Whose choice? *Yours.* No one can determine the direction or function of your brain but you. It's going to grow and change, you might as well dictate the direction.

How does this brain of ours work? We hear about how trauma causes damage to the brain; exactly how does that happen?

In an article by Kelly Green Jennings, ND, MSOM in Naturopathic Doctor News and Review, titled *Trauma, the Amygdala and Post-Traumatic Stress Disorder: Part 1* she illustrates the three primary layers of the brain impacted by trauma in a simplistic form.

"The modern human brain is composed of three distinct, albeit interrelated and interdependent, layers." The brainstem, the most primitive layer, controls all motor and vital functions necessary for survival and homeostasis, including arousal, reproductive drive, sensation, instinctual movement and impulse.

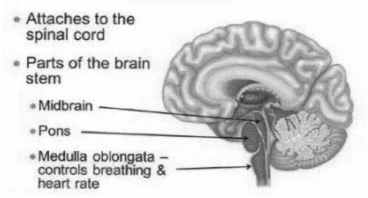

Brain Stem

- Attaches to the spinal cord
- Parts of the brain stem
  - Midbrain
  - Pons
  - Medulla oblongata – controls breathing & heart rate

The next layer, the limbic system, anatomically surrounds the brainstem and encompasses the capacity for parent-child bonding and enduring family units. It regulates the perception of our experience of incoming sensory information, memory, some social behavior and learning, and is associated with the *expression* of emotions, including the desire for social-emotional contact.

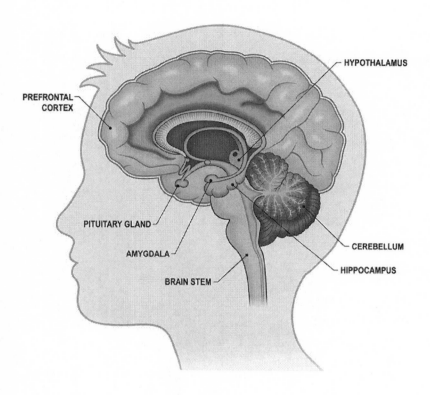

The third layer is the neocortex, which enables cognition, comprehension, self-awareness, decision-making and conceptual thinking[14].

---

[14] https://ndnr.com/neurology/trauma-the-amygdala-and-post-traumatic-stress-disorder-part-1/

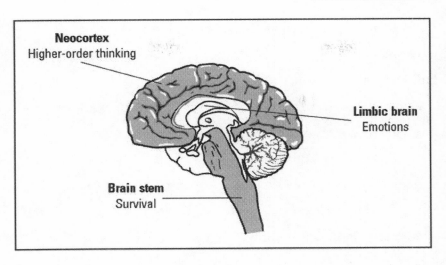

The limbic system and neocortex are dependent on our environment and our interactions with others in order to develop. The contact we have with others determines how these parts of the brain mature. Trauma primarily impacts the limbic system, which is comprised of four parts:

The thalmus, which regulates your sensory experiences.

The amygdala, which is responsible for emotion, and is highly activated when incoming sensory information is highlighted with emotional content.

The hippocampus, which is responsible for memory and converts short-term memory into long-term memory.

And the hypothalmus, which is responsible for regulating your automatic nervous system, such as fight or flight. It determines when to release hormones such as adrenaline. It also regulates other drives like hunger, thirst, sleep and sex.

I remember these by thinking of a Hippo with a HAT on. Hippocampus, Hypothalmus, Amygdala, and Thalmus. Each is closely intertwined with and dependent on one another.

While the brain stem is fully developed at birth, the limbic system needs a lot of social, emotional, perceptual and cognitive stimulation during the first several years of life for normal and healthy development. So, what happens when our environment is abnormal and neglectful, or traumatic, during that critical time?

Some neural connections wither and die while others persist that should atrophy. Copious amounts of research have proved that during the first three to five years of life when the limbic system and neocortex are maturing, a nurturing environment is essential for sustaining and shaping a healthy human being.

In reality, few of us have a perfectly healthy and nurturing environment. Not everyone with a difficult upbringing, however, has had a traumatic upbringing that would cause significant brain damage. Knowing God's original intention for our mind allows us to grasp what happened when sin entered the world, and I believe it will light a fire under us to leap for Jesus' restoration and redemption.

From birth, the amygdala guides infants and toddlers to recognize the familiar and secure boundaries of their world while increasing their sense of attachment and sensitivity to affection, mood and environment.

This tiny part of the brain helps us to recognize fear and the sensations associated with fear as well as provides us with the ability to express it. As we grow, we discover the difference between what is safe and unsafe through the eyes and reactions of our caretaker. We build trust.

Trauma violates those boundaries and destroys that trust. What was once safe suddenly becomes unsafe, and it leads us to question all things, and especially all people. It doesn't matter how safe or secure things seem anymore, because when our life and body is violated to the degree that trauma inflicts, nothing can be trusted anymore.

The amygdala itself is a composite of four differing clusters of neurons. The central nucleus is most closely linked with the brainstem, which is highly involved in manipulating the body's response to emotional stimuli through the autonomic nervous system. We face a new circumstance, and this new information is poured into the amygdala. The amygdala relays the information to the hippocampus, which stores memories. The hippocampus tells the amygdala, *Hold up! This is like that one time!...* and the central nucleus of the amygdala then activates our brainstem. This is why when we see someone that reminds us of our abuser, our palms start to sweat, and our hands start to shake.

Follow me here: *The amygdala enhances memory depending on the profoundness and emotional value of an event.* Since the amygdala reminds us not to repeat mistakes, a condition such as PTSD can cause the function of the amygdala to dysfunction. It often presents with low-grade to paralyzing state of fear manifesting in both physical and psychological symptoms.

Regardless of whether the threat is real or not.

This is a very important thing to remember when it comes to trauma. The trauma (a heightened emotional event) literally damaged the amygdala and its ability to discern between what is safe and unsafe, what are healthy and unhealthy boundaries. In a traumatic event, the brain has, in a way, been hijacked by primitive areas that are essential for survival. The very tools God gave the brain to function in times of survival have taken over long after they're needed. This changes the relationship amongst these areas of the brain from one of cooperation to a struggle for control that leads to hyper-vigilance, impulsivity and overall dissatisfaction.

When trauma occurs, the hippocampus freezes the memory in a sort of hold. One of two things happen with the memory of the trauma. Sometimes there are "holes" in the memory of the traumatic event, and sometimes the memories are incredibly vivid and always present. So, when the amygdala leaps into overdrive the hippocampus digs through its memory bank and finds a very vivid picture of the trauma and backs up the amygdala. Or it picks up the tiniest of details supporting the amygdala's warning to the threat, labels it legitimate for the sake of self-preservation and stores it away in the trauma-like box for future reference.

I can remember believing that if a man was safe that actually made him more dangerous. My brain was convinced that the closer a man was in relation to me, the kinder he seemed, the bigger of a threat he was. It was my older brother, my stepfathers, my mom's boyfriends, my closest friend in the Marine Corps, and then my husband, who sexually assaulted and raped me. My amygdala took each new occurrence to my hippocampus, which then stored each experience, as it's designed to do, as evidence that if a man was deemed "safe" then he was very dangerous and couldn't be trusted. Strangers were more approachable and trustworthy compared to people I knew, because strangers had never assaulted me.

On the flipside, sometimes holes in the memory mean the hippocampus can't find anything at all to support the amygdala's heightened response. It's not that the event didn't happen, but that the event created such a heightened state of fear the hippocampus malfunctioned, unable to retain the details of the memory. I picture a risk-management officer behind his desk frantically looking through files unable to find what he's looking for while his office mate is screaming about a very real threat outside their door. What do we do?! He finally chucks the files and says, "Forget it! Run!"

We accumulate our fears in "flashbulb memories" stored in the amygdala, which in turn keeps the brain and body hyper-aroused, prepared for the next attack. Whether the hippocampus can help or not, the amygdala is essentially running its own show. The thalmus part of the limbic system is responsible for relaying sensory information and acting as a center for pain *perception*. Perceived pain is as real to the thalmus as actual pain.

This is an important element to consider for people who have experienced trauma. Sensory pain from past trauma - such as a rape, a battle wound, a car accident, etc. - is stored in the mind and is as real, to the person, in the memory of it as the actual moment of it. For some people who experience flashbacks of the trauma, the thalmus has stored the memory of pain with the memory itself, and the perception of that pain is as real as the intensely vivid memory stored in the hippocampus. Because the limbic system is so interconnected - think a tangle of toxic wires instead of separate boxes - each system operates in self-preservation sharing and cross sharing information to keep the person safe.

Even though there is no real threat anymore. The brain is responding to a story of an old threat as if it is currently happening and cannot separate the story from present reality.

While the amygdala is taking in new information and the hippocampus is handing out old information, the thalmus is receiving and perceiving all the sensory aspects of past and present while the hypothalmus is regulating the automatic nervous system, the fight or flight urge we face in the body, releasing hormones such as adrenaline according to the *perceived pain* the thalmus is feeding it. The hypothalmus also regulates other drives like hunger, thirst, sleep and sex, which is always working to bring about homeostasis in the body.

Unfortunately, this means the brain is sending signals it doesn't need to send. It's operating on a perception, on what could happen, on the lingering pain of what did happen, and on the illusion of the pain being present.

Trauma causes the amygdala and hippocampus and the rest of the limbic system to malfunction. Rather than operating properly for true health and wellness they are, instead, in survival mode in response to a perceived threat. This means the rest of the body is therefore operating against God's original design in response to the messages sent by the limbic system.

Studies have shown that long-term, ongoing stress *as a result of severe and chronic PTSD* can ultimately permanently damage the hippocampus. For some people, symptoms of trauma include nightmares, flashbacks and unbidden thoughts that can be triggered by seemingly ordinary events. Some people may dissociate or shut down aspects of their personality. Together, it's these experiences that manifest themselves in what has come to be called post-traumatic stress disorder. It's important to note, however, that not everyone who experiences a traumatic event is diagnosed with PTSD.

What is post-traumatic stress disorder exactly? And what determines who is diagnosed and who isn't?

Post-traumatic stress disorder is an anxiety disorder that develops in relation to an event which creates psychological trauma. It's diagnosed when symptoms cause clinically significant distress or impairment in social and/or occupational dysfunction for a period of at least one month[15]. According to an article in *Theravive*, an online mental health awareness and therapist network, symptoms of PTSD can include:

Re-experiencing the event: recurrent memories of the event, traumatic nightmares, dissociative reactions, prolonged psychological distress.

Alterations in arousal: Aggressive, reckless, or self-destructive behavior, sleep disturbances, hypervigilance.

Avoidance: Distressing memories, thoughts or reminders of the event.

Negative alterations in cognition and mood: Persistent negative beliefs, distorted blame, or trauma-related emotions; feelings of alienation and diminished interest in life.

I wasn't diagnosed with PTSD until I was in my early twenties. I suspected I had some form of post-traumatic stress disorder, but when I was diagnosed, my doctors called it *complex*-PTSD.

My first thought was, is that even a thing? Am I just so messed up they can't even slap a basic label on whatever it is I have? They have to add the "complex" part to make sense of it?

---

[15] https://www.theravive.com/therapedia/posttraumatic-stress-disorder-(ptsd)-dsm--5-309.81-(f43.10)

As it turns out, the DSM-5 conceptualizes post-traumatic stress disorder as a single, broad diagnosis, whereas the International Classification of Diseases (ICD-11) offers two "sibling" disorders: PTSD and complex PTSD (also called CPTSD).

My doctors gave me an ICD-11 CPTSD diagnosis. Further personal research provided more insight to understand the difference. ICD-11 CPTSD was distinguished from ICD-11 PTSD by higher levels of dissociation, depression, and borderline personality disorder. Diagnostic associations were higher with depression, anxiety and suicidal ideation and self-harm for ICD-11 CPTSD compared to DSM-5 PTSD[16].

Essentially, the symptoms resulting from repetitive traumatic events in the twenty-odd years prior to my diagnosis were severe enough to be classified as complex post-traumatic stress disorder according to the International Classification of Diseases.

What did this look like?

I lived in a fatalistic present, certain the trauma of years past was going to repeat itself in my future. I felt trapped in the events. By the time I was diagnosed I'd been raped more than half a dozen times since I was a child, and sexually assaulted more times than I could count. The perpetrators were people intimately involved in my life. Several years after I was diagnosed, after I thought I had the worst of my symptoms managed, I took a leap of faith and got married. Shortly after we were married, the cycle of sexual abuse began again, and eighteen months later we were divorced.

---

[16] https://www.ncbi.nlm.nih.gov/pubmed/29577450

I had chronic insomnia, broken up only by sleep ravaged by nightmares so bad they wouldn't try to make horror movies out of what I saw in my sleep. I stayed away from my family unless I felt confident in my ability to shut off the parts of me triggered by them and my surroundings. If I could shut it off, at least for a few hours, I would go home and weep, wrecked by panic attacks. I went through every day hyper vigilant of my surroundings. I couldn't go onto a college campus without being paralyzed by fear walking across an open quad - so I took distance learning courses and got my degree online.

Physical touch felt like slithering snakes inside and outside of my body. I felt a surge of sick pleasure that made me want to vomit while simultaneously longing for more. I hated men. I wanted to connect with people, but the very desire brought forth so much shame I was perpetually suicidal. I was confused and angry and grieved by God, because I cried out to him as a child as the abuse continued. Day after day.

More than anything, however, I hated myself. In this state I subconsciously made dozens of vows and judgments that, until recently, all but damned the direction of my life.

Vows and Judgments in the Mind

Believe it or not, it's not the reality of what happened that determines our values and belief systems about ourselves and the world, but what we *decide* to believe about what happened. We all have a story, but it's the story we tell ourselves that determines the course of our life. Often, we spend more time telling the worst version of our story, and we wonder why our lives are in such disarray. If you speak poorly about yourself, others or your situation enough times you will begin to believe it as truth. You forget about the good, however small. Eventually you end up acting as though it is true, essentially creating a self-fulfilling prophecy.

I call these vows and judgments.

While pain is a simple byproduct of living in a fallen world, what we tell ourselves about pain and the catalyst to that pain, determines how we face life in the future.

If I walk through a sliding glass door and end up with eighteen stitches across my forehead, that hurts! A perfectly normal response would be, "I'm never doing that again!" The simple statement, "I'm never..." is a vow. Why did I make that vow? I judged that walking through a sliding glass door is painful. This is a true judgment!

However, this judgment and vow could lead me to making sure no house I live in ever has a sliding glass door in its design. I might be extra careful when visiting friends who have sliding glass doors. My caution isn't due to the door being a threat, but *my belief* about the *possibility* of what could happen based on an experience with a sliding glass door.

Let's make this more appropriate to our topic of trauma.

I was first molested by my older brother before I could string more than a few words together in a sentence. I was raped by him when I was nine years old, and then sexually assaulted by a handful of my mother's boyfriends and treated very sexually inappropriately by my stepfathers. I was then raped in the Marine Corps several times by men with the responsibility for protecting me. I then married a man who, shortly after we said our "I do's" used his sexual addiction as an excuse to rape me.

After all of this, I made the judgment: all men are sexual animals.

This then led to the vow: I will never let a man touch me again.

This judgment and vow led to hypervigilance, insecurity and an unreasonable amount of fear regarding every man I ever met - especially the ones that were supposed to look out for me. They definitely couldn't be trusted. As a result, my behavior toward men became rude, unkind, sarcastic, manipulative and downright mean sometimes. I took what men had done to me in the past and judged every man based on the trauma caused by other men.

My symptoms of PTSD ran rampant and were perpetuated by my vows and judgments. What I believed intensified what surfaced.

That's not a way to live.

I was miserable, I was constantly afraid, and I couldn't address these issues until I was willing to look at the vows and judgments I'd made that were not of the mind of Christ. They were in direct response to my trauma, which led to a tainted heart condition that bled into behavior that was not a reflection of the heart of Jesus.

These are some common bitter root judgments and their potential corresponding vows. I believed most of these, and it was in this belief system that kept me trapped and enabled my mind to maintain its toxic circle. Whether you own one or all of these, or you have some of your own that don't make this list, your situation isn't hopeless. God can and does save us no matter how deep the pit of our own thoughts.

As with the evidences of trauma, don't borrow what isn't yours. Simply acknowledge what may be an inner judgment and vow you've operated under. If there are more that aren't on this list, I encourage you to write them down. We can't move in a new direction if we don't acknowledge that we're going in the wrong one today.

Judgment (I believe/I expect) (Therefore...) The Inner Vow

No one cares about me (...) I will have to take care of myself.

I can't trust anyone (...) I will never trust/open my heart

People let me down (...) I always have to do things on my own

Life is unfair (...) I will never be able to change things

Nobody likes me (...) I will be unfriendly first

I am ugly (...) I will hide myself

I am dumb (...) I will never succeed/never learn

All women are critical (...) I will never be vulnerable to them

I am no good (...) I will act out of my evil impulses

I don't deserve God's blessings (...) I will do it on my own

It's not safe to feel (...) I will never feel/be aware of my feelings

People betray me (...) I will never share my feelings with anyone

Dad never listens to me (...) I will make sure that people listen

Mom is controlling (...) I will never let anyone control me again

People don't accept me (...)I will put a wall around myself

Christians are hypocrites (...) I will not trust Christians

Pastors are authoritarians (...) I will not come under my pastor

Dad is a poor provider (...) I will always have money

Mom and Dad are terrible parents (...) I will never treat my kids that way

Mom is weak (…) I will never be pushed around and bullied

Dad is a horrible alcoholic (…) I will never drink/do drugs

Anger hurts people (…) I will never be angry

Men are abusive (…) I will never let a man touch me again

Dad is out of control (…) I will never be out of control

Mom and Dad don't love me (…) I will never let anyone love me

Men don't cry (…) I will never show my emotions

My opinions never matter (…) I will not share my emotions

People always go away (…) I will not give myself totally to anyone

My life is chaotic (…) I will always be logical and in control

It's not safe to grow up (…) I will never grow up/never mature

My needs will never be met (…) I will meet my own needs

Dad abandoned me/rejected me (…) I will not need anyone

I will never please a woman/man (…) I will not try/I will do everything I can to please

These are common judgments, common vows.

You'll find no condemnation on this side of the page for you having them. When I first discovered this list, I'd highlighted almost every single vow and judgment before I sat down to weep at my depravity!

We have to know where we are if we're going to have any idea of where we're going.

Beloved, you are the daughter of a King, clothed in Christ. You, having been baptized in the Holy Spirit, are now one with Christ, which means you have the mind of Christ (1 Corinthians 2:16).

Having the mind of Christ means you no longer need to operate out of your own strength and wisdom. You get to operate out of His! Not sure what's His and what's yours? Ask!

"If you need wisdom, ask our generous God, and he will give it to you. He will not rebuke you for asking" (James 1:5, NLT).

"But if you remain in me and my words remain in you, you may ask for anything you want, and it will be granted!" (John 15:7).

"Ask, and it will be given to you; seek, and you will find; knock, and it will be opened to you" (Matthew 7:7, ESV).

My friend, one of the most beautiful things about the God we get to serve is that He values your free will far more than you do. He is a gentleman. He will not force anything upon you - not even the answer to the question you long for most but refuse to ask.

I joyfully invite you to ask Him what His thoughts are for you. What are His thoughts toward the traumatic history you experienced? What does He say about your enemies, or about pain? When you have the answer, which is most often found in His Word, you get to choose to believe that, or choose to continue operating in the vow and judgment you've made.

I admit, the illusion of self-protective vow is quite convincing. But if you've lived in it long enough, you're beginning to see those vows that looked as a giant brick wall to keep out pain is starting to look a lot more like a prison you created for yourself.

When you begin to see the truth and take down the wall, it can feel terribly vulnerable. A bit like running naked through town. Thankfully, God has given us a weapon to equip us for the battle that comes when our self-protective wall is removed. No longer do we rely on vows and judgments to defend us, but His Word.

160

What does that look like exactly?

The Overcoming Mind

You are not a victim.

You can control your reactions to life. You always have a choice. Controlling our responses to negative situations is the difference between a healthy mind and body, and a sick mind and body. Choosing your perspective about past experiences as well as current circumstances determines the difference in your mental, emotional, physical and spiritual health.

In Christ, we do not have a spirit of fear, but of power, love and self-control (2 Timothy 1:7). The first step is believing you have this Spirit. If you don't, you need Jesus. In surrendering your life to Him He gives you His Holy Spirit as a gift! Girlfriend - take it!

It is impossible to help yourself apart from Jesus Christ.

Any effort to help yourself apart from Him will fall flat and disappoint - eventually - because you're trying to attain what cannot be attained apart from Jesus. Wholeness and completion and love (self-love and love for others) apart from the one who *is* love, complete and whole, is impossible. It will always fall short.

If you're too angry at God to receive any gift from Him - get the anger out and then take the gift. Move on. Your anger is paralyzing you and keeping you right where the enemy wants you: stuck. You certainly can't pull this off on your own, because the multi-billion-dollar self-help industry is incomplete. Yes, there are many helpful tools that allow us to help ourselves, but all the visualization and verbalization misses the basic elements required for success and change: God himself. You can't have successful living without the Creator of successful living residing inside of you in the Holy Spirit.

Our free will, another gift from God, is what enables us to choose God's path, or Satan's. Remember, there is a battle for your heart, and it begins in your mind.

So, what is it about our mind that makes this impossible task of standing in victory with Christ possible?

Dr. Caroline Leaf has done extensive research in this area and I highly encourage you to read her book *Switch on Your Brain* to get more insight and clarity about the science behind this information. Much of the information in this book is based on her research.

She writes, "Scientists are discovering precise pathways by which changes in human thinking operate as signals that activate genetic expression, which then produce changes in our brains and bodies. Our genetic makeup fluctuates *by the minute* based on what we are thinking and choosing. Clearly, then, following the advice of Philippians 4:8 will have a profound healing and regenerative impact on our bodies and minds by affecting our genetic expression: 'Finally, brothers and sister, whatever is true, whatever is noble, whatever is right, whatever is pure, whatever is lovely, whatever is admirable - if anything is excellent or praiseworthy - think about such things' (NIV)" (*emphasis mine*).

She goes on to write, "Genes may create an environment within us in which a problem may grow, a predisposition, but they do not produce the problem; we produce it through our choices. Our choices act as the signals that unzip the DNA."

Bottom line, what we choose to focus on will dictate what DNA we create within ourselves. Our genes are constantly being remodeled in response to our life's circumstances, and how we choose to respond to those circumstances dictates the direction of that remodel.

We are not victims of our biology.

You are not a victim of your circumstances. You are not a victim of your parents parenting skills - or lack thereof. You are not a byproduct of your environment. You are a co-creator of your destiny right beside your Abba Father.

He leads, but we must choose to let Him lead. We've been designed to create thoughts and it's by those thoughts we live every moment of our life in word and deed.

The scientific power of our mind to change the brain is called *epigenetics* and spiritually it is as a man thinks, so is he (Proverbs 23:7). The way the brain changes as a result of mental activity is scientifically called *neuroplasticity*. And spiritually, it is the renewing of the mind (Romans 12:2).

While we may be predisposed to certain things because of decisions made by our ancestors, we are responsible to be aware of those predispositions, evaluate them and choose to get rid of them. Choose to think differently. Choose to speak differently. Choose to live differently.

I love the way one person put it: think of your thoughts like various paths. There are six-lane highways and deer trails. Your brain is naturally lazy and will take the easiest route, unless your mind tells it to do otherwise. If you spent three hours watching the news and three minutes reading your Bible, your brain will take the route that has the most foot traffic.

What you feed grows, and if your thoughts are food for your mind, then whatever you think on will multiply.

The brain can get worse by constantly focusing on a problem, or it can get better by understanding how to eliminate and replace the problem. The brain changes as a result of mental activity.

Let's look at this in context of trauma.

"In post-traumatic stress disorder (PTSD), neuroplasticity has worked against the person. He or she has experienced a crushing mental event that fundamentally changed the meaning of their life and altered the brain structurally because of the neuroplasticity of the brain. During the trauma, the person's mind was not thinking in soul harmony (Colossians 3:15, AMP), so consequently he or she did not choose, process, or react correctly to the event making the thought that became wired in a jumbled toxic mess. As the person relives the event over and over, it wires itself deeper into the mind, becoming a main filter and disrupting normal function. Flashbacks - reliving the bad memory many times a day - strengthen the circuit, making it worse and more debilitating.

"The overriding concept is to apply neuroplasticity in the *correct* direction by rewiring the event with the positive thinking of Philippians 4:8... Thus, the person consciously chooses, preferably under the leading of the Holy Spirit, to bring the memory into consciousness where it becomes plastic enough to be changed. This means the physical substrate of the memory becomes weakened, vulnerable, malleable, and able to be manipulated. The person then chooses to replace the crushing mental event with the implanted word of God, which saves the soul (James 1:21). The person, as though an outsider looking in through a window, will observe the toxic, traumatic memory as a weakening and dying experience but, at the same time, observe the new healthy experience that is growing. In practicing this daily, the person wires the healthy new thoughts ever more deeply into the mind[17]."

As someone who continues to walk this out, I know the fear that rises at the idea of choosing to bring the memory of the traumatic event into consciousness. This is why it is imperative to have the guidance of the Holy Spirit, and the support of wise and Spirit-led people mentioned in an earlier chapter. You can't do it alone, and you certainly can't do it without Jesus Christ.

The enemy would have you believe that you can, but I will tell you from experience - you can't. The consequences of bringing a traumatic memory to the surface without the guidance and assistance and protection of people who love you, of the Holy Spirit who knows you completely, is asking to deepen a wound that already feels unbearable.

People can have excellent intentions and lack wisdom. "If anyone longs to be wise, as God for wisdom and he will give it!" (James 1:5). "There is a way that seems right to a man, but its end is the way to death" (Proverbs 14:12; 16:25). True wisdom comes from God alone.

The enemy wants to destroy you. The trauma you've faced is evidence of that already. He doesn't care what you rely on as long as you don't rely on Jesus Christ. The easiest substitute for God is self. Max Lucado put it well when it said, "Lack of God-centeredness leads to self-centeredness." Self-centeredness is never esteemed and always,

---

[17] Leaf, C. (2015). *Switch on your brain: the key to peak happiness, thinking, and health.* Grand Rapids, MI: Baker Books.

ultimately, fails. Only in Christ do you have the power to change the makeup of your mind and be restored in perfect relationship with the Father, in the original design God intended for your mind and body to be.

Bottom line, however, is if you don't believe - in Christ - you have the power to change, then you won't.

Healing can happen overnight but change often takes place over time and continual persistence. *Don't quit because you don't see immediate results.* The mind that has endured trauma went through a horrific experience, whether it was one occurrence of over the course of a lifetime. It doesn't matter whether it's been five hours or fifty years since it happened. It will take time, patience and intentional rewiring to restore what was broken.

It will take habitual meditation on God's word, persistence in His way, to take what was meant for evil and give God the freedom to use it for good (Genesis 50:20). It's by meditating on God's Word that our way is made prosperous (Joshua 1:8).

This isn't just about memorizing scripture or theoretically trusting God to make things right.

We must catch our thoughts as they come to mind, which means we must pay attention to what we're thinking about. "We demolish arguments and every pretension that sets itself up against the knowledge of God, and we take captive every thought to make it obedient to Christ (2 Corinthians 3:5, NIV). "Give attention to my words; incline your ear to my sayings. Do not let them depart from your eyes; keep them in the midst of your heart; for they are life to those who find them, and health to all their flesh" (Proverbs 4:20-22).

When we purposefully catch our thoughts, we can control the brain's sensory processing, rewiring, the neurotransmitters, the genetic expression, and the cellular activity in a positive *or negative* direction. We choose. I think of it like railroad tracks. Every time a thought comes to mind, we decide whether the direction of our thought will continue on a negative track or be rerouted to Christ-centeredness.

The final element to this is action.

Action completes the cycle of breaking down and building up thoughts. James 2:26 tells us faith without works is dead. Your brain becomes what you focus on, and what your brain has become produces what you say and do and how you feel mentally and physically.

It all starts in your mind.

Evidence of Trauma and Being Real

A quick recap:

You know how God designed the brain to function.

You know the physiological consequences of trauma on the brain.

You know your responsibility and the power you have in Christ to change your thought patterns, which will change the actual DNA of your brain and bring about healing.

You know that having PTSD isn't the end of the world, and you can be healed because you have access to the Healer. You're still breathing, so God still has a plan.

You know that the thing that separates you from healing lies primarily in your belief and choice.

We're going to take a brief look at the evidence of trauma. Brief, because I don't want to dwell on the consequences of sin as there is no life in that pattern of thinking. It is important, however, if you work with or have a personal relationship with someone who has had trauma in their life. Perhaps you suspect and are concerned about their current lifestyle. Having an awareness of the fruit of trauma can help us have compassion when we see those exhibiting those behaviors, and prayerfully move toward showing them the Healer.

No person can be forced into healing. You can't make a person want healing, and you can't force a person to accept the gift of healing. It's something they have to come to on their own, but your witness as having been healed of the symptoms of trauma and your love for them in spite of the difficult behaviors resulting from their symptoms, can be an enormous aid in guiding them toward our Jehovah Rapha, God who Heals.

Trauma is not black and white. It's not something you can fit into a box. In the years I've been working through my own trauma and helping others walk out healing in their own, I've learned that the damage caused by trauma is determined by the individual who experienced it. It manifests in many ways. This can depend on the temperament God gave you, the details of the circumstances and the age in which you lived out those circumstances, your coping skills, resilience, prior history and the care you received after the trauma took place.

But healing is possible in every situation.

Healing is not determined by anything other than the One in whom you place your hope and trust for healing. There are many therapies, but only one Cure. There are many doctors, but only one

Healer. The deeper the trauma lies, unaddressed, the more subtle the physical evidences of that trauma. Not all these means someone has endured trauma, but it's safe to say they are possible side effects of the physical body manifesting the trauma.

While not conclusive, it is worth exploring and discussing with those willing to share. Some of these are easily explained. The more chronic and unexplainable the symptoms, however the more it's worth considering the relationship to possible past trauma. Being willing to open a conversation about these symptoms can lead to a connection of trauma, and Lord-willing, to healing.

There are many types of trauma, and many books that focus on those types of trauma. Instead of dwelling on the trauma, my desire is to dwell on the Healer and provide you with guideposts of walking out healing on your journey, no matter what trauma you've faced.

Some of the evidences of trauma are not difficult to see with the naked eye.

Other evidences are less obvious.

Proverbs 15:13 says, "A happy heart makes the face cheerful, but heartache crushes the spirit" (NIV). Having a crushed spirit affects us emotionally, physically and spiritually but most of us are not aware of this crushing as an effect of a spirit weighed down by trauma. We see it as "just the way it is," or "I've always been this way" not realizing that this isn't true.

Trauma settles in our hearts and minds, which is transposed in our behavior, in one way or another if it isn't resolved. Unresolved trauma produces itself in the following "fruit." Use common sense in reading this list. If you haven't eaten breakfast and you feel pain in your stomach when you read about stomach pain, it's likely you're simply hungry. Don't borrow trouble, but be honest about what persisting, unreasonable and unexplainable symptoms you've experienced or are experiencing that could be a result of trauma. The body tends to manifest externally what's happening internally. This list is far from exhaustive, but it allows for a place to begin.

Invisible and Visible Fruit

- Changes in sleep patterns
- Loss of hair, changes in color, texture, etc.
- Easily startled
- Unexplained aches and pains: extreme weariness, Fibromyalgia, inflammation, arthritis, headaches/migraines, sinus problems, TMJ
- Reproductive difficulties: endometriosis, excessive menstrual bleeding/pain, infertility
- Frigidity/Promiscuity
- Cardiovascular system: Heart disease, blood pressure, breathing difficulties
- Bones and Bone Marrow disease (Proverbs 17:22; 18:14)
- Immune System: constantly fighting infections, colds, etc., long recovery times, autoimmune disease, cancer
- Bowels: Irritable Bowel Syndrome, colitis
- Kidneys: Urinary tract infections, kidney disease
- Stomach: Ulcers, chronic acid reflux
- Sensory organs

- Memory: conscious, sub-conscious, body memory
- Dreams
- Nightmares
- Lack of dreams
- Flashbacks
- PTSD

It's important to note that God does not take away our memories of the trauma. Nor does He change history in any way. He does, however, change the effect of history. Anytime we revisit our past apart from the redemptive blood of Jesus, we revisit a lie. When we believe the lie, the memory of the past apart from the redemptive work of Christ, we reinforce and strengthen the liar and give him a tighter grip on our present.

It strengthens the vows and judgments and keeps us outside of the truth of scripture, and therefore outside of the protection of God's Word and will.

God is a god of truth and He desires truth in us. This means we don't deny the bad thing that happened, and we don't pretend or imagine it was something else. I don't pretend I was snuggling with a giant teddy bear when I remember the trauma of my brother coming into my room at nap time to sexually harm me. I acknowledge it for the sin it is, the harm that was done, and thank God that He sent His son to bear the pain and burden of that sin against me and take *all* the condemnation that went with it.

This means I no longer have to live condemned because of what my brother did to me. I get to live in the state of being a beloved daughter of a just King who knew someone had to pay for what my brother did to me, and that I needed to be rescued from that suffering. So, He sent His Son, essentially, He sent Himself, to pay the price for that sin, and to be my defender and rescuer. Rather than carry the chains of condemnation, I get to wear the robe of righteousness being clothed in Christ (Galatians 3:27).

This means that instead of denying the past, we can talk about it. We share what we can with a trusted individual who allows the Holy Spirit to set the pace. Give the Holy Spirit permission to reveal the things that have been hidden or forgotten that may be a stumbling block in moving forward.

If you're exploring this for yourself and nothing comes to the surface, don't push it. Again, *don't borrow trouble*. If God has decided you don't need to remember then take it as a blessing and move on! If you can't remember, then let it stay dormant! Often in our attempt to *make* memories surface we end up creating a memory that never actually took place. If it's not there, it's not. If it is, let it be there and stand under the redemptive blood of Jesus.

Acknowledging the past, facing the trauma, doesn't mean we have to re-live the trauma. The pain of the past does not need to be repeated in order to be healed. Jesus bore that pain for us on the cross (Isaiah 53:4-5) and it was by His wounds we are healed (1 Peter 2:24). We don't need to re-experience our wounds in order to be healed. We simply need to recognize the wounds we have faced, the scars we do carry, in order for His suffering to have its full effect in our life.

The memory itself doesn't hold any power to destroy or cause harm. That's the lie. The truth is our past becomes our testimony of God's goodness and love. Not the trauma itself, but the healing Christ did on the cross for us today so that our trauma no longer gets to hold us captive. We've all been broken. Only Jesus heals, and He came in order to heal the sick. If you can't admit you're sick, then why would you need Jesus at all?

The Truth of Your Identity

Your primary weapon is so simple a child could wield it. In fact, you must become child-like in order to use it (Matthew 18:2-4).

It's truth. The truth alone will set you free (John 8:32).

In case I haven't drilled it home well enough yet: your decision to surrender the lies in exchange for the truth will determine your healing. The lies created by trauma, for the truth of who Jesus says you are in Christ. The lies we create because of our experiences, exchanged for the truth of what Jesus is doing in us in the spirit-realm to be manifested in the physical as we walk in love void of fear.

The life you choose to lead, determined by what you decide to believe, determines your destiny.

It's not complicated.

Who you believe you are is the thing that drives you to choose what kind of life you'll live. No circumstance, good or bad, can dictate the direction of your life. How you choose to live in response to your circumstances, and by what values and truths, determines the course of your life. You may not be where you planned to be, but you can be who you want to be - who you were destined to be. Who you believe you are bypasses everything else set up to help you succeed, or fail, and becomes the lifeline to which you can cling through anything thrown at you. Most of us are programmed to believe what our caretakers tell us. They are our entire world from the very beginning in the birth canal to about the age of six. Those formative years are pivotal in shaping our identity.

But no matter what we've been told about who we are, no matter what we've been programmed to believe, we get to decide whether or not we want to live by that definition, or by the definition of being a son or daughter to the King of kings. You can be in your seventies reading this for the first time, and it's just as possible to change who you believe you are. The only thing that stops you is your willingness to believe.

One common theme I've noticed in my years of working with women and teenagers who have been victims of trauma, is most of them come from severely broken homes. Parents who have no grasp of their own identity pass on the messages they exist on to their children. They start with a shaky foundation. They endure trauma, and the foundation shatters.

Squeeze a lemon and lemon juice gushes out. Squeeze a grapefruit and you get grapefruit juice. Too many parents have immeasurable pain and bitterness inside, and children are excellent at revealing their flaws they try so hard to hide. Threatened, parents lash out at their children and what comes out is what's been there all along: self-hatred now targeted at their child, resentment, fear, doubt, insecurity, etc.

The child grows up with such things being normal, and they adopt them as a way of life while never knowing the truth of who they are. Being blind to the truth doesn't change the truth.

We all have a choice.

I lived in Okinawa, Japan while I was in the Marine Corps and discovered it is typically the number one or number two rated country with the oldest people on it. It's not uncommon for men and women to live to the age of one hundred here. This gave me a beautiful bit of exposure to generational differences. The oldest generation still remembers World War II and the atrocities that happened on the island of Okinawa during the war in the Pacific. Many are still very angry and resistant to an American presence (more than 10 military bases occupy the island that is 63 miles long and 4 miles wide). The next generation, what American's call the baby-boomers, are more open to an American presence but primarily from an economic standpoint. They see the benefits the American military has on their country economically and are willing to set aside whatever resentments may still exist for a greater purpose.

Millennial's are far more removed from the influence of the oldest generation. They see the benefits of the American military presence economically and are willing to get to know Americans individually on a more personal level as well. They've integrated some American cultural habits while not abandoning their own and are more likely to be seen having coffee or a beer with an American than their two older generations. The last generation, Gen-Z, the teenagers and younger, are almost completely opposite their great-grandparents in their desire to adopt all things American into their lives. They adhere to Okinawan culture out of respect and honor to their family, but you'll find them enamored with American pop culture, media, clothing lines and celebrities in ways the previous three generations are not.

Within each generation a choice was made that bypassed the individual's upbringing and cultural norms. In both directions someone either chose to hold fast to their resentment, or reject it, regardless of what the generation after and before decided to do. A decision was made about who the individual was going to be.

So, who are you?

It's important to note that we are never able to just decide our identity in a way that wipes clean the slate of what we began with. For years I determined that I was going to be strong, fierce and I would accomplish amazing things. I was going to prove people wrong - that I could do anything I put my mind to!

Not realizing that my very determination to make these decisions about who I was going to be was in direct response to who others said I already was! If I was too emotional than I was adamant I would be tough as nails because apparently being too emotional was a bad thing. I didn't decide to be tough because I thought being tough was a good thing all by itself, but because being sensitive was received as a negative trait. I was simply reacting to a negative response with what I thought would bring me less pain, not because it was something I thought was good or would help me in my future or was even true.

So, I became something I wasn't sure I really wanted to be because I thought it would achieve a less negative response than being too sensitive to emotions. Only to find out that being tough as nails is isolating and painful in a way all on its own. By my early twenties I found myself too afraid to let my emotions show up out of fear of being rejected again, and my tough approach was turning my heart into stone and turning away people away with whom I wanted to be in relationship. Now what? Was there something in between?

It was about this time that I decided to change from being a believer in Jesus to being a follower of Jesus. Hearing how He provided the way, the truth and was the life I sought after grabbed my attention. I was dying inside, and I knew it. I grabbed his robe with both hands and when I came out of the waters of baptism... I was found, but still felt lost. I knew I was on solid ground, but I also knew I had a very long way to go to get where I wanted to be.

I belonged to Christ, and yet I still had every vow and judgment I ever made wreaking havoc on my soul. I was saved, but the sanctification process was just beginning.

I thought I knew what it meant to surrender, but the full extent of that would, by God's grace, come to me in pieces as I was able to handle them. The next eight years of my walk with Him has been one of a whole lot of trial, even more error, and an abundance of grace and mercy that drowned all of it.

What I've discovered in those years is why I decided to write this book. The Word of God promises healing of mind, body and soul so I refused to settle for only one of those to be healed - I wanted it all! I still have much to learn, but I will say the pivotal factor, the final shift of the puzzle piece that tied everything together was wrapped up in one vital, and painfully simple, concept:

My identity.

It's not enough to call myself a Christian. It's not even enough to do all the things I'm supposed to do as a Christian. There are 623 laws and 10 commandments in the Bible and only one man was ever able to fulfill them all. The only thing that changes everything and brings the healing promised in scripture is Christ and the cross. What He did for you and me, so we can be who we were destined to be, and already are, in the eyes of our Father. If I can help you wrap your heart and mind around who you already are, the decisions you make in response to that identity will change everything about you and the life you live.

Trauma will no longer be a wall, but fuel for the plan the Father has for your life. It will be the place from which Jesus rescued you from, rather than the place you're continually trying to avoid and hide from yourself and the world.

It's only when you know the truth of who you are to God that you'll be able to move forward.

So many of us are aware of this, and yet at the root of our intellectual knowing is a question we're often too scared to ask or say out loud. "God, are you good? Do you even care that this is happening (or has happened) to me?"

When we know who we are to Christ, we'll know the answer to that question. We first need to establish that the Word of God is truth - every bit of it. It is the first part of the armor Paul tells us to put on (Ephesians 6:14) before anything else because every other piece of armor hangs on the truth.

That truth, that extends beyond our intellect, is God. We must be willing to let go of everything we know (intellectually) to know (experientially) who He is, and in turn who we are. We can't pick and choose which of His words are true based on our understanding and wisdom. He is truth, regardless of our ability to grasp it. If we decide the Bible is true in one part, then it must be true in all.

In Christ, you have a very clear identity. The following list was pulled from Neil T. Anderson's book *The Bondage Breaker*[18] and is just a few examples of who God says you are. I encourage you to go to the scripture in your own Bible, or on an app on your phone, and don't just take my word for it. Then, speak your identity out loud.

I am Accepted:

1 John 1:12	I am God's child.
John 15:15	I am Christ's friend.
Romans 5:1	I have been justified.
1 Corinthians 6:17	I am united with the Lord and one with Him in Spirit.
1 Corinthians 6:20	I have been bought with a price - I belong to God.
1 Corinthians 12:27	I am a member of Christ's body.
Ephesians 1:1	I am a saint.
Ephesians 1:5	I have been adopted as God's child.
Ephesians 2:18	I have direct access to God through the Holy Spirit.
Colossians 1:14	I have been redeemed and forgiven of all my sins.
Colossians 2:10	I am complete in Christ.

I am Secure:

---

[18] Anderson, N. T. (2006). *The bondage breaker.* Eugene, Or.: Harvest House.

Romans 8:1-2	I am free from condemnation.
Romans 8:28	I am assured that all things work together for good.
Romans 8:31-34	I am free from any condemning charges against me.
Romans 8:35-39	I cannot be separated from the love of God.
2 Corinthians 1:21-22	I have been established, anointed, and sealed by God.
Colossians 3:3	I am hidden with Christ in God.
Philippians 1:6	I am confident that the good work that God has begun in me will be perfected.
Philippians 3:20	I am a citizen of heaven.
2 Timothy 1:7	I have not been given a spirit of fear but of power, love and a sound mind.
Hebrews 4:16	I can find grace and mercy in time of need.
1 John 5:18	I am born of God and the evil one cannot touch me.

I am Significant:

Matthew 5:13	I am the salt and light of the earth.
John 15:1, 5	I am a branch of the true vine, a channel of His life.
John 15:16	I have been chosen and appointed to bear fruit.
Acts 1:8	I am a personal witness of Christ's.
1 Corinthians 3:16	I am God's temple.
2 Corinthians 5:17-20	I am a minister of reconciliation.

2 Corinthians 6:1	I am God's coworker.
Ephesians 2:6	I am seated with Christ in the heavenly realm.
Ephesians 2:10	I am God's workmanship
Ephesians 3:12	I may approach God with freedom and confidence.
Philippians 4:13	I can do all things through Christ who strengthens me.

I don't know about you, but the first time I read that I was a little skeptical. My whole life has been filled with messages of the exact opposite.

The enemy surrounds us with deception - in our relationships, our circumstances, the media, and every other nook and cranny he can sink his little teeth into. He will do whatever it takes to convince us the lie is the truth and when we doubt him, he'll use intimidation to bully us into believing him. In one of Graham Cooke's podcasts on being a spiritual warrior he said, "Intimidation is the normal tactic of the enemy. The antidote of intimidation is always the intimacy that we have with the nature of God."

Intimacy. Knowing Him, with the same knowing that happens between husband and wife.

As someone who spent most of her life seeing intimacy and terror as synonymous, this has been one of the most difficult things to grasp. Intimacy with God is the antidote of intimidation. When I know who I am to the Father in Christ, and have experienced that intimacy with the Father, intimidation falls flat.

The enemy is crafty. He sows his lie with a kernel of truth, and he uses things we already trust to add credibility to the lie, so it's often very difficult to discern what is God and what isn't. *This is why relationship with the Father, intimacy with the Son, is so vital.*

It's only when you know the voice of Father in an intimate relationship with Him that you'll be able to recognize the difference between God's voice and the voices of the world and the enemy and yourself. The only thing that can help us differentiate between the truth of the Word and the lie of the enemy is knowing the voice of our Father (John 10:27). The only way to know His voice is to spend time with him, and like any relationship spending time takes time. We can't expect the investment of an hour produce the fruit of ten hours.

We need to remember that the enemy only has as much authority in your life as you give him. As intimidating as he can appear, the world is covered in his fingerprints of destruction, sorrow and pain, it's not the actual events that destroy us.

It's how we decide to receive and respond to those events.

If you know, beyond a shadow of a doubt, who you are in Christ, and you stand securely in that identity, there is no power in heaven or on earth that can derail you. In Christ, your authority is far above the enemy's and while he may be able to wipe out everything you have, take away everything you cherish and strip you down to nakedness (consider the story of Job), he still has no authority outside of what you give him.

The enemy can't take away a future you don't give him.

If your identity is wrapped up in what God says about you - you are His temple, you have not been given a spirit of fear, the evil one cannot touch you, you are God's workmanship, you are complete in Christ, you are God's child... then you'll face loss and be pressed and persecuted, but you won't be crushed or abandoned (2

Corinthians 4:8-10). You'll have security in knowing the One who created the entire world in seven days will take care of you and your family, and though much was lost, He promises He will give you everything you need.

Everything means everything; emotional, spiritual and physical.

Nothing is more foundational and essential to your freedom than your belief in your identity in Christ. We've already seen how science has proved that what you believe has a direct influence on how you live. If you believe you are a helpless victim of Satan or circumstances, bound to be in bondage the rest of your life then you'll act like it and fulfill the very thing you believed. Essentially, it's your own belief that makes it a reality! Why not choose something different to believe in? When we change what we believe and live in that belief with our words and our actions, our lives change.

I know this is difficult to grasp in its simplicity.

Is it just about what I believe? *Yes.* Because belief determines your thoughts, and your thoughts become your words and your words become your actions. It's not about denying trauma and the very real effects of that trauma. Nor is it about minimizing or diminishing that trauma, but about owning the reality of what happened and letting the rock of Christ be the foundation upon which you stand as He shows you what He will do with what the enemy tried to use to destroy you. What He says about you cannot be stained by the trauma. Who He says you are cannot be diminished by trauma.

Having been baptized into Christ you are now sealed for eternity in heaven, given the Holy Spirit as proof of that seal - a sort of wedding ring tattooed on your heart (Ephesians 1:13-14). You are also now given the power to walk according to the Spirit, and not according to your old ways - the ways of the flesh (Galatians 5:16). Old habits can now die off because you have a new way revealed in the Word of God, and the Holy Spirit of life enabling you to take those steps as you grow in maturity in Christ (Ephesians 4:11-14).

With continual, persistence in thinking like Christ, speaking life, and then walking it out.

How does this grasp of our identity make any difference in your current circumstances?

"Each of us can go only as far as God has given us permission to go. Our authority grows as our maturity in Christ grows. By knowing who God is for us we never have to be afraid of our circumstances[19]." It's not an overnight experience, but a process of sanctification that takes time, patience and an absolute refusal to give up. The enemy won't like you changing your mind, and I can almost guarantee he'll start throwing even more at your feet to convince you of the lie he's had you convinced of for years, but the power and control remains in your hands.

Not God's, but yours.

We tend to think that God needs to be the one to make change. Truthfully, He's already given us all the tools and power we need. It's up to us to use those tools and trust He's going to come through the way He promises when we act. It's not His power apart from us, nor is it our power, but His power through us.

Consider a light switch. If you walk into a dark room, you can call the power company all day and tell them to turn the power on.

---

[19] Cooke, G. (2004). *The language of love: hearing and speaking the language of God*. Grand Rapids, MI: Chosen Books.

They're going to tell you that the power is already on, *you have to turn on the light switch!*

Flip the switch and trust the light will appear.

Act, and trust that God will respond the way He promises He will.

The fact is, if we are in Christ, we've already won the battle against the enemy and everything he throws at us - including trauma. The victory is already in our hands. There's nothing left to do but stand on that promise. That's why in Ephesians 6 as Paul talks about putting on the armor of God, he doesn't tell us to charge into battle. He simply tells us to stand firm and fight from our place of victory. We're never told to rebuke the enemy; we're told to submit to Jesus and resist the enemy. Submit to the truth Jesus says about you and resist the lies the enemy has for you by standing on the infallible Word of God.

The sword of the Spirit, God's Word, is the weapon we use to cut down every lie the enemy that tries to use to shove us off our rightful place beside our Father. We focus on that, on the truth, not on the lies, and watch the power of His Word work on our behalf.

For most of my life I've believed that any man I ever let close to me will only, inevitably, fail me. Not only that, but the ones that should matter most to me will do the worst. Any man meant to be a protector will do the most harm. They can't be trusted. They'll rape and/or sexually assault me, they'll ignore me when I cry out for help, they'll treat my pain as an inconvenience, they'll consider me a burden, they'll lie and do whatever it takes to do whatever they can to hurt me, and there's nothing I can do about it.

As I developed my relationship with Jesus, I began to see that I was limiting how close I was allowing myself to get with the Lord because I believed that He, too, would do what every other man had already done. Vows and judgments were severely limiting my life.

I was allowing life experience to determine my future. As I began letting God inch closer - he's a gentleman and will not go where you will not let Him - I began to learn what I'd believed and experienced my whole life wasn't necessarily the truth. It was a very real experience, but my past didn't have to be my future. My experience with men as a direct reflection of their failing to live out their true identity in Christ, not a reflection of the character of God. Nor a reflection of who I was.

Several years ago, I met a man and I fell in love. He was kind, a gentleman, dependable, took care of me, enjoyed me and never pushed me the way other men had in my past. He wooed me with his words and his charm and his willingness to do just about anything for me. Eighteen months after we met, he asked me to marry him. I was terrified, but I took a leap of faith and said yes. I was scared he'd end up just like every other man in my life and the more I prayed about it the more I kept hearing God say, "Trust me."

I began to believe that my husband would be different. From what I could see in my relationship with this man up to that point, he was a godly man who loved the Lord and wanted a righteous marriage. Anyone who tries to follow scripture and has the humility to admit when they're wrong is worth a chance, after all. What more could I ask for?

As I write this, eighteen months after we got married, I'm in the process of a divorce. Things began to change a few months into our marriage. The man I thought I married turned out to be a facade. He openly admitted to tricking me into marrying him, withholding things from his past that he knew would have stopped me from marrying him had I known the truth, as well as things he was still involved in. When the sin of his sexual addiction and pathological deception came to light, I did everything I could think of to try to get us help. He refused to repent and tried to make the struggle in our marriage about my being too damaged from my past to make our marriage work.

To say that I began a downward spiral is an understatement.

After a decade of trying to rebuild my mind to healthier, biblical thinking, I felt his deception threaten to destroy the work God and I had done in me. I felt his betrayal rip open the wounds of my past as though they happened yesterday. What made this situation worse in every way, in my mind, was I had entered a covenant relationship with this man. There are very few biblical reasons for divorce and even if I did have biblical reason, God still hated divorce. Was God going to punish me by keeping me in a marriage that tore apart the very thing I'd spent the last decade trying to build? Is every man like this? Will every man I entrust myself to eviscerate me?

Will God?

What followed was a very dark and difficult season. One that I can say I'm walking out of, after nearly a year since my divorce. In that year, however, God's faithfulness amid blinding pain and tears has been overwhelming. I began taking my dog on long hikes through the woods near our house, praying and crying out to God for clarity and understanding. More than anything, however, I begged, pleaded and demanded for God to show me who He was and who I was to Him.

Prove it! I shouted on more than one occasion.

I'd been learning and growing in learning to love others for years but was still stumbling through the process of learning how to be loved. How to receive love from the Father. The enemy has given me reason after reason to believe I am unlovable. My husband's betrayal was one giant rock on a very big pile.

In the midst of all this God asked: "Who do you say that I am?"(Matthew 16:15).

The most helpful thing in my present circumstances has been, strangely, irrelevant to my circumstances. It occurred to me that no matter what I face, no matter what happens in the world or what the enemy does to me, none of it will change who Jesus is and what He's already done on the cross.

If I believe, then nothing can take that away (Romans 8:38-39). The only thing that can separate me from the love of Christ is my refusal to accept it.

Not even the betrayal of my husband can take away the sacrificial love Jesus has already given me, proving my value and worth to the Almighty, my heavenly Father. The only thing my husband's betrayal reveals, is his own lack of understanding of what Jesus has done for him.

What will you believe? Who do you say Jesus is?

Who do you say you are?

Contrary to popular opinion, time does not heal all wounds. Time can work as an anesthesia to the wounds, and time can help you forget the details of the wounds, but the wounds remain. It doesn't matter if you ignore a broken arm, it will remain broken until you decide to do something about it. Otherwise it will heal in such a way that it will never function the way it was designed to in the first place and there will always be an ache; an understanding that something just isn't right.

The heart is no different.

You have every right to be free from bondage. You were never designed to live in suffering and pain, and while you have learned to function during it, you were created with a much greater and more fulfilling purpose. You were created to live in love; whole and complete.

Discerning the truth takes time, patience and desire, but it is possible. His Word says you already have a place in victory that you don't have to fight to get to - you're already there.

Take a moment to rest in that.

Then and Now

We're not meant to have the whole picture. If we did, I don't think we'd give God much of a chance. We're meant to have the next step, and then the step after that. When scripture says His word is a lamp to my feet and a light to my path, it isn't talking about streetlights that flood the next ten to twelve feet. It's literally talking about a small flame from an oil lamp in your hand that provides *the next step*.

Sometimes I look back on my journey and I wonder how on earth God got me from where I was to where I am. How did he do it? I couldn't go through an entire day without a severe panic attack. I couldn't sleep, and when I could the nightmares were horrific. I became dependent on medication to get through the day. As mentioned earlier, the safer someone appeared the more dangerous they were. I would try to ensure people liked me but didn't want - or at least didn't try - to get too close to me. The one person I did allow close enough became a twisted, demonic, homosexual relationship, claiming to act in love when it was in direct contradiction to the Word of God.

I threw myself into various addictions to numb or avoid the perceived pain of memories that were triggered by the most unexpected events. I drank far too much and was borderline a functioning alcoholic. I smoked cigarettes compulsively. I cleaned. I shopped. I gave up drinking (as much) to exercise obsessively. When that stopped being as effective, I worked constantly, averaging seventy hours a week while going to school full time. I stopped sleeping. I became a Pharisee, determined to learn everything about the Bible and about God to be right before Him, only to fail miserably and yet still desperate for what I was reading in His Word and yet having no idea how to grasp it.

Unfortunately, even this wasn't enough to stop the flashbacks, the nightmares, depression or cynicism. No amount of avoidance made my anxiety disappear, nor did it help my incredibly short fuse. The smallest things infuriated me or drove me to choking sobs that made absolutely no sense in context.

The more I read the Bible the more I shifted my focus to serving others. I joined ministry after ministry and served in my church. I traveled around the world doing humanitarian work. I was striving, sprinting as fast as I could, away from the memories, the pain, the shame and the gut-wrenching guilt for the ways I responded to the pain. I hurt people as I held myself and others to impossible legalistic standards.

I felt broken, cut off from God, and every effort I made to make myself better, to make myself get over what had happened, simply led me down a self-destructive path disguised as self-preservation. I thought I knew who Jesus was, but I was absolutely and undoubtedly lost as to the truth.

It wasn't until I joined a group of women who loved Jesus, had an intimate relationship with him, and were devoted to sharing the love of Jesus that I began to see. I saw the love of Christ in their eyes and I would start to cry for no reason. I couldn't explain it, but I encountered Jesus through them. As I sought to know what they knew, I began to have ears to hear the truth. On a mountain top God invited me to rip up a root of unbelief, to be willing to sacrifice all I thought I knew and trusted and depended on, to have the truth instead.

"Will you trust me?" he asked.

As I write this, that was nearly two years ago.

It's been two years of confession, repentance, and learning how to be who God says I already am. Renewing my mind to the truth of scripture. Losing everything I thought mattered, to gain everything that really did matter.

I'm learning how to live in a place of dependence on God, being still and waiting for Him to do what only He can while I rest in who He says I am. I'm complete in Christ, but I'm far from finished. I'm whole because He is whole, but I am still being sanctified. I am righteous because I'm covered in the blood of Christ, but God is far from done with me yet.

My hope is that as you read the following chapters you'll learn from my mistakes, my hang-ups and take the truth to heart. If you don't remember anything else from this book, remember that what you believe about who you are will determine your entire future. There's what God says, and there's everything else. The only thing that matters is what He says.

CHAPTER SIX
GETTING RIGHT FIRST

Your Book in Heaven

Did you know that you were predestined before the foundation of the world?

Did you know that before you were even an inkling in your parents' eyes, before you were even conceived, your entire life, moment-by-moment, was written by God in a book in heaven?

Or that as you were growing in your mother's womb, it was the Lord Himself who was knitting you together (Psalm 139:13)?

Or that on the cross He carved your name on the palms of His hands and would have died there even if you were the only person on the planet - ever (Isaiah 49:16)?

Beloved, you are so incredibly treasured it's simply unfathomable. You are God's workmanship, His masterpiece, and He gave up His perfect Son before you were born because He knew you'd be here one day. He knew you'd be taken away from Him the moment you came into this world and took your first breath of sin-filled air. He has always been, and always will be, forever pursuing your heart. Even if you already have an incredible relationship with Him, it's nothing compared to what He has for you tomorrow, or ten years from now, or fifty years from now.

You have a book in heaven that He personally wrote. As a writer, this just tickles me. I like to believe God used a quill made from the feather of one of His own wings, and hand-wrote every moment, using His own blood and tears as the ink. He painstakingly considered every element of life, anticipating and preparing for every work of the enemy and established every back door and way of escape the enemy wouldn't have any clue about. I can imagine His smile, his laughter, and His sorrow, as he depicted to the Holy Spirit what He would have to do to help you grasp the depth of His love for you.

Perhaps the most beautiful, and the most terrible part of this book is that it contains every detail of pain and sorrow, love and joy.

The enemy is aptly named the Accuser, because that's what he sets out to do. While he can't read our thoughts, he's been at this job of lying, stealing, destroying, killing and accusing for quite a while. He can see what even we can't. He is constantly pointing out the holes in our character, the stains on our hearts and the multitude of reasons we fall short and don't deserve a relationship with the Most Holy God, much less His defense.

Apart from Christ, the enemy is right. We don't deserve this relationship, and every person who's ever taken a breath falls short of the glory of God (Romans 3:23).

But Jesus. He stands beside the Father interceding on our behalf (Romans 8:34). His blood covers us and makes us righteous.

Even better than this, when He calls us and says to come to Him for rest, He also says, "Take my yoke upon you. Let me teach you," (Matthew 11:29a). Earlier he calls us to seek the kingdom of God above all else, *and his righteousness*, and we'll have everything we need (Matthew 6:33).

The kingdom and his righteousness. His righteousness, not our own. His doing, not ours. His purity, not ours. His right-standing with the Father. It's only in what He has done that we can stand before the Father at all. Part of your book in heaven involves the entirety of your guilt being wiped clean - past, present and future. You get to live from a perpetual state of *now* that never becomes tomorrow and is never stained with yesterday.

When you understand that God wrote your entire life, your whole book is planned out, suddenly there's something to discover. Life is no longer about me deciding what I'm going to do with my life, and more a matter of getting so close to the heart of God I get to discover what He planned for my life and the love that consumes every moment of that plan.

This doesn't mean you don't have choice. It means we get to choose to align ourselves with that book and his sovereign will, or not.

So, what happens when we slip? We all do. What happens when we find ourselves being accused, whether we deserve it or not? How do we get out from under that oppression? How do we get back on track?

God's Responsibility

God's purity demands an eradication of sin. To obliterate all of it from the earth. The fury we feel toward the one who stripped us of our dignity, eviscerated us of our humanity by stealing our delight and joy in desire is a microcosm of the fury God feels toward the sin itself. But God, in his infinite mercy, does not allow Himself to destroy humanity though she's steeped in sin. In His unfathomable grace, He chooses to restore us instead. He harbors a divine compassion for His children we can't begin to fathom.

It's important to remember that *anything* not of God in word, deed and motive, is sin. While there are degrees of sin, God must either wipe out all sin or continue to be patient in seeking and waiting for as many to come to Him for salvation and restoration as possible. He does work out all things for the good of those who love Him - if we let Him. In order to do this, it means walking through the agony of our shame, pain, and grief with God so He can bring us healing in relationship with Him.

Healing isn't on the other side of God, or through God, but *in God*. Healing isn't a removal of the effects of sin or the sin itself, but rather an intimate relationship with the One who overturned the consequences of sin by becoming sin and raising from the dead. He showed that even the consequences of sin are no match for the power and love of God. God's goodness is displayed by sending His Son to suffer on our behalf.

We don't have to suffer - Jesus did it for us.

2 Peter 2:24 says "He himself bore our sins in his body on the tree, that we might die to sin and live to righteousness. By his wounds you have been healed" (ESV). Notice it reads "have been" - past tense. Not 'will be' or 'can be' but *have been*.

Jesus made it very clear in his last breath on the cross: "When Jesus had received the sour wine, he said, 'It is finished,' and he bowed his head and gave up his spirit" (John 19:30). There's nothing left to do. Jesus did it all.

Does this mean we'll never experience pain? No. The Lord spoke to Ananias about Paul saying, "For I will show him how much he must suffer for the sake of my name" (Acts 9:16). Later Paul said, "For I consider that the sufferings of this present time are not worth comparing with the glory that is to be revealed to us" (Romans 8:18). And again, "For it has been granted to you that for the sake of Christ you should not only believe in him but also suffer for his sake, engaged in the same conflict that you saw I had and now hear that I still have" (Philippians 1:29-30).

Suffering is part of the journey. However, Paul found peace in all circumstances that surpassed the understanding of the physical world. "Do not be anxious about anything, but in everything by prayer and supplication with thanksgiving let your requests be made known to God. And the peace of God, which surpasses all understanding, will guard your hearts and minds in Christ Jesus" (Philippians 4:6-7).

A few verses later Paul goes on to say, "I know how to be brought low, and I know how to abound. In any and every circumstance, I have learned the secret of facing plenty and hunger, abundance and need. I can do all things through him who strengthens me" (v.12-13).

Paul's contentment wasn't in doing anything that would make sense or result in physical action on this side of glory. He prayed, gave thanks to the Lord, made his request known and had faith in what was already done. The strength of Christ in him is what gave peace and the ability to be content. It's not a passiveness, but an active faith trusting in what has already been done on the cross.

What does this mean practically?

Choose life. Choose to believe. It's so simple, and yet it's so difficult for us to comprehend the simplicity of such faith because it's a level of self-denial that is, apart from the power of the Holy Spirit, impossible.

The Courts v. the Battlefield

When we find ourselves in a place of persecution, need, pain and fear we must go before the Judge. We start by praying. Prayer opens the doors to the court room and places us in the seat of the defendant.

God is our Judge (Psalm 76:8-9; 89:14) and He is a righteous one. This means He cannot bend the laws He created in order to execute judgment. There must be a penalty for sin, just like there must be a penalty in any courtroom for someone who has broken the laws of our government.

In Revelation 19:11 we read about the vision John had of Jesus return: "Then I saw heaven opened, and behold, a white horse! The one sitting on it is called Faithful and True, and in righteousness he judges and makes war."

This order is important. He judges, and then he makes war. This "judging" is referring specifically to a judicial activity, like what we see happen in a physical room. The action, or battle, takes place after the court date. We need to step into the court room before we think of stepping onto the battlefield. If we haven't gotten the verdict from our Father, the Judge, before we go into war with the enemy, we are sure to lose.

Satan is roaming the earth looking for those he can devour (1 Peter 5:8). He can only devour those he has legal reason and the whole reason he's walking around is to gather evidence to accuse and be granted legal right to destroy. Sometimes this is why we see bad things happen to good people. Somewhere in their life or ancestry the devil finds a legal right to bring destruction. Our response to persecution shouldn't be to jump into the battlefield, but to go to the court room. When you sit in the courtroom and accept the gift of redemption and salvation, of no condemnation through Jesus taking your punishment on the cross, you set fire to the evidence. Jesus took your punishment, so there's no longer any reason you can't receive what God has destined for you.

Bad things happen in a fallen world. This is the devastating effects of sin. Bad things happen to good people. Evil is rampant. Just turn on the television and you'll see it.

Because we were born in sin, we are no exception. Every one of us deserves hell. Anything good that happens apart from hell on earth is evidence of God's mercy and grace.

Records show I was first sexually abused when I was three years old, and it continued and got worse until I was a teenager. How does a child *deserve* sexual abuse? No child deserves it. Unfortunately, children are not exempt to the consequences of living in a fallen world. I will say that the abuse I endured as a little girl contributed to my selfish-ambition, bitterness and hard-hearted character. When I was old enough to know the difference between right and wrong and make decisions about who I was going to become, it became my responsibility to repent of the effects of that trauma.

The abuse was never my fault, just like your abuse was never your fault. However, what we do with that trauma is in our hands alone. It is this response the enemy grabs hold of as evidence to God to withhold the destiny He has written in our book of life.

No matter how justified we are, no matter how right it seems to hate the one who harmed us, no matter how good it feels to withhold forgiveness, it is always outside of God's will. If we're unwilling to walk in the will of the Father, we're unwilling to accept what His Son did for us, and therefore we condemn ourselves. God, as a just and righteous God, has no choice but to allow the enemy to wreak havoc because we are unwilling to accept the defense the Judge Himself offers us through His Son on the cross.

If we lean on ourselves and justify our sinful actions with good intentions or comparisons ("at least I'm not like Hitler") we condemn ourselves because no one is righteous or justified before God (Romans 3:23; 8:8) no matter how good we are. By accepting God's defense for us, it means we have to lay down our own. Our justifications for our behavior and attitudes must be put at the foot of the cross.

If, however, we look to Jesus as our defender, and we accept the covenant relationship He extends to us, the covering of His blood shed for us by the perfect Son sent to slaughter on our behalf, every punishment that we ever deserved lands on His shoulders and we are set free. There is no condemnation for those in Christ (Romans 5:7-11; 8:1). So, when we step into the court room in prayer, it's our job to first repent and be reconciled to God.

This happens in prayer.

When Jesus taught about prayer, he referred to it as an intimate relationship with the Father (Matthew 6:5-15), and a friend approaching a friend (Luke 11:1-13). It's not meant to be fancy, but honest. Not drawn out and elaborate, but truthful. Instead of prayer being a battlefield, he put prayer in a judicial setting (Luke 18:1-8).

If the enemy is roaming the earth looking for evidence to accuse you, such as sin, then he must bring those accusations to the Judge. If there must be a penalty for sin, and God is just to punish sin, then He is just to punish us for our sin. *However,* for those of us in Christ there is no punishment because God has already executed judgment on His own Son on the cross.

This means that when the Accuser puts us on the witness stand and shouts at us all the reasons we fail and fall short and don't deserve the blessings of God, He's right. We, however, get to choose our defender.

1 John 1:9 reads, "If we confess our sins, He is faithful and just to forgive us our sins and to cleanse us from all unrighteousness." God is faithful and just. Faithful to the covenant He made with us through his son Jesus. A covenant is a legal entity. Because He is also just, He also administered justice into place.

Robert Henderson, in his book *Operating in the Courts of Heaven,* puts it plainly:

"God can therefore legally show us mercy because a legal precedent has been set from the cross that allows the Lord from His covenant and justice to be merciful. His mercy is a result of his justice. When we meet the legal requirements of confession, God is freed to legally forgive us of our sins. But the forgiveness released to us is found in the just nature of God. Because of what Jesus did for us on the cross, God can now legally forgive and cleanse us when we meet the legal requirement of confession. The cross of Jesus grants God the legal and just right to forgive and cleanse. We are, in essence, executing what Jesus legally purchased for us. But without our confession and repentance that legally puts forgiveness, cleansing and restoration in place, the work of Jesus is for nothing, even though He completed His job. Having a legal decree and executing it into place are two different things. This is why repentance is so important. Our repentance grants God the legal right to display and show His mercy."[20]

So, before you get on the battlefield and start warring with the devil about your "rights," have you stepped into the court room?

No one can stand for you like Jesus can. He is our only mediator (1 Timothy 2:5) and the thing about a mediator is that he or she must be fair in order to execute their position. A mediator must see both parties' positions. Jesus understood God's demand for holiness, purity and righteousness and understood that these standards could not be compromised in any form or fashion. God demands His people be holy (1 Peter 1:15-16) and He never diminished that demand. He simply answered those demands Himself in Christ and gave us the grace to empower us to live a holy life as His Son is holy.

When you receive the pardon for your sin because of what Jesus did on the cross, you're then able to walk away from condemnation, shame and guilt and live in the freedom of being in right standing in your relationship with the Lord. Jesus answered the penalty for your sin, so the enemy has nothing to hold over your head.

---

[20] Courts of Heaven

The means that when a desire stirs in your heart for a dream, and a list of reasons why you don't deserve such a blessing scrolls through your head, you can set fire to the list and go after the dream. Jesus paid the penalty for that list, so you don't have to.

When you go on a date and imagine having a happy marriage, you can rejoice that it's possible. When the enemy accuses you of being too broken, stained and ruined because of a promiscuous past or a sexual trauma, you can stand under the covering of the blood of Jesus who carried all condemnation on the cross so you don't have to.

This isn't a one-shot deal. Jesus is constantly working and praying on our behalf (Hebrews 8:6). None of us is without sin, and while we can't spend every waking hour of the day before God searching our hearts, we can seek His guidance as to whether the enemy has a foothold in any area to which we need to repent and make obedient to the Lord.

Here's the key portion of this: repentance isn't just a matter of speaking and thinking but doing. Faith without works is dead (James 2:17), therefore our actions must be lining up in response to our hearts.

God can't intervene until we've given him the legal right to do so, which means we need to repent. We cannot compare our lives to this world when we're judging what is and is not all right. We have to compare ourselves to the scriptures, to God's standard, and repent where we fall short.

This isn't about being perfect, but about bearing the fruit of righteousness that comes with keeping repentance (Luke 3:8). It's about having a constant awareness of your lack and Jesus' willingness and ability to complete what you, alone, cannot.

For many years I used alcohol to "take the edge off" of difficult days. Unfortunately, being a victim of trauma, most days were difficult days. When I was going through my separation and divorce, I found alcohol slipping into my day earlier and earlier rather than waiting for the sun to set or dinner to come around. The excuses got longer, and I justified my drinking by saying I could hold my alcohol well and I wasn't making any stupid decisions.

One day I looked in the mirror and I saw the reality of what I'd allowed myself to become. I saw how I was sabotaging the plans God had for my life and I realized if I were to ever face accusations, I had nothing to stand on. God couldn't defend me, because I was too busy defending myself. I couldn't stand under the blood of Jesus because I was refusing to repent.

Until I did.

There was a conflict in a ministry I was part of that continued to grow. Nothing I said or did made the situation better. During that season I was convicted of my need to repent of my drinking even though it was unrelated to the conflict. A couple of months after I quit drinking this person resigned from the ministry and the conflict that was causing so much turmoil in my life disappeared with her. Had I continued in my drinking patterns they would have added to the conflict and she would have had every justifiable right to accuse me. Once I repented, however, Jesus took the penalty for the sins I'd committed against myself and Him, and there lies no condemnation.

Lack of results from our prayers does not necessarily mean we need to put more effort into something. More effort without additional wisdom usually produces nothing more than exhaustion.

Speaking from a vast amount of experience in this area, striving produces frustration. Revelation produces fruit.

Jesus himself had a book he came to fulfill (Hebrews 10:5-7). As we discovered earlier, you also have a book written in heaven only you can fulfill, and there is a plan and intention of God to bring heaven to earth (Matthew 6:10). It's now up to us to decide if we're going to do what heaven intends.

The beautiful part about this is that even when we have good intentions and fail, God gives us more opportunities to fulfill our purpose. He doesn't write us off because we fell short a few times. If we're going to completely miss the intention and desire that God has for our lives means we must be consistently rebellious in the face of God's faithful dealings of us.

If you find yourself frustrated because you feel as if something is resisting you from stepping into what you were made for, it could be that the Accuser is "presenting evidence to God the Judge of all as to why He cannot legally grant to you what is written in your book. Satan knows that if we get what is in our book, then we will do massive damage to his devilish empire in the Earth. He uses accusations against us to stop us from stepping into all that heaven ordained[21]."

Check into the court room. Agree with your Accuser, repent, and put on Christ.

Real Relationship: Getting Started on the Right Foot

---

[21] Courts of Heaven

When we think about repentance, it's often we think about the outside behavior. We need to stop smoking, drinking, yelling, gossiping, lying.... Unfortunately, when we only look at our outward behavior, we're neglecting the root of the sin in the first place. Like chopping off the limbs of a very large weed, until we pull it up at the root, more limbs are going to grow.

We need to get to the heart of the issue.

This means we must realize the foundation we've laid in which our problems taken root.

Who are you? Who is God?

Until you have the answers to these questions, and established the relationship between the answers, you are forever going to be hacking away at your sin with a machete.

What you could be doing, is ripping up the root so you can focus on producing fruit.

The beauty of what God did for you in Christ goes so far beyond what I can address in this book. However, I will tell you that what happened on that cross not only paved a way for you to find complete freedom from your sin, but from your shame as well. The enemy's sole purpose is to blind you from the truth - you are free, forgiven, redeemed, and there is a very specific plan for your life in which God will use every ounce of your pain and past for a purpose.

Truly. All of it.

Your job, and mine, is to accept the gift God has given through His Son and walk in relationship with Him.

For many of us the idea of relationship is frightening. It's vulnerable. It's exposed. It's dangerous. As beautiful as it appears on the surface, it means we must grant full access to another being with what's happening in our hearts. We see the condition of our hearts and wince.

Our Father, who created our hearts, and already knows what we refuse to show Him, rejoices over us with singing (Zephaniah 3:17).

Looking on the inside is difficult, no doubt about it. It's confusing. While our heart is deceitful above all things (Jeremiah 17:9) and we're told to guard our heart (Proverbs 4:23), we're still called to navigate it. This is impossible without God's help. Who better to ask for help than the One who created the thing we're trying to figure out? With Him, we can understand what was impossible to grasp on our own. When depression sinks in and slowly erodes our energy, when the sudden urge to do something stupid leaps to the forefront of our mind, when we try to communicate love and fail miserably, we have to stand confidently on the Word of God, that it will guide us no matter what we come against.

While we may never "figure out" all that we desire, we can rest in the Creator who tells us we don't have to, and we can have peace that literally transcends understanding (Philippians 4:7).

You are loved by a mighty God who created all things for His glory and your good. You are cherished by a King who has every resource at His disposal and every answer to your questions. God is good, all the time. His goodness is not dependent on your feelings or your circumstances.

We can only experience the victory we read about when we are willing to begin right here: in relationship with our amazing Father in heaven, through whom we can see very clearly through His Son who was an exact mirror of the Father (John 14:9).

Our thirst for a relationship that's tension-free and filled with deep, loving acceptance isn't wrong. This is normal. It's what we were created to experience, first and foremost with Jesus. We were all created with a God-sized hole in us that we're constantly trying to fill. Only in relationship with Jesus is that filled, and from there God uses everything at His disposal to demonstrate His love for us - first and foremost through the cross (Romans 5:8).

The problem is, as people we want to run our own lives. We don't like the idea of submission because, for many of us who have experienced trauma, submission means punishment and fear. Except in Christ there is no fear in love because perfect love drives out fear (1 John 4:18), which means that in a real, loving relationship with Jesus you don't have to worry about facing the same abuse you faced in the past. You don't need to throw up walls of self-protection.

Our longing is legitimate, and it can be met in Jesus Christ.

God isn't impressed with our outside cleanliness. Have you ever noticed that no matter how "good" you get you still feel as if you're falling short of where you "should" be? We dress ourselves up with good deeds and expect God to be impressed. Instead, he taps at the door of our heart and whispers, "I want what's in here."

More effort isn't the answer.

He just wants to be in relationship with you; to do life with you and love others through you. This relationship is not a comfortable one, because knowing God means constantly living in the unknowable. His thoughts are not our thoughts, nor His ways our ways (Isaiah 55:8-9), so to live securely in His love for you means His love, and all His love entails, is the only thing you can be sure of. In his book *Inside Out*, Dr. Larry Crabb puts it beautifully:

"We have to either be comfortable (both internally and externally, but especially internally) or live to know God. We can't have it both ways. One choice excludes the other."[22]

A relationship with Jesus isn't comfortable, but there is no securer place. There's comfort in the discomfort, because you realize that as you live to know God you are constantly in the hands and will of the One who loves you wholly and completely and is always looking out for your well-being.

We tend to come to Christ for relief, which isn't wrong. However, if we seek Him for relief rather than a determination to believe, to hope, and to love we've missed it. Deadening the pain of unmet longing does not make the longings go away. Trust me - I've tried.

Knowing Him and being in relationship with Him doesn't make your hurts go away either. Sometimes, in fact, the closer I draw near to God and the more I press into Him, the sharper the pain. I've realized it's not the pain that's intensified as much as it's my thirst for Him. Pain reveals where my thirst for Living Water is most intense, and as I press in further and respond in obedience to what He calls me to do - pray, read His Word, cry, repent, ask for help, declare truth, worship - the thirst is slowly quenched.

Those of us who have become exceptional at deadening the pain of unmet longings inevitably become dangerously vulnerable to developing compulsively sinful habits. The unrecognized and largely unfelt ache in her soul still demands relief, which makes us a prime target for being hooked by the enemy into sin that provides

---

[22] Inside Out

momentary relief and a sense of fulfillment that leads to a mental, emotional and spiritual prison.

We must be willing to engage in relationship with the One who meets every need and allow Him to provide the resources to meet our longings. We must let Him in if we're going to be able to walk out of our turmoil, because only He can lead us out of the darkness. He is the light.

Everything We Need

The beauty about Jesus having already gone before you is that there really is nothing left for you to do.

He's completed every requirement required by the laws His Father established, in holiness and righteousness. He's satisfied every law and commandment. He's loved wholly and completely. He's paid the penalty sin is due. He's provided the example we're to follow. He's left us the Holy Spirit to guide and empower us.

Everything we need to be who we're called to be is already is in place and within us.

The relationship He desires to have with us is entirely for our benefit. By accepting what Jesus did on the cross to free us from condemnation and secure our place in heaven, we've begun a relationship the way a wedding begins a marriage. It's far from the end. As we get to know our Father in heaven through Jesus Christ and our growing intimacy with the Holy Spirit, we learn how to work with God instead of against Him. We learn how to walk in line with His will through grace rather than trying to get it right all the time. We have the freedom to fail and it's that unlimited love that moves us to desire holiness and righteousness because we understand how much we've been forgiven. We can look at those relationships that have caused us so much harm and walk out what used to be impossible. We can love and have compassion on those who are lost and hurting themselves and others in their hurt rather than judging and condemning them. We see the forgiveness God gives us and are quick to extend it to others, regardless of where they are in life.

We learn to see Jesus in every aspect of life, no matter how small, and find joy in places we normally wouldn't have considered because we realize joy has a name - and it's Jesus.

We can live in peace because the Prince of Peace lives inside of us in the Holy Spirit.

We can forgive because we already have been forgiven.

We no longer need the forgiveness of others, nor do we have to bow under their condemnation, because we have already been pardoned.

In Christ we already have the victory. When doubt seeps in I always go back to Romans 3:4, "Let God be true, though everyone were a liar" because as Paul writes to Titus, "God cannot lie," (Titus 1:2).

I lay this foundation of knowing who you are, who God is, and the fact that there is a war for your soul because it is fundamental. Everything that follows apart from this foundation can easily turn into a religious to-do list. There are beneficial disciplines to learn, armor to wear, hazards to be aware of, deliverance to be had and miraculous healing to take place. However, if you don't know who you are, and who God is, and the fact that all these things are meant to be byproducts of *being* a daughter or son to the Most High King, you'll miss it.

Victory is in Christ; not in what you accomplish.

Victory is in who you already are in Christ; not in what you do for Jesus.

Victory is in what was done long before you were even born to contribute to it! It's not in what you have to offer.

Victory is a matter of accepting the truth, every day, and living from truth, not striving toward it.

Everything that follows this page are merely meant to draw you back to Jesus and what He's already done on your behalf. Remember: it's not about you. It's for you.

CHAPTER SEVEN

IDENTIFY THE TOOLS AT YOUR DISPOSAL

Prayer

Prayer was never meant to be a one-sided conversation. We look at what we see happening in churches and often it's a pastor or church staff member standing in front of everyone, speaking to God on behalf of the congregation. We go into our bedrooms and we fold our hands, bow our heads, and talk to the air wondering if anyone is listening.

How does the pastor seem so confident? How does he know what to say?

What if we approached prayer the way God intended for it to be approached as demonstrated in scripture?

Rather than looking to our church leaders to teach us about prayer, as helpful as they can be, how about we look at Jesus as our teacher and what He said about prayer?

On the sermon on the mount, Jesus was speaking to a crowd of people and said, *"When* you pray..." When. Not if.

Prayer is an expected part of relationship with Jesus. How can any relationship grow if one party isn't willing to engage in listening and talking?

Jesus went on to say in this part of his lesson to not be hypocritical in your prayers. Don't pray to be seen and show off but pray to God when no one else is around to see what you're doing. Don't throw up a bunch of religious sounding phrases, or words that you don't understand. Pray honestly. Pray humbly. Pray for God's will to be done on earth as it is in heaven. Ask for your needs to be met today and let tomorrows be met by tomorrow's prayer. Forgive and ask for forgiveness. Pray to be delivered from evil, which is all that seeks to steal, kill and destroy, and to not give in to temptation (Matthew 6:5-13).

Prayer was never meant to be a to-do list for God. Nor was it intended to make your life easier. It was meant to elevate our thinking from worldly circumstances to a kingdom reality. Prayer was meant as a weapon (Ephesians 6:18) to empower us and others to live in the grace extended to us from our heavenly Father and defeat Satan's schemes against us.

Prayer was designed as our personal, direct line to God.

Through Christ and in Christ we have the Holy Spirit dwelling within us, who enables us to be one with the Father. Prayer not only lines our hearts up with His desires, but it also deepens our relationship with Him. That's why Paul tells us to pray continually, to not be anxious but (in everything) by prayer and supplication with thanksgiving, let your requests be made known to God (Philippians 4:6).

Jesus was a man who often spent an entire night praying (Luke 6:12). Though he was one with the Father in heaven, he was still fully man and his prayers went on for hours. Paul prayed constantly, consistently and persistently (Romans 1:10; Ephesians 1:16; 1 Thessalonians 1:2). David, a man after God's own heart, petitioned God in prayer more than thirty times in the Psalms (Psalm 17; 86; 90; 102; 142). Zechariah prayed for his barren wife Elizabeth (Luke 1:13), and Anna prayed for the long-awaited Messiah for decades before she got to meet him (Luke 2:37).

Jesus' most famous prayer, and probably the greatest example of prayer, is recorded in John 17.

"Father, the hour has come; glorify *your Son* that the Son *may glorify you*, since you have given him authority over all flesh, to give eternal life to all whom you have given him. And this is eternal life, that they know you the only true God, and Jesus Christ whom you have sent" (John 17:1-3, ESV, *emphasis mine*). Jesus begins His prayer by declaring his identity in the Father and the purpose the Father has given him.

When you pray, begin with who you are and who God is.

So, who are you? In Christ you are all that Jesus is. You are a son. You are a daughter. Declare your purpose in your prayer and thank God for that saving purpose. There is no trauma that trumps your being a son or daughter in Christ. No pain can prevent you from glorifying the Father, because His grace and mercy is bigger than even your suffering.

Getting punched in the face at school as a child doesn't make you less of a son when you get home and your dad wipes your nose clean. Being teased in the locker room after volleyball practice doesn't make you less of a daughter when you get home and tell your mom how it hurt. You're still a son. You're still a daughter.

What happens when it's your dad who beat you or raped you? What happens when it was your mom who didn't defend you, but pimped you out for drugs?

You're still a son. You're still a daughter.

They simply didn't know how to be a mother or father. The weight is laid on our shoulders when we must unlearn the patterns of receiving incomplete, even abusive "love" and learn how to accept a love that's perfect, pure, whole, self-sacrificing, and complete from the perfect, pure-loving Father. And His patience is eternal.

Jesus ends his prayer with his desires.

"Father, *I desire* that they also, whom you have given me, may be with me where I am, to see my glory that you have given me because you loved me before the foundation of the world... I made known to them your name, and *I will continue to make it known, that the love with which you have loved me may be in them, and I in them*" (v.24, 26, *emphasis mine*).

What Jesus desires more than anything is to make known the greatest love in existence, and the name behind the One who loves this way. For that love to manifest in everyone in relationship with Him, and then to each other.

In your prayers begin with who you are and who God is. Rest there. Reflect, as Jesus did, on what God has done and what He is doing now and thank Him for it. Even if it's something as simple as giving you the breath in your lungs to wake up this morning and get to work on time. Some days that very act is a miracle.

Then ask for what you want. Be honest.

Sometimes prayer is clean and straightforward. Sometimes it's a bungled mess.

God takes both.

Personal Example

I went on a hike the other day, wrestling with this complex mess of life and the seemingly clean lines of scripture. Warring with God's promises, confused by the explosions that seemed to be happening in the waiting process, frustrated with my efforts to just do what God was telling me to do and being met with opposition.

I'd take a leap in repentance, celebrate the victory God gave me, and then be knocked off my feet mere days or weeks later by something completely out of my control. I remained on the rock, but I had the wind knocked out of me.

My own words of encouragement and hope to others sounded like a penny in a tin can to my own ears. How could I stand firmly on the promises of prosperity (Jeremiah 29:11; Ephesians 3:20) when I couldn't pay my bills? When leaving my ministry to get a full-time job was out of the question because I knew the ministry is where God wanted me to be? How could I talk about this purely, wholesome, amazing love that was bigger than my dwindling bank account, the physical pain from my car accident, the loneliness of approaching holidays as a divorcee, when that very love was terrifying me?

Almost as terrifying as being without it.

I walked, practically trampled, through the woods on my hike as I wrestled with it all. After more than a half an hour of fighting tears and my mind spinning in circles, I saw a scene flash before my eyes from the movie the Shack, with Octavia Spencer and Sam Worthington.

Sam's character, Mack, is in a wooden rowboat in the middle of the lake. Jesus told Mack to take the boat out while Jesus finished a task. Suddenly, the boat starts to break apart and sink. Mack is stuck, and there's nothing he can do, no where he can go to save himself.

He hears Jesus' voice, "Mack, it's okay."

"What's happening? Why are you doing this?"

"It isn't me, Mack. It's in your mind."

"You told me to come out here." He's sinking faster.

"Look at me, Mack. It isn't real. Look at me. Keep your eyes on me."

Mack looks and sees Jesus walking on water, his gaze fierce and calm as he slowly approaches the sinking boat. Mack looks away and Jesus repeats, "Look at me, Mack. Keep your eyes on me. It's okay. It's all right. I won't let anything happen to you."

Mack looks at Jesus and keeps his focus there, the steady voice of Jesus reassuring him. Suddenly, everything *is* all right. The boat wasn't breaking apart after all. He wasn't sinking.

I could all but here a similar voice in my mind. "Look at me, Samantha. Keep your eyes on me."

But...

"Look at me. Keep your eyes on me. I'm right here."

Jesus.

Kind.

Merciful.

Loving.

Tender, joyful, hopeful, passionate, zealous, a protector, initiator, the one and only sacrifice for me to have everything that mattered...

I felt as if I were gasping for air.

He reminded me of the briefest of seconds when he met me in worship or in silence. Singing a song of praise and in my mind I danced with the Father with more joy than made sense in my circumstances. In my mind I wasn't anywhere near my pain - I was with my Father, dancing and laughing and racing him through fields of glory.

He reminded me of moments of slow dancing with him in tears, moments he held me so close I could almost feel his heartbeat as he whispered, "I love you." He reminded me of a particularly dark moment on the same trail a year ago when I was at my wits end. He brought me to a clearing off the path, the sun warming my face.

He told me I needed to know how loved I was if I was going to endure what was coming. I needed to know and believe he loved me. He drew me into the stars, billions upon billions of blazing balls of light and color pulsing in the velvet sky, the two of us soaring through the stars like eagles. We dove deep into the ocean, and where it should have been cold, I was warm even as we explored the deepest crevices. We drifted and raced beside the most magnificent sea creatures, twisting with whales and weaving through vibrant wreaths of coral. In a blink we raged along the surf and up a magnificent cliff to a place he often takes me, even today. A place where the sun is forever in between night and day, day and night.

The sunset reminds me of a painting, alive with color and energy, vibrating with a song using words of praise I've never heard before, so perfectly blended it almost sounds like the purest silence. A single tree clings to a cliff, it's growth it's enemy as it always seems on the precipice of falling, and yet somehow growing stronger as it fights. The flowers and the waving grass are in an eternal dance with the One who created them.

And my Father, standing before me holding my face in His hands with tears in His eyes as he tells me, "All of this is nothing compared to how much I love you. This beauty pales in comparison to how beautiful you are to me every day. Even on your worst days. You need to know who you are, and you are everything to me, Beloved. Everything."

As my most recent hike continued to march on, darkness encroached like a predator. The sun was setting.

"Look at me," God seemed to say, reminding me of the love he poured out over the last few years. These weren't days or weeks of bliss. They were minutes, spread out over the course of months of trying not to be consumed by fear and doubt.

"This," he said drawing me back to what only happened between just the two of us, "*This* is real."

Who I am.

Who He is.

His whole desire - me.

His whole desire for me - Him.

Shivering in the dark, I thanked Him for what He'd done, and though I didn't understand I thanked Him for what He was doing.

Whatever He was doing had to be good, because that's who He is, regardless of what's happening around me.

My hike came to an end, and though (emotionally) I was exhausted and didn't *feel* better, it was as if I'd found a ledge to stand on in the cliff I was clinging to.

Prayer isn't always neat and tidy. It can be, but it doesn't have to be.

When words fail on our end, and when they do it's all right, we have a Savior interceding on our behalf (Romans 8:34; Hebrews 7:25). We have the Holy Spirit, interceding for us with groaning of His own, helping us when we don't have words to say.

Prayer, to put it simply, is your heart spread before the Father and allow Him to meet you there.

To respond.

Meditation

When God commissioned Joshua to take over after Moses died - no small shoes to fill - he began by giving Joshua some very important instructions. He made some equally important declarations that Joshua was going to need in order to have the courage to do some of the things God was going to ask him to do.

Among them, God said, "This Book of the Law shall not depart from your mouth, but you shall meditate on it day and night, so that you may be careful to do according to all that is written in it. For then you will make your way prosperous, and then you will have good success" (Joshua 1:8, ESV).

Meditate on the book of the law. That book of the law was not only the ten commandments, but the 613 laws that proceeded from the ten commandments. God was telling Joshua that if he meditated on this book day and night, he'd be more likely to walk it out and would therefore be prosperous. Anyone who has tried to live a perfect life knows just how impossible it is, which is one of many reasons Jesus is so incredible.

He did it.

He managed to live his entire life keeping every law and commandment, being without sin for his entire 33 years, before he was crucified. He was the pure lamb sent to slaughter for our sins. His perfect life made a way for us all to be unified with the Creator who has no sin in Him.

We still need God's Word. If Jesus fulfilled the book of the law, and meditation on the book of the law is what leads to prosperity and success, wouldn't it be safe to say that instead of meditating on the law itself it'd be better to meditate on the one who already fulfilled the law?

David wrote many times in his psalms that he was determined to meditate on the laws of the Lord, his statutes and precepts (Psalm 119). He was a man after God's own heart. If we desire to be the same, we ought to have the same intention.

There are two different kinds of meditation.

Eastern meditation focuses on emptying your mind.

Biblical meditation focuses on filling it. Biblical meditation means taking scripture and mulling it around in your mind. The Hebrew word used in the Joshua 1:8 scripture is *hagah*, which means to moan, growl, utter, speak or muse.

How appropriate that when meditating on scripture we're encouraged to moan and growl? I can count many times I've read a passage and wanted to groan at the difficulty of carrying it out! As I continue to speak it, utter it, growl it out through clenched teeth of flesh and soul, His grace enables me to chew on what I would have choked on without Jesus having done it already before me.

In 1 Timothy 4:13-16, "Until I come, devote yourself to the public reading of Scripture, to exhortation, to teaching. Do not neglect the gift you have, which was given you by prophecy when the council of elders laid their hands on you. Practice these things, immerse yourself in them, so that all may see your progress. Keep a close watch on yourself and on the teaching. Persist in this, for by so doing you will save both yourself and your hearers." This word "practice these things" in the ESV translates to "take pains with these things" in the New American Standard and "Meditate upon" in the King James Version.

This word in the Greek is *meletao,* which means to care for, practice, study.

Meditate.

If we're not seeing God's Word for what it is, we can quickly grow bored with it. The words lose their impact, the messages their meaning, and we find ourselves reading the same passage over and over again untouched by the very words of our God and King. When you meditate on scripture, you're taking the living word that is sharper than any two-edged sword (Hebrews 4:12) and dividing the true intentions and motives of your heart. Meditating on scripture stores it up in your heart to be able to discern what is the will of the Father and empowers you to move forward with direct instructions from the Lord of all.

You can prosper, not because your circumstances are suddenly better, but because being victorious in Christ you can stand on what Jesus has already done that you can't do alone. You can rest on the bed of promises that reminds you this is not all there is. You also have the tools to discern what may or may not be the wisest next step in your life. You can hear the Lord when he says, "This is the way, walk in it" (Isaiah 30:21).

Fasting

One thing I appreciate about fasting is its ability to quickly get my mind on what's most important. A fast is a personal choice, and one where the motives of the heart are as important as the act itself. There is no right or wrong way to fast, except when it comes to the motive of the heart. Isaiah makes it clear in his message from God in chapter 58 verses 1-11.

"Cry aloud; do not hold back; lift up your voice like a trumpet; declare to my people their transgression, to the house of Jacob their sins. Yet they seek me daily and delight to know my ways, as if they were a nation that did righteousness and did not forsake the judgment of their God; they ask of me righteous judgments; they delight to draw near to God. 'Why have we fasted, and you see it not? Why have we humbled ourselves, and you take no knowledge of it?' Behold, in the day of your fast you seek your own pleasure and oppress all your workers. Behold, you fast only to quarrel and to fight and to hit with a wicked fist. Fasting like yours this day will not make your voice to be heard on high. Is such the fast that I choose, a day for a person to humble himself? Is it to bow down his head like a reed, and to spread sack clock and ashes under him? Will you call this a fast, and a day acceptable to the Lord? Is not this the fast that I choose; to loose the bonds of wickedness, to undo the straps of the yoke, to let the oppressed go free, and to break every yoke? Is it not to share your bread with the hungry and bring the homeless poor into your house; when you see the naked, to cover him, and not to hide yourself from your own flesh? Then shall your light break forth like the dawn, and your healing shall spring up speedily; your righteousness shall go before you; the glory of the Lord shall be your rear guard. Then you shall call, and the Lord will answer; you shall cry, and he will say, 'Here I am.' If you take away the yoke from your midst, the pointing of the finger, and speaking of wickedness, if you pour yourself out for the hungry and satisfy the desire of the afflicted, then shall your light rise in the darkness and your gloom be as the noonday. And the Lord will guide you continually and satisfy your desire in scorched places and make your bones strong; and you shall be like a watered garden, like a spring of water whose waters do not fail."

People were abstaining from food, which is the technical definition of fasting, but their hearts were selfish. They fasted to receive from God, rather than fasting for a change of their own hearts.

This discipline is designed to humble yourself before God and be reminded of our need for and dependency on Him. The goal isn't to increase our status before God because, as we've already established, nothing you say or do can increase or decrease your value to Him.

You are already victorious, loved and wholly forgiven.

Fasting is a means of humbling ourselves before God and seeking his face. An outward act expressing inward humility before God, not as a means of obtaining recognition from others.

Sometimes, like a helium balloon, when we get too full of ourselves and too caught up in the winds of life, we start to drift away from what really matters. Fasting is like tying a weight to our string pulling us back to the reality of who we are - already rooted in complete love in our Creator. There's no need to chase every idea and desire carried on the breeze.

It reminds us that while we have very real needs - such as the need for food - it's God who provides and sustains us. Apart from him, we really can do nothing at all.

Offerings

There is a tithe, and then there is an offering. A tithe is a tenth portion of something given to God. In most cases this is in reference to a financial giving.

An offering is in addition to the tithe. Not necessarily financial, it is always an excess of a tithe. In every act of giving we're called to give with a cheerful heart (2 Corinthians 9:7) because we're following and imitating someone who gave his life away because he loves us so much (John 3:16). God doesn't need our money. He makes it clear, however, that we can't serve two masters, or we'll hate one and love the other (Matthew 6:24).

In the old testament there were several different words used for offering, including the Hebrew words *zebah* meaning sacrifice (Exodus 3:18), or *minha* meaning gift, such as in a grain offering (1 Kings 10:25; 2 Kings 20:12; Psalm 45:12). In the New Testament "offering" is referred to in Greek as the word *doron,* which means gift or present (Matthew 5:23-24; 23:18-19; Hebrew 5:1; 8:3-4) and *thysia* referring to a sacrifice (Acts 7:41-42; Hebrews 10:8).

Notice that in both the Hebrew and the Greek the word offering is both a gift and a sacrifice.

We give gifts because we enjoy the act of giving. We give a gift with a smile. It's a desire, a delight in us to do so.

A sacrifice might feel painful in the moment, but it's a choice we make because whatever we're sacrificing for is always worth what we're sacrificing. A mother may wince at passing up an exceptional sale on winter coats her size, but she doesn't regret that decision when she sees new snow boots on her children's feet. She smiles because what she gave, she gave in love. What she gave up, she did so in love.

This act of giving an offering to God is both a gift and a sacrifice.

What's most interesting is that our offering is more of a gift to ourselves and the sacrifice is paid by God alone. He made the ultimate sacrifice so we wouldn't have to. Every sacrifice we make, every offering we give, is acceptable only because Jesus went before us to give the ultimate offering. He paved the way, showed us how, and made every offering acceptable because what he gave bridges the gap between us and the One we're giving to.

I once had an Isuzu Rodeo that I loved. This little used SUV was mine for only a couple of years before it crossed that ominous

200,000-mile mark and it started showing its age. I drove that thing all over the Pacific Northwest. By 205,000 miles, however, I knew it was just weeks away from sputtering and dying. A mechanic friend of mine drove it around with me for a short bit and said he wouldn't try selling it for more than five hundred bucks. It wasn't worth the work it needed.

Unfortunately, I didn't have the funds to purchase a new car. Not even a new, used car.

Then the parents of a friend of mine informed me they were getting a new SUV and wanted to know if I wanted their old Cadillac. As a gift. It had 50,000 less miles on it than my Rodeo, was a year newer and in much better condition. The blessing knocked the wind out of me. Of course, I said yes, thanked them profusely and put my beloved Rodeo up for sale.

When I first considered listing it, I thought I'd try my luck at selling it at $1,000. I had time to sell it, nothing needed to happen immediately, and maybe I'd get lucky and manage to pocket $750 for a car a mechanic said wasn't worth $500.

As I was about to list it and enter the price, the number $1,200 came to mind.

"Really, Lord?" I asked.

Again, the number was solid and firm in my mind: $1,200.

Shrugging, I listed it for $1,200.

Within five hours my Rodeo sold, and I had $1,200 in my pocket. That evening when the offering plate came by, I put in more than the tithe I would have normally put in from the sale.

The extra I gave was what I decided in my heart to give. It was a sacrifice. But the gratitude I felt for what God had already given and knowing that the money I put in the bucket was going towards work that would honor him and further his kingdom, I was able to give it gladly.

I can say with confidence that there has never been a time God has not provided for my needs. While it may not always look like what I want, I have never been without shelter, food, clothing and a means of transportation. Trusting him in those moments and choosing to give an offering even when you aren't sure what you have to give, shows trust in who God is as our provider and loving Father and friend.

It's worth noting that an offering doesn't necessarily have to be financial. Sometimes an offering involves sacrificing your time in a busy week to cook a meal for a family in need. Sometimes it's sitting with your child without your cell phone, though you're expecting an important call, to listen to him talk about what he did at recess. It could be waking up in the middle of the night to rock the baby to sleep because your spouse has been sick with a cold all day. When we choose to give up something we don't have to give up, in order love and serve someone else because we remember what Jesus has already sacrificed and offered up himself, the offering then is for God and not for the other person.

It's not about paying God back as much as it's about paying his love forward. In so doing, we do end up loving him in return for his love.

This tool of giving an offering forces our minds outside of our own little circle of self. It forces us to think beyond ourselves to the needs of others. When we do this, the storms of life that seemed so big earlier in the day are drowned out by the life and heart of a human needing God's love.

Let's face it: there's never been a day one of us has not needed someone to share the love of God with us. I don't know about you, but I can't get enough of it. I'd never take someone's sacrifice and tell them they can keep it because, "I've had enough love for today."

Every willing offering we make, regardless of how it's received, is not only storing up treasures in heaven (Matthew 6:19-21), but it's also drawing you into the greater kingdom perspective we need to operate in victory.

Humility

What exactly is it?

C.S. Lewis wrote, "Humility is not thinking less of yourself, it's thinking of yourself less."

International Standard Bible Encyclopedia expands on this. In referencing the "humble" and "humility," other words show up like "poor" (Psalm 9:12; 10:12), "meek" (Psalm 10:17; 34:2; Psalm 69:32), and "afflicted" (Isaiah 2:11; 10:33).

In other areas it's translated as "lowliness" (James 4:6; 1 Peter 5:5).

When looking at those who have demonstrated lives of humility, both publicly and privately, I've noticed several things. They're often teachable, servants, loving, grateful, confident, responsible and optimistic.

Humility is a character trait that acts like a reality check. It gives, serves, loves and receives what's already been given from God himself. There's no need for pride and self-exaltation because it's already been done in Christ. When we glorify lift him up, humbling ourselves in the process, we are, in turn, exalted as a natural byproduct of glorifying Christ. It's why James tells us that if we humble ourselves before the Lord we will be exalted (James 4:10).

Remember, our identity is in him. In him, we are already victorious. When we humble ourselves apart from him, recognize that apart from him we truly can do nothing, and we exalt the one with whom we are one, we then are exalted in the process. It's because of Jesus.

Humility isn't about bowing down before others, but about bowing down before Christ. It's not about making ourselves less than those around us, but about glorifying the One within us.

Forgiveness

I love Peter and his questions. His outside voice sounds a lot like my inside voice.

After Jesus had finished teaching about what to do if your brother or sister in Christ sins against you (Matthew 18:15-20), Peter immediately asks, "Lord, how often will my brother sin against me, and I forgive him? As many as seven times?" (v.21).

The question is really - how many times do I have to forgive him before I don't have to forgive him anymore? How many times do I have to let him off the hook before he finally gets what's coming to him?

"Jesus said to him, 'I do not say to you seven times, but seventy times seven'" (v.22). He goes on to tell a story of a man who owed a king an astronomical debt and then was forgiven the debt. Forgiven, the man approaches a servant who owed him a much smaller amount and demanded the debt be paid. When the king heard about it, he called the man to him, put the debt back on his record and threw him in jail until the debt could be paid. Which, if you think about it, would never be possible - how does a man pay off a debt when he's stuck in prison?

Jesus tells Peter, "So also my heavenly Father will do to every one of you, if you do not forgive your brother from your heart" (v.35). How many times? As many times as you're wronged.

The point Jesus is making here is that we are the man, and our Father in heaven is the king. Every one of us has been forgiven a debt that is impossible for us to pay back. No amount of good deeds or righteous living makes it possible for us to pay back the debt sin gets us in. Whether you're a murderer, a drug addict, a white-collar criminal or whether you simply refuse to trust God - we all owe the same debt. We are born in sin. Sin is us missing the mark of perfection God demands as our perfect Creator in order to be in relationship with him.

It sounds harsh, until you meet Jesus. God knew it was impossible for us to pay such a debt, so he sent himself, his only Son, to do what we couldn't so we could be reunited with him again.

When you realize how much you've been forgiven - not only of your past but of your present and future sins - forgiving others becomes nonnegotiable. If we don't forgive, how can we accept forgiveness? Our debt to God is always bigger than any debt another has toward us.

Consider that for a moment. Anything your abuser ever did to you pales in comparison to the sin you committed against your heavenly Father. Any judgment you want your abuser to face, or I want mine to face, is less than the judgment we deserve for what we've done to God.

We're called to walk in love. To let all bitterness, wrath, anger, slander, malice and bitterness be put away. To be kind, tenderhearted, and forgiving of one another as God is toward us (Ephesians 4:31-32). Forgiveness doesn't let mean the other person gets away with what they've done. It simply means you let go of their throat and let God do what God does best.

As his love has been extended to you, no matter what terrible things you may have thought or done, He extends that same forgiveness and love toward the one you've abused. If you don't accept that love and forgiveness and turn to Christ, you'll face judgment for your sins against him because you rejected the only door to saving grace. If your abuser rejects the love and forgiveness of Jesus, he or she will face their own judgment.

God doesn't need your help to judge them. But he'll take your help to love them.

Forgiveness shakes off the weight of judgment we were never meant to carry. It unlocks the chains that hold us to that person we're refusing to forgive. It allows us to let go and walk in the freedom we were designed for.

Forgiveness does nothing for the person who's harmed us, but it does everything for us and our relationship with our heavenly Father.

Praise and Worship

When I began to realize the power of praise, I was (quite literally) brought to my knees.

This is probably my absolute favorite tool in my bag. It's like my duct tape to all things broken. If I have no idea what to do or how to fix something, I bring out the praise. It may not necessarily fix what's happening but if my heart is all over the place praise has a way of strapping it to God's quick.

David, a man after God's own heart, wrote an entire book of the Bible full of praises to God. Psalm after Psalm exalts the Lord. Even in the Old Testament battles were won simply with praise.

In 2 Chronicles 20, King Jehoshaphat is told "a great multitude is coming against you from Edom" (v.2). He was afraid, set his face to seek the Lord, proclaimed a fast and assembled an entire city to seek the Lord. His honesty is a relief for those of us who aren't sure how honest we can be with God. "O our God, will you not execute judgment on them? For we are powerless against this great horde that is coming against us. We do not know what to do, but our eyes are on you" (v.12).

I've lost count the number of times I've been in that position and cried out, "Lord, help! I'm powerless! I don't even know what to do. Tell me!"

The Spirit of the Lord comes upon Jahaziel, a Levite, and he tells the king to not be afraid, "for the battle is not yours but God's... You will not need to fight in this battle. Stand firm, hold your position, and see the salvation of the Lord on your behalf, O Judah and Jerusalem" (v. 15, 17). I love what Jehoshaphat does next.

"Then Jehoshaphat bowed his head with his face to the ground, and all Judah and the inhabitants of Jerusalem fell down before the Lord, worshiping the Lord" (v.18).

Nothing had been done yet.

They hadn't gone before anyone in battle. God hadn't come through yet. He simply promised them they'd be all right and King Jehoshaphat set the example and worshiped the Lord for the promise.

This is probably one of the most difficult parts of worship. How do we praise God when nothing has changed?

We lift our voices in praise because the character of our God is not determined by our circumstances. Things don't need to be going well for us to praise him because he is worthy of praise no matter how good or bad our situation. On the surface it looked as if Jehoshaphat and his people were going to get slaughtered. God said it wasn't going to happen.

It was up to the king to decide what he was going to believe. Was he going to cower in fear because of how things looked, or was he going to trust what God said was going to happen? Trust in the Lord isn't the absence of fear. It's taking a step in obedience even when fear is shouting in your ears.

We don't worship God because things are going good for us. We worship him because He is good no matter what's happening to us or around us. We worship him because his promises are true, and his love endures forever. Because he is worthy to be praised.

The next morning Jehoshaphat had to face the army from Edom.

"And they rose early in the morning and went out into the wilderness of Tekoa. And when they went out, Jehoshaphat stood and said, 'Hear me, Judah and inhabitants of Jerusalem! Believe in the Lord your God, and you will be established; believe his prophets, and you will succeed.' And when he had taken counsel with the people, *he appointed those who were to sing to the Lord and praise him in holy attire, as they went before the army*, and say, 'Give thanks to the Lord for his steadfast love endures forever.' And when they began to sing and praise, the Lord set an ambush against the men of Ammon, Moab, and Mount Seir, who had come against Judah, so that they were routed. For the men of Ammon and Moab rose against the inhabitants of Mount Seir, devoting them to destruction, and when they had made an end of the inhabitants of Seir, they all helped to destroy one another. When Judah came to the watchtower of the wilderness, they looked toward the horde, and behold, there were dead bodies lying on the ground; none had escaped."

Jehoshaphat put the worship team on the front lines of the army going into battle. The worship team sang, and sang, and sang.

By the time they got to the front lines, the army they were expected to see was already dead. God had followed through with his promise and defeated the army that threatened to come against Jehoshaphat and his people.

Was worship what saved them? No. God saved them. Their praise honored the one who saved them. Their praise glorified the one who was greater than their circumstances.

Praise changes our heart.

Even when our mind knows there's nothing to fear, our heart may tremble. Praise engages our heart in a way knowledge and prayer don't. Prayer and reading and meditating on scripture are essential parts of our walk with the Lord, but they engage the mind.

God inhabits the praises of his people, so when we praise, we are inviting him to dwell with us. We swing open the doors of our hearts to say, "Lord, regardless of what my heart feels and believes, I will praise you. I will honor you and glorify you because regardless of how I'm feeling or what's happening around me, you are still good, and you are still God."

Confession and Repentance

A woman caught in adultery is thrown at the feet of Jesus. He has every right, based on one of the 613 laws his Father gave to Moses after the Ten Commandments, to stone her and kill her for her sin. Scribes and Pharisees, religious people fully aware of the laws this woman had broken, picked up rocks to stone her and asked Jesus what his thoughts were about this woman and the law (John 8:1-6).

Jesus bent down to write something in the sand and as he wrote, they continued to ask him what he thought should happen to the woman. If he disagreed with the law then he was not the Son of God he claimed to be, and they would have justification to kill him, too. If he stoned her, then he would have upheld the law, but Jesus didn't come to uphold the law, but fulfill it and abolish it on the cross.

Instead he stood and said, "Let him who is without sin among you be the first to throw a stone at her."

Every person slowly dropped their stones and walked away.

Jesus then doesn't condemn the woman but has mercy and tells her to leave her life of sin.

When we confess with our mouth the sins we've committed, we accept responsibility for it. Only when we accept responsibility can we receive the gift of forgiveness and repent. You can't repent from what you aren't willing to confess.

When we own our sinful attitudes and behaviors, we can then change our minds from the ways of this world, which are demonic in nature, to having the mind of Christ. We are unable to fulfill the laws and commandments. Paul says we're condemned not by Jesus, but by the law of Moses (John 5:45). When we try to fulfill what we were never meant to fulfill, we live under a cloak of shame and condemnation for falling short.

When we engage in the law of liberty, the Word of God met with the gospel of Jesus Christ, we are free (1 Peter 2:16). Confession has power. It's by confessing with our mouth that Jesus is Lord we are saved (Romans 10:9), and confessing our sins that God is faithful and just to forgive us (1 John 1:9).

Repentance brings us back into alignment with God and his will for our lives.

Being Still

"Be still before the Lord, and wait patiently for him," writes David in the 37th Psalm. In the Passion translation the verse reads, "Quiet your heart in his presence and pray; keep hope alive as you long for God to come through for you" (Psalm 37:7).

Like many people, I'm not great at being still.

Too many years of entrusting my heart, livelihood and basic needs to others, only to have them drop the ball, taught me if I wanted something done (especially if I wanted it done well), I needed to do it myself.

My mother enjoys reminding me my first sentence was, "I do it."

Independence was encouraged, even expected, as I grew older. When I realized I couldn't do something after all, I would finally ask for help and often be met with the response, "Figure it out."

So, I'd try harder. Fail better. Try harder still. Fail better. I finally reached a point of figuring out what I was so determined to learn or accomplish, or if I really couldn't figure it out, I'd decide I didn't want it that bad after all and move on.

The concept of being still and waiting for someone else to do what I couldn't was entirely foreign to me.

To be helped was to act, and someone would assist toward the goal. It was rude, even punished, to stand around when there was a job to do or to ask for help and "make" the other person do all the work.

The only time I can remember being told to be still was when it involved punishment.

God didn't start tackling this concept of being still until I was in my late twenties.

I went to a conference in the high desert of Oregon with a bus load of women I do ministry with. One afternoon in the cold, clear day with snow-capped Sisters' mountains beaming at us in the distance, a dear friend stood beside me and said, "Sam, you really need to just learn how to be. Stop trying to *do* all the time. Just be."

I looked at her as if she'd grown two heads. "I don't know what that means."

Life was doing. My life was day after day of making sure I was doing everything I could to be the disciple of Jesus I knew I was supposed to be. I wanted to do it. I enjoyed serving. I enjoyed reading my Bible and praying and telling people about Jesus.

And yet for some reason my time at the conference and being met with the love of Jesus head on made me feel like I was trying to drink from a fire hose. I was wrecked. My philosophy on doing for Jesus was suddenly turned inside out and didn't make any sense.

What did it mean to just *be*? How do you *be* without doing something to get there or stay there?

"Be still and know that I am God," (Psalm 46:10). Be *still*. The Hebrew word for this is *"harpu,"* which means to cease striving. The "and know" Hebrew word is *"udeu,"* which means to be sure.

"Cease striving and be sure that I am God."

If he is God, eternal and infinite in every way, then everything in his hands is possible. Scripture even says that all things are possible with God (Mark 10:27). So, when something is impossible for us, even difficult for us, God commands us to just be still. Stop striving. And know that he is God. Be sure of who he is. When you know who he is there's no need to strive and run from task to task and race down your to-do list and figure out all there is to do to make this thing possible, because he's God and already has it figured out.

We strive for one of two reasons. Either (a) we're prideful and want it done a certain way, or (b) we're insecure, which is just another form of pride, and don't believe God is going to take care of it. Either we want to do it ourselves to receive the glory, or we don't believe that God loves us to the degree he says he does and will do what he says he's going to do.

If we're facing pride, we need to go back to the cross.

Nothing we do is ever done on our own strength. Like a five-year-old hand-washing a semi-truck, every effort we make in life falls short of accomplishing the goal. Our Father is following behind us doing the real work. Everything that's possible in our lives is made possible because of Jesus. Every good and perfect gift is from the father and it's he who gives life to the full in every area. We do nothing on our own.

If we're facing insecurity, we still need to go back to the cross.

The failure of others to take care of us, to meet our needs, to even love us, is not God's fault. We cling tightly to what we want to protect, run circles around it patching up the broken bits while the Healer stands with his hand out asking if he can make it better. But that means letting go and being still while we wait for him to do what only he can do.

CHAPTER EIGHT

DRESSING FOR THE EXPEDITION

Breastplate of Righteousness

The breastplate was a large bronze plate of armor fitted on layered linen or leather adding for extra protection. It was a solid piece, which didn't allow much for flexibility, but it did allow for the ultimate protection. Nothing was getting through this piece of bronze, which is why I think, of all the types of torso armor Paul could have referred to he was specific about calling it the *breastplate* of righteousness.

Unlike scale armor, mail armor, or segmented armor, which had breaks and slats to allow for flexibility, the breastplate was a single piece of bronze. Less flexibility, but more protection.

The breastplate of righteousness is no different. There isn't room for flexibility. If you're looking to allow unrighteousness in - you must take off the entire slab of armor. Nothing is going to slip in by accident. In order to be out from the breastplate of righteousness, you must willingly step out from under it.

Belt of Truth

The belt of a Roman soldier's attire, unlike the belt as we know it today, had nothing to do with holding up a pair of pants. The belt in the first century went around the shoulder, cross-body, and around the waist and had one purpose: to carry weapons. Archaeologists say that the belt often had metals and precious stones on it as well to indicate the rank of the soldier who wore it.

Spiritually speaking, Paul calls it the Belt of Truth.

It's doesn't hold anything up. Rather, it's the piece that our weapons hang on. Our greatest weapon in spiritual warfare, the Sword of the Spirit, hangs on truth and truth alone. Lies break. Eventually, they fall apart and no weapon hanging on a lie will hang there forever.

Truth stands. Truth cannot be shaken. Truth doesn't change or shift or crack under pressure. It is resolute, and it does not fail. This is why Paul tells us that the piece of armor that does little to protect, is as essential as every other piece because it is the only thing our offensive weapon can hang on and last the duration of the battle without faltering. If our weapon has faltered, it's because our belt of Truth is not securely fastened.

If the belt of Truth isn't securely fastened, it's because we've cinched it together with a lie. Every time we draw the weapon and put it back in its place, the blade is dulled by the lie. It must be called out for what it is and replaced with Truth or our Sword will be rendered ineffective because of the lies that have damaged its integrity.

Helmet of Salvation

The Roman helmets of the first century were relatively the same, depending on whether it was a montefortino, coolus or imperial gallic helmet[23].

They were all made from iron, brass or bronze, and they all had cheek plates and neck guards. The helmet didn't only protect the brain, but the vulnerable parts of the body closest to the brain; the neck and face. As the soldiers' helmet protects the brain, so the helmet of salvation protects the mind.

Our mind is the greatest gift God gave our earthly bodies. The ability to desire, analyze, discern and choose are some of the things that set us apart from his other creations. As evidence in a previous chapter, our mind is mightier than our brain. Our mind can determine the cells the brain produces, which results in a change of our very DNA.

When we're secure in our salvation, certain of who we are as sons and daughters of the King of the universe, nothing can stop us. When we have the Holy Spirit, we are saved and therefore are given the Helmet of Salvation.

It's our choice to put it on.

I like knowing things. I like understanding things better. I like it when I have the answers. It gives me a very comfortable sense of security that I love to nest in.

God loves to pluck me out of my nest.

---

[23] https://historyplex.com/ancient-roman-armor

It's not intellectual knowledge that protects our mind, it's knowing experientially we're saved. It's not insight and wisdom that guards our mind; it's resting and relying on what Jesus did on the cross to save us from our sin. Therefore, all can be saved - it's based on what Jesus did and not what we can retain or understand! In order to have the peace that surpasses understanding we must be willing to give up our right to understand and surrender our desire to understand.

We must be willing to let go, be willing to not know.

All those questions that begin with "Why" can be expressed but must be surrendered. Maybe there will come a day God will answer. If he does it will come at a time when you're not so desperate to know them. Maybe he'll answer them sooner rather than later.

In my experience, however, the questions I want to know and the things I desperately want to understand have no bearing on the most important question of all: am I saved?

When I can answer that with a resounding yes, confident and firm, I realize the answers to the other questions have no impact on that primary question. They don't make a dent in it - no matter what the answer is.

When we are saved by grace, and we grasp who we have become in Christ, the power we carry within us is inconceivable. Jesus himself said that when we have the Holy Spirit, we'll be able to do even greater things than he did (John 14:12). It's why in Paul's letter to the Ephesians he writes that God (inside of us) can do immeasurably more than anything we ask, think or imagine (Ephesians 3:20). It's why Jesus tells his disciples that with God *all things* are possible (Mark 9:23).

The Holy Spirit is God's Spirit inside of us, empowering us and enabling us to do all things.

The same Holy Spirit that rose Lazarus (John 11:43-45) and Jesus (Luke 24:3) from the dead.

The same Holy Spirit that cast out demons, healed the sick, and turned one of the greatest terrorists in human history, Saul of Tarsus, into (arguably) the greatest disciple of all time: the apostle Paul.

We are saved by grace, and that salvation is a helmet that protects our mind from every lie of the enemy, others and ourselves. When we go back to the basic fact that we are saved by grace, everything else is put into perspective. Keep your helmet on, and when the questions bombard you like sword thrusts to the neck, go back to the armor - are you saved? Do those questions change the answer to the most important question?

Gospel of Peace on Your Feet

Every Roman soldier had the same sandals on his feet.

It didn't matter what their rank was, every soldier was expected to wear the same *caligae*. They were boots with heavy, thick soles and hobnails. Made of leather, laced from the center of the foot to the ankle, sometimes up the calf, the open design ensured air could pass through to prevent blisters from forming. In order to charge into battle undeterred by what they stepped on, these were an essential part of the armor.

Paul tells us to put the gospel of peace on our feet. As an educated scholar, he was well versed in the scriptures from what we know to be the old testament. He's specifically referring to Isaiah 52:7, "How beautiful on the mountains are the feet of those who bring good news, who proclaim peace, who bring good tidings, who proclaim salvation, who say to Zion, 'Your God reigns!'"

Even amid battle, even while wearing the helmet, the breastplate, the shield and the belt that holds our sword, we're called to have our feet fitted with the gospel of *peace*. To approach every enemy with the good news of the gospel of Jesus, who bring good tidings and proclaim salvation to those who persecute us. When we're facing an argument with our spouse, no matter how big or small, and we feel the sting of offense and bitterness wedge its way into our heart, we shove it aside and step in peace rather than retaliation. When we find ourselves on a break at work, surrounded by people gossiping about a co-worker's poor job on a project, we choose to take a step of peace, rather than participating in sowing discord.

Proclaiming peace is a choice. Bringing good news is an active decision. One we all must take every day. We're either walking in peace or disruption. I think most of us tend to spend our time looking for a vacation, or the end of the workday, or that glass of wine after the kids have gone to bed to be our peace.

Our peace is within us. His name is Jesus Christ and he is the Prince of Peace. When we choose him, speak life, share the good news of salvation, we are walking in peace. We don't have to wait for it to come. It already *has* come. We make the choice to walk it out. It's easier said than done, especially when we've created habits of speaking ill of others and ourselves, complaining and rolling our eyes when someone inconveniences us.

Like the *caligae*, I like to think the open design in our feet being fitted with the gospel of peace is to allow the air of offense to pass through to prevent our hearts from blistering.

How's your heart?

Shield of Faith

There were two primary shields used by Roman soldiers during the first century when Paul wrote his letter to the church in Ephesus. The first was a round shield, the Parma, which had a thirty-six-inch diameter and was made of iron and wood. This was used often on horseback because of its smaller size. It was excellent at deflecting arrows, sword grazes, and providing quick, defensive moves. It provided the bare necessities of protection for the flexibility and mobility needed while on offense.

When Paul wrote his letter to the Ephesians and mentioned the shield of faith, I don't believe the Parma was the shield he was referring to.

The second shield, the Scutum, was tall and rectangular. It was roughly four feet high and between twenty and twenty-five pounds. Before going into battle the soldier would wet the entire front of the shield to be able to extinguish flaming arrows shot at them by the enemy. One of the most effective tactics used with the Scutum was called the *testudo* or tortoise formation.

The soldiers would gather close and the front row of soldiers would align their shields in front. The soldiers behind would align their shields on top, protecting the entire group from flaming arrows and other projectiles. This formation made them virtually invulnerable to any attack.

When Paul mentions the Shield of Faith, this is the image he intended to convey.

Our faith is a shield that covers us from head to toe. Faith acts like a force field that prevents the arrows from even touching our breastplate of righteousness or helmet of salvation. The shield is big enough that it doesn't need to be held up all the time in order to be effective and it literally extinguishes the flying fiery arrows. It's light enough to be mobile, but sturdy enough to be able to withstand the most effective weapons.

When one soldier is too weak to hold his shield, his fellow soldier's shield is big enough to provide him cover. When the wounded are unable to hold their own shields above themselves, the soldiers with strength create the *testudo* and suddenly a wood and iron shield has been created above and in front of the wounded.

Sword of the Spirit - the Word of God

Roman soldiers had not only a sword at their disposal, but a lance and dagger as well.

Paul, however, made a point that the only weapon Christians had in spiritual warfare was the 20-24-inch-long, double-edged sword soldiers used for close combat with the enemy.

This sword is the only offensive weapon in the array of armor Paul says is essential for our fighting and standing firm in battle. This sword is the Word of God (Hebrews 4:12). In the beginning was the

Word and the Word was with God and the Word *was* God (John 1:1). From Genesis to Revelation, the words of God himself both recorded and not recorded (John 21:25 tells us there were many, many more words of Jesus spoken) is the weapon we have against the enemy.

We see God speak and the entire world is created in seven days. From nothing to everything we see in front of us, the Almighty God made what never was suddenly become what is using nothing more than His words (Genesis 1:1 - 2:3).

We see Him do miracles in nature, stopping violent storms in their tracks with three words, "Peace! Be still!" (Mark 4:39). We witness Him raise the dead with the simplest of commands, "Lazarus, come out!" (John 11:43). It's not the words themselves, but the one from whom they originate that give them power.

This is why we can ask for anything *in Jesus' name* and it will be given (Matthew 21:20-21; John 14:12-14). When it comes from the mouth of Jesus, and seeks to glorify the Son, it will be done.

Miraculous healing happens in the name of Jesus (Acts 3:6).

Demons, oppression, and all things evil *flee* when we turn to Jesus and stand firm in His name, trusting in His words (Mark 9:16-27; Luke 8:30-33; James 4:7).

Every Roman soldier, before they go into battle, trained with their sword.

We need to have the same diligence and wisdom. This doesn't mean we go around thrusting scripture in the face of people we meet. Like a child playing with a real sword, it can cause unnecessary harm. We need to know it before we use it.

From 2007 to 2011 I served in the United States Marine Corps, and one thing became abundantly clear: training never ended.

From our run first thing in the morning to the way we held our food trays to the angle of our feet and the speed with which we responded to an order, every second of every day was training us for what was to come when we would inevitably face combat.

I didn't fire my weapon on the firing range until almost two thirds of the way into training, but I carried that rifle just about everywhere I went. I learned how to take it apart and put it together again as if it were as familiar as an old Lego set. There was little fear in me when I finally loaded the magazine and put a round in the chamber. I knew my weapon. I knew how it felt and I knew what it was capable of, down to the feet a round would travel in various weather conditions. I'd exercised and had been disciplined with my weapon, so my arms and shoulders didn't tire from holding it in various positions while firing live ammunition.

By the time I fired my first shot it neither surprised nor intimidated me. I felt as if we were a team doing exactly what we were meant to do.

The Word of God is a sword. Like any weapon, the more familiar you are with it before you must use it, the better you are at using it when the time comes. Read it in the morning. Meditate on passages in the shower before work. Listen to scripture in praise and worship songs on the radio. Roll it around in your mind and use it in discussion with others. Ask others how they read and interpret the passages you spent time on that morning. Hold it up against the circumstances in your life and see how you can better shift your heart and attitude to do what it's calling you to do. Send it in a text message to someone you care about. Write it down on a white board by your front door. Journal about it in a notebook.

By the time you face persecution and need your weapon sharp and ready to slay the enemy, you've spent so much time with it you know it by heart. Your mental muscles aren't weak at drawing it out. Your mind is prepared and quick to dance around the enemy like a boxer in a ring. Because the Word of God never fails (Isaiah 40:8).

CHAPTER NINE

IDENTIFY HAZARDS

Wrong Directions - Lies

A victim believes the lies.
A victor believes the truth.

For almost a year I lived just outside of Baltimore, Maryland. One of my favorite getaways during this season of life was to take weekend trips to Washington D.C. I loved the history in this city and how easy it was for me to disappear in a crowd of people. On one of those trips I had access to a car, and I was on my way to pick up a couple of friends from a Thai restaurant in Dupont Circle.

I was given verbal instructions and I wrote them down, including the names of streets and which left and right to take and when. However, when I got behind the wheel during D.C. traffic at seven o'clock in the evening, the directions I was given did not lead me to the restaurant. Somehow, I managed to find my way across a bridge and into a part of town that deemed bars on the windows as a necessary household accessory. Most of the people who lined the streets stood by broken down cars or pimped out Cadillacs, or they walked very quickly with their heads down. They frowned when they saw the young white woman behind the wheel and a few even reached for the waistband of their pants.

"Okay," I said under my breath as I locked the doors and sped up. "Let's find a new route."

I managed to find my way out of there and ditched the directions I'd been given. When I got to a safer part of town lined with shops I pulled over, used a map and made a few phone calls before I finally managed to find the restaurant I was trying to get to.

It turns out the person who'd given me directions wasn't sure he'd given me the right directions when he told them to me. He apologized but shrugged it off. I don't believe he understood just how potentially dangerous the situation could have been. I learned then: I need to make sure I can trust the source.

Certainly, the directions need to be accurate, but first: who is telling me where to go?

When we make decisions in life, we're essentially choosing the road we're taking toward an eventual destination. What we believe dictates the decisions we make in life. Our mind, therefore, needs to act like a sieve and let in only that which leads us to truth.

The enemy is cunning. He knows you're probably smart enough to reject a blatant lie, but you'll likely consider this lie if it's woven into truth. I knew the Thai restaurant was in Dupont Circle, and the first few steps I'd been given did lead me in that general direction. And yet, it was wrong. Even though it seemed right.

Do you notice the whisper in the back of your mind when you approach a group of friends who disperse as soon as you arrive? *They don't want to hang out with you. They don't want you around.* It may look that way, but what if the conversation really did happen to end and each of them had a place to be?

Do you feel that twist in your gut when your spouse's eyes linger in the general direction of a younger and seemingly more attractive woman? *He's checking her out. He's attracted to her. Should I be worried? Is he even attracted to me anymore?*

And you miss the truck for sale right behind her.

I'm part of an equine ministry and we currently serve teenage girls in recovery once a week. I love these kids with a passion, and I know is the Lord is loving them through me. There have been times, however, I'll speak up about something I know the Lord wants me to say to these girls and the response from other staff and the girls falls flat. *Did I hear you right, Lord? Am I losing my touch? Should I even be doing this anymore?*

Perhaps the flat silence is the weight of God's word landing on the hearts of those listening, squashing any retaliation or rejection of what He told me to say.

When a thought comes to your mind begin by asking: Who told me that?

Can what you're listening to support the Word of God? If not, let it go.

If it isn't true, it's a lie. If it's partially true, a lie is nesting inside. Truth makes no compromises. Truth does not waver or falter. Truth leaves no room for interpretation.

A lie can seem like a detour sign that will eventually get us back on track. It's okay for now, it makes the journey more comfortable, even if it is a bit longer. A longer paved road is a lot better than a short dirt road for some. However, the comfort we grasp by accepting directions from a source that does not care about our well-being and provides a false sense of security for a time, eventually leads us into dangerous situations.

I was told, enough times, from a very young age and throughout my teen years, that I can be a burden sometimes. It was a statement made by people I cared about, and it was said with such emphatic disdain I believed it must be true. It wasn't until I was well into my twenties, I realized that just because someone important said it, and other important people treated me like it was true, doesn't necessarily make it true.

It just makes it what people said and did.

The truth is who your Father says you are. He says you are the joy set before Him (Hebrews 12:2), you are His friend (John 15:14), beautiful (Song of Solomon 4:7) and His son/daughter (Romans 8:14).

Who you believe you are will determine every decision you make in life, starting with what you believe. Whose opinion matters more to you? Whose words carry more weight to you? What do you *want* to believe above all else? If you ensure your mind is guarded and guided by the Words of God, both His written word in scripture and his spoken word by the Holy Spirit, you are sure to remain in victory and on the path toward your destiny - no matter how sporadic or chaotic your circumstances get.

I don't believe any of us wants to believe the terrible things people say about us, and about people who do things like what we've done. It's just difficult to believe anything else. Difficult, but not impossible.

The rubber meets the road at our choice.

The fact is, anything less than what God says about you is a lie. Those words are wrong directions careening you toward a rough neighborhood. Get off that road and back onto the path of righteousness that you have in Christ.

His Word, His directions, never fail. They act as both a guard and a guide. Circumstances may get dark, relationships may get difficult, but neither has an impact on the victory you have as a son or daughter of the Almighty God, the Creator, who loves you.

How do you tell the difference between being on the right path and the wrong one? If the quality of our circumstances and relationships aren't the indicator, what is?

His Word. Period.

Whether we're believing that truth is evident in the condition of your heart. You know you're on the wrong path, following the wrong directions, when dark circumstances draw up despair. When the hardships of life are accompanied by hopelessness. When the loss of a loved one, or a job, leaves you devastated when it could have stopped at grief, or even disappointment. In no way am I claiming victory and truth always wear a smile. I am saying that victory is in our choice to believe truth even when we're not smiling.

Paul was in prison when he wrote these following words in his letter to the church in Phillipi. "Rejoice in the Lord always. I will say it again: Rejoice! Let your gentleness be evident to all. The Lord is near.

Do not be anxious about anything, but in every situation, by prayer and petition, with thanksgiving, present your requests to God. And the peace of God, which transcends all understanding, will guard your hearts and your minds in Christ Jesus" (Philippians 4:4-7, NIV). In order to receive this peace that transcends understanding, you must be willing to give up your right to the answers to all the questions you have that leave you confused.

His Word stands.

Answers don't bring peace - Jesus does. Paul's peace wasn't in his circumstances or in his relationships with people. It was in His relationship with Jesus. He was in prison, abandoned by just about everyone he cared about, and utterly alone behind bars. Not to mention, He was in prison for sharing the gospel! He hadn't even committed a crime worthy of such a punishment!

Still, he rejoiced. He spoke of being content even in those circumstances (Philippians 4:10-14).

We're encouraged to ask questions, to rant and wail and lay our heavy hearts at Jesus' feet, but to then let go. If He deems it appropriate for us to have the answers, He'll give them, but more often than not He desires us to trust Him, to meet us where we are in our lack and fill us with Himself. Truth brings peace that surpasses understanding - and that truth has a name.

His name is Jesus.

Relying Too Much on Past Experiences - Shame

A victim believes she is bad.

A victor knows she is in Christ, who is good.

I over analyze. A lot. I'm working on it, but I can create an entire storyline from one silent conversation between two people over coffee. The twitch of an eyebrow in response to someone clearing their throat, the clenched jaw when a bag brushes up against a table in passing, the tapping of a foot or pencil, or even the blank stare out the window can all compile into an elaborate plot for a book that would take three months to write.

This is great for helping me write novels.

This is terrible when I let it contribute to relationships.

The last few years I've been working at being more open and vulnerable with people closest to me and being willing to let love in. I've been working on sharing what I think or desire when I may have elected to stay silent in the past. While this vulnerability used to act as an invitation to receive criticism, even mockery, healthier relationships today and a clearer understanding of who Jesus has helped me to understand those past experiences were more evidence of the condition of the hearts of others. The words you speak are like pulling back the curtain on the condition of your heart (James 3:5-6).

The simple act of confessing, "I'm afraid" and asking for a hug absolutely terrified me. Such confessions to my husband turned into ways for him to manipulate the very clear limits we'd initially agreed upon in our marriage - specifically in the bedroom. The manipulation became abusive, and it was subtle enough I didn't see it until I was hip-deep in it.

When my marriage started to spiral and the reality of how unhealthy our relationship became clearer, I became terrified of physical touch. I spent almost a decade in counseling to help me overcome it before; and here it was again. It was as if every sexual trauma from my childhood and my years in the military came crashing down on my mind. Suddenly every hug or tender gesture from anyone became sexual in nature and, therefore, a threat. I jumped when a hand was put on my shoulder, I winced when my husband reached for my hand.

I was consumed with shame, and cynicism stained my perception.

Frustratingly, at the same time I longed for pure physical touch that would bring comfort rather than fear. I yearned to be hugged, to crawl into the lap of someone who wouldn't take advantage of me or see me as a threat but help me feel safe. I had such a deep desire for emotional support the war of desire and shame about tore my soul in two. It got to the point I couldn't bear to look at myself in the mirror, nor could I stand to be closer than three feet of another human being.

One night, after a FaceTime with my stoic husband that made me realize our marriage was really at an end, and the next step was to file for divorce, I had a breakdown. At nearly eleven o'clock at night I found myself at the kitchen counter of a friend's house with a bowl of ice cream and a cup of hot tea in front of me. Her husband of almost thirty years watched television in the living room while I poked at the ice cream with a spoon, tears filling my eyes.

All I could see was my husband's apathy, his bored expression over the screen of my phone because he couldn't be bothered to drive thirty minutes to meet me face-to-face to tell our marriage was over. Despite my debasing myself to keep him happy, because I thought a good Christian wife did whatever her husband wanted in the bedroom to keep him happy, I'd disappointed him. I'd failed him. Despite my efforts to heal from past trauma, to him I was broken beyond repair. No longer his problem, he'd get satisfaction elsewhere.

I felt sick.

With tears streaming down my face, the quiet interrupted by the faint murmur of the television in the next room and the clink of silverware on dishes, I felt the urge to run.

Yet I was rooted to my chair. The presence of my friend was both comforting and oppressive. I kept seeing my husband's face and I wiped my eyes. "How can you even bear to look at me?" I whispered.

I felt her glare like a knife to the heart. "How can you even say that?"

When I met her eyes, however, they swam in tears for me. Suddenly it was as if I saw a crack in the foundation I'd built regarding my beliefs about people. Not everyone I meet is out to take advantage of me, and those who aren't out to take advantage are not all looking at me as if I'm a soiled rag.

Some really do just love me.

By the time her arms came around me, it was as if she'd bypassed the wall I'd carefully built to protect myself. The love she offered in a hug held me together even as I fell apart.

When we rely on our past experiences to determine our future, we're bound to make our future exactly like our past. We live in fear, seeking that which proves our fears are relevant and therefore reinforce the walls we put around us to protect us from following the directions we know we're supposed to follow.

When we refuse to believe that we are lovable, indeed we are loved and have become love in Christ, regardless of how we feel, we continue to stir the stew of shame. When we lean on the experiences of our yesterdays to determine our value, we strip the cross of its power. When we stand on our trauma as the defining moment, or moments, that have made us who we are, we spit in the eyes of Jesus and all he sacrificed to rescue us from such lies.

"Love your enemies," we read. We remember how our efforts to love our enemies didn't go well in the past and we listen to the lie that says we don't really have to do that, and we sidestep that road for another that looks like it - Tolerance.

"Ask anything in my name, and I will do it," we read. We remember the dozens of times we asked for things from God and He seemed to ignore it or not hear us, so we stop asking because we assume God isn't listening. We neglect to consider the possibility that we might be asking with the wrong motives, or even perhaps that He's getting things in place to answer our request better than we imagined.

When the shame of yesterday determines our today, we create a tomorrow of recurring shame. Shame multiplies in the dark, so every choice made to hide intensifies the hidden emotions. There is no darkness in light, so when we let light in, the shame that hides in the dark is washed away by the blood of Jesus who bore the weight of all of our condemnation; what's been done to us and what we've done to others.

I'll admit that sometimes the past can be very convincing. Once again, it's one of the tactics of the enemy who knows your heart much better than you do. He's cunning, and he knows you'll choose a false sense of safety over the transparency and vulnerability of pure love any day. Until you know how secure that love is, such love is as terrifying as it is freeing.

When I mention shame, I'm not talking about conviction. Conviction is from God and draws us into the light of confession and repentance. Shame keeps us in the dark. Conviction says, "What I said/did was sin and I feel bad about having said/done it. I'm going to change and walk in who I am in Christ because who I was when I said/did that thing is not the real me."

Shame says, "I am bad. Because I'm bad I do bad things and since I'm bad I have been rejected."

When Jesus died on the cross, He scorned shame. He destroyed it. In Him there is no such thing as shame because you are as He is - perfectly loved, whole, pure, free and powerful. In Christ you are all that you were designed to be walking out a purpose He determined for you before you were born. Walking outside of that purpose does not cause shame.

Shame is about identity, and failure has no impact on your identity. Your identity is about who Jesus is and what Jesus has done and how He's chosen to give it all to you because *He* is that amazing.

So instead of leaning on what others have said and done before today, look at what Christ is doing and will be doing in you and through you. Seek His face today and watch him transform tomorrow.

Too Much Trust in Self - Pride

A victim believes he or she is above failure.
A victor knows he or she needs Christ because He alone cannot fail.

My mother takes great pride in telling the story of my first sentence.

"I do it."

I wish I could say that I'm much more Mary than Martha these days, but old habits die hard. It wasn't very long ago I spent four hours taking apart my dryer to replace a heating element. I had that appliance in dozens of pieces all over my hallway floor and managed to put it back together without a single extra screw leftover. Thank you, YouTube.

When walking out my journey with Christ, however, my "I do it" mentality has cornered me more than it's helped me. For almost two years I was determined to not trust another person with my walk. I'd spent so much of my life allowing others to determine what was going to happen to me, what was best for me, and it hadn't worked out like I'd hoped. I swung to the other side of the pendulum and kept any advice and input at arm's length. I read scripture and made my own conclusions about what it meant without asking for input. I applied certain scripture the way I thought it was meant to be applied according to my experiences and found myself entrenched in sin I'd justified by saying it "felt good" and "seemed right."

Feelings are like the little indicator lights that come up on the dashboard of your car. They give you a heads up about what's happening in your spirit and soul. When you depend on them to make decisions, they will always inevitably lead you astray (James 1:15; 2 Peter 3:3). Our emotions were not meant to be the deciding factor in what happens in your life. Your emotions are more like the red flag that lets you know something is amiss and it needs to get right again.

We need to be realistic about what's wrong, because putting a band-aid on a sucking chest wound might seem like a solution, but it ignores the reality of the situation.

As mentioned in a previous chapter, we are not designed to walk this journey of life alone. When we face trauma, our self-protective reflexes leap into overdrive and suddenly our desire to avoid pain motivates every decision we make. Even these desires to avoid pain, while they sound like a good idea, are detrimental.

Pain is inevitable. We choose whether it will be the pain of regret and the consequences of sin, or the pain of growth.

You've heard the saying; pride comes before the fall. No matter how smart you are, you're not smart enough to see the whole picture. No matter how talented you are, you're not skilled enough to go through life entirely on your own. No matter how much money you have, no amount of money can make you entirely self-sufficient because what you buy is dependent on others to provide it.

We must drop the pride if we're going to avoid the fall that follows it. We need the Lord, and we need each other.

Not Trusting Your Guide - Fear

A victim acts like everyone is out to hurt her.
A victor knows, in Christ, nothing can.

"When the Spirit of truth comes, he will guide you into all truth, for he will not speak on his own authority, but whatever he hears he will speak, and he will declare to you the things that are to come" (John 16:13, ESV).

When you've been baptized in the Holy Spirit, which is different than being baptized with water (Acts 1:5), you receive the indwelling of the Holy Spirit. This means the Spirit of the God who created all things, of the Son who lived a perfectly holy life and was raised from the dead, takes up residence in you.

You have access to all things. Jesus himself said it was to our advantage that he go away because in leaving He made it possible to send the Holy Spirit (John 16:7). "(Holy Spirit) will glorify me, for he will take what is mine and declare it to you. All that the Father has is mine; therefore, I said that he will take what is mine and declare it to you" (John 16:15).

All that the Father has belongs to Jesus, and the Holy Spirit takes what belongs to Jesus and declares it to those who have the Spirit living inside of them. You have access to all truth through the Holy Spirit. He is not only the one who empowers and enables us to do all things, but He guides us into all truth. We can stare at devastating facts and He will guide us into the truth woven between or in the facts.

Fact: I was raped as a child.

Truth: I have been purified because I hope in Christ who is pure (1 John 3:3).

Fact: I have sinned in ways that would make some people's ears bleed.

Truth: I have cast off the works of darkness and put on the armor of light (Romans 13:12), and nothing can separate me from the love of Christ (Romans 8:38).

Fact: I have lost everything, multiple times, apart from a few suitcases with clothes, my dog and my faith.

Truth: I have learned in whatever situation I am to be content. The secret of facing plenty and hunger, abundance and need, is in Christ who strengthens me (Philippians 4:11-13).

Our circumstances do not dictate the direction of life. That thing you're most afraid of doesn't have to or get to define the course of your life. Our response to those circumstances, which is directed by what we believe, does. If you don't trust the One Guide who knows all, has access to all truth, and paves a way through every circumstance, you will live a life marginally satisfied at best, and miserable at worst.

Perhaps you're in that space of safe living, where you enjoy your relationships but there isn't much depth. The whisper to take a leap of vulnerability calls, but fear keeps you rooted. Rather than take responsibility for your own insecurity, you try to minimize our external world, so you don't have to feel that fear and pain. You put a fence around that thing driving your fear, rather than facing it and disarming it with truth.

Perhaps you're at the end of your rope and aren't sure whether it's worth it to keep trying. The dull ache for closeness sharpens as you see an opportunity to connect with people you've been wanting to get to know better, but fear of rejection drives you deeper into yourself. Rather than ask someone to coffee, or go on a walk in the park, you claim you can't and shut down.

Suddenly the words, "I can't," become a mantra that leaves no room for possibility, connection, passion or joy. True joy comes from freedom to love and be loved, and in freedom there is always risk. The fear of risk drives us into all the reasons why we can't, when they're masking the reason we won't - we're afraid because we don't trust our guide.

Here's the truth: the Holy Spirit is not a spirit of fear. He is a Spirit who gives you power, love and self-control (2 Timothy 1:7). Every risk leads to possibilities, and every consequence to those possibilities is out of our control. Rather than deal with our issues of control we speak as though we can't make a choice, or we limit the choices we have. When we face a situation with multiple choices, and most of them are unappealing, we're quick to choose the least painful and claim "well, I didn't have a choice!"

Truthfully, there were multiple choices and the one you picked had the least painful outcome. Just because we don't like the choices and the consequences that can result from them doesn't mean we don't have a choice. We fear what may come as though we don't get to decide how what may come impacts us. We assume that because something bad happens it must devastate us. The idea that we have no control over our response to painful circumstances isn't true.

We're so quick to make ourselves into victims because we're afraid. We may not get to control the consequences of our decisions, but we always have a decision to make. We may not like the consequences, but we do get to control our responses to those consequences.

We have a lot more control and responsibility than we'd like to admit. Unfortunately, rather than focusing on self-control we've zeroed in on controlling others and our circumstances, which are the two things we don't have any control over at all!

When we have the Holy Spirit as our guide, we have access to all truth, which means nothing when it comes to changing other people and changing our circumstances to suit our preferences.

But it means everything when we're willing to change ourselves.

When we stop focusing on everyone else, and everything that has hurt us or could hurt us, and we start looking at Jesus and asking him to change us - suddenly the Holy Spirit becomes a partner in the most incredible transformation we'll ever experience.

There is no fear in love because perfect love drives out fear (1 John 4:18). We can only know that perfect love when we know the one who is love. Trust him.

Distractions - Unhealthy Habits

A victim allows a habit to rule her.
A victor rules her habits.

Not all of us have experienced some massive form of trauma. For some of us, our lives have been normal, even mediocre. Nothing incredibly traumatic or incredibly amazing has happened. It's easy to fly under the radar and think you're doing fine. However, you don't need to be wrapped up in strongholds to be ineffective in the kingdom. The enemy sinks his teeth in unhealthy habits just as easily.

In fact, Paul writes about some of these in his letter to the church in Galatia. "Now the works of the flesh are evident: sexual immorality, impurity, sensuality, idolatry, sorcery, enmity, strife, jealousy, fits of anger, rivalries, dissensions, divisions, envy, drunkenness, orgies, and things like these. I warn you, as I warned you before, that those who do such things will not inherit the kingdom of God" (Galatians 5:19-21, ESV).

Have you found yourself wearing certain clothes to the office to attract the lingering gaze of men you work with to boost your self-confidence? Do you have a habit of yelling or having fits of anger with your children when they're not behaving the way you think they should? Do you find yourself envying your friends who have better paychecks, better husbands, better homes, better cars, better... than you? Itching for a cigarette or a piece of chocolate or carbs or a drink when the day gets difficult?

Why is it that one never seems to be enough? And after a while, even two or three falls short?

These habits are like distractions that can cause us to swerve into oncoming traffic or into the ditch. They're what take our eyes off the road. The problem is that when you create a habit, you get more confident in your ability to multi-task in that habit. When you first started texting and driving you were hesitant to write more than a one-word answer. I bet you can manage an entire paragraph now while you're driving down the road and hardly bat an eye.

You can manage an entire lifetime and never get in a car accident because of distracted driving. The goal of driving, however, isn't to avoid accidents. It's to get to your destination and enjoy the journey on the way. Distracted driving is now illegal and there's a reason for it. One distraction may not seem like a big deal, but we don't do life that way.

The distractions we allow ourselves seem harmless, but they're not.

The works of the flesh are things we all deal with entirely separate from the spiritual battle we face. The enemy doesn't have to work very hard. He simply puts things in front of us our flesh already wants and lets us do the rest. When we give in, we're entertaining a distraction from the life and desires and purposes God has for us. How can you see signs God is giving if you're too focused on numbing the offense you decided to take on? How can you see the one who could use your help, if you're too busy trying to get a man to notice and flatter you? How can you press into the Lord, deepening and maturing your relationship with Him, if you're too focused on distancing yourself from pain?

What unhealthy habits do you engage in that distract you from the purpose God has for your life? What unhealthy habits hinder your intimacy with him and enable your victim mindset? The mentality that says you don't have a choice, and that you're helpless? Distractions can sometimes make us feel like we're in control, but they're as fleeting as a feather on a breeze and they always leave us empty.

When we allow our habits to rule our lives, we're allowing ourselves to become a victim.

Choose your habits. Everything we do with our time, no matter how small, either propels us toward Christ or away from him.

Intentional Detours from the Route - Unbelief

A victim says, "I can't."
A victor knows Jesus already has.

"Therefore, as the Holy Spirit says, 'Today if you hear his voice, do not harden your hearts as in the rebellion, on the day of testing in the wilderness...' Take care brothers, lest there be in any of you an evil, unbelieving heart, leading you to fall away from the living God... And to whom did he swear that they would not enter his rest, but to those who were disobedient? So, we see that they were unable to enter because of unbelief" (Hebrews 3:7-8, 12, 18-19, ESV).

This isn't about perfection. It's about belief.

What do you believe?

Far too often we dodge that question and claim the direction of our lives has less to do with what we believe and more to do with the reality of what we can and can't do. As though there's an invisible barrier dictated by some unforeseen force that determines just how far we can go, how much we can accomplish, and who we're destined to be.

Rather than address our beliefs, such as who we say God is - is He all-powerful? Sovereign? Good? - we ignore them completely and start using the "c" word.

I can't apply for that job.

I can't move to that city.

I can't go talk to that person.

I can't ask for help.

I can't apologize.

I can't change.

But we can. We use can't as the end to every argument, the cut-off to all possibility and the stand-still to all movement forward. We use it to hide, to avoid, to run and still maintain our dignity in the process. "Can't" implies forces outside of our control are preventing us from doing the very thing we want, or should, do.

Even worse, who we're meant to be.

What if the outside force is nothing compared to the One within you (1 John 4:4)? What if what you believe about the Holy Spirit is what determines who you are, and what you can do in this life?

We throw out "can't" because we don't want to admit that the risk is simply greater, the cost higher, than what we're willing to sacrifice. What if, to own your responsibility to not try, to not sacrifice, you substituted, "I can't," with "I won't?"

I won't apply to that job.

I won't move to that city.

I won't go talk to that person.

I won't ask for help.

I won't apologize.

I won't change.

When we're stuck in "can't" we're focused on our own ability and what change and risk will cost us. What if everything that mattered most to you wasn't wrapped up in success, a dream job, good standing in your community, or looking good in front of people? What if all that mattered was the relationship you had with the One who created you. The One who died to save you. The One who knows exactly what you were purposed to do, designed to accomplish, and molded to become? What if that relationship mattered more than anything you might lose by following the directions of One who's sole aim is your good?

Suddenly the word "can't" seems foolish.

What you believe about Jesus, who you say He is, is the most important decision you'll ever make in your life. That belief opens the door to eternity and the purpose you have today, tomorrow, and every day after. Jesus isn't looking at your history or your resume to determine what your value or purpose is in life. He's already determined it, and it includes the mess that came before today. It includes the joy that came before today. There's not one wasted moment if your life or mine.

Not one.

So every excuse we draw up as a reason why we *can't* is a lie because that excuse is obsolete in the grand plan the Father has for your life and has had since long before you were born. The most beautiful part of it all, is that anything you've been designed to do, regardless of how impossible it may seem, is possible.

With the power of the Holy Spirit inside of you, the same Holy Spirit that raised Jesus from the dead, nothing is impossible. We look at death as the absolute end. The most final of finalities. Nothing can defeat death.

But Jesus did.

When your time to breathe your last breath arrives, there is no stopping it. Unless you believe in the one who defeated death, Jesus Christ, and then death becomes a long nap before you're resurrected in eternal life. Any harm others may have caused you is harm only to the flesh and soul that is being sanctified, washed clean and transformed, refined in fire.

When you believe in the One who defeated death and crushed Satan's head, there's nothing the enemy can throw at you that can make any mark on the plan God has for your life, and the identity you have in Jesus Christ.

Nothing.

No rape. No loss of limb. No emotional or spiritual torment. No loss of a loved one. No harm you may have caused others. No abuse you endured. Nothing can take away who you are in Christ. Ever.

The only decision you need to make, is to believe and confess that Jesus has already done all that you can't do. Therefore, in Him, you've already accomplished everything that mattered, and are being equipped to do what you have yet to take on.

CHAPTER TEN

HAND OVER THE MAP AND FOLLOW YOUR GUIDE

What Your Counselor Provides

Even with all of this in place, every box checked, there is no guaranteed outcome to this thing.

We're human, and we're dealing with other humans, which means our efforts to walk in victory will turn out flawed at best. A mess doesn't equate to failure, but humanity. This isn't to discourage you, but to remind you that walking out this journey religiously and expecting a specific outcome is to set yourself up for disappointment.

I've done it.

The more I studied the Bible, the more I did what, I thought, Jesus wanted me to do in a performance-based mindset, the more disappointed I became. He promised to work out all things for my good... it's been weeks, months, of doing what he said I needed to do, *so where was the good?*

I questioned God's goodness and faithfulness to His word. He said He'd never leave me or forsake me, so when I was in the trenches of despair and grief, my marriage nothing more than a pile of dust at my feet, where was He? When I was left to sell or give away the pieces of my home, I carefully put together just eighteen months ago, my life reduced to a 5x5 storage unit and a few suitcases for probably the fifth time in the last ten years, where was God's provision? Was I to be an example of God's word, *literally*, when it said to follow Jesus was to possibly have no place to lay your head? I was faithful, I was repenting, I was doing everything I was supposed to be doing!

Admittedly, there were more than a few times I would pray and have nothing more to say than, "God... what the hell are you doing?"

I read the Bible with an "if I, then God" perception. If I do this, then God will do this. If I give to the church God will provide for my needs. If I love people, whether they deserve it or not, God will ensure I am loved and cared for as well. If I am faithful and trust God, it'll make Him happy and He'll bless me. I neglected to consider the fact that God was a being with a mind and plan and purpose of His own and, under no circumstances, was going to fit into the box I defined for Him. Even if that box was made up of scriptures. Especially if those scriptures were twisted to suit a belief system that did not support His character.

God always fulfills His word, and He will never contradict His word. We cannot neglect to consider God's timing, and what he might be doing in the waiting process. Sometimes the season of anticipation can feel like a waste. It's not.

When we walk out this journey in relationship with the Father, saved by Jesus and having received the indwelling Holy Spirit, we are not only sealed for eternity, but we have a Guide for this life. One who knows every step of the journey and is telling us what step to take next - if we're willing to listen.

It's been a challenge convincing myself that the brief three years I had with my husband - including the time spent dating him - wasn't wasted. I can say beyond a shadow of a doubt that those years were a season God was growing me in learning how to have a relationship with Him. Desperate, I quickly realized my religious and formulated walk with God was not going to get me through this season. I needed a relationship with the Lord that went far deeper than what I had when I said my vows.

Especially as things became more difficult and my world turned inside out. Everything I ever told myself about how to be safe in this journey with Jesus was crumbling into dust with my marriage. My faith in doctrine and duty wasn't enough to withstand this refining fire.

I cried out and clung to the Holy Spirit to do what I couldn't. I was not going to survive the devastation of my separation and divorce. There was no way. Not when it took so much faith to say "I do" in the first place. The hurt was too deep, the betrayal too destructive... everything I'd worked to remove from my thoughts the last ten years came sprinting to the forefront of my mind. My ex-husband was proving true all that I tried so hard to believe was a lie.

I'm unwanted.

I'm a lost cause.

I'm disgusting.

I'm incapable.

I'm dirty.

I'm unworthy.

I'm nothing...

It was only in relationship with Jesus through His incredible gift of the Holy Spirit that I was able to, in time, refute these lies and stand on the truth of who I really am in Christ.

You cannot walk out this journey on your own. It's not enough to even have the right support system or to wear all the right armor or to even have the directions in your hands. Without a personal relationship with the Guide who knows exactly the route to take, and the hazards on the routes, and the ways of escape in times of trial, and every resource known and unknown to mankind at His disposal to help you... without Him you're lost.

He provides so much more than I could ever put in this book - perhaps that's another book for another time. The following are a few of the resources your Counselor, the Holy Spirit, provides in this journey of choosing victory in Christ.

Grace

Grace does not exist as a means of allowing you to sin and get away with it. Grace is a gift that God gave to enable us to do the impossible things God requires of us to do in His word. Love your enemies? There is no possible way to love the one who has murdered your child - not if we're speaking in strictly human terms.

When, however, you have a relationship with Jesus Christ and the Holy Spirit resides in you, you are given a new heart that is capable of loving people the way Jesus loves them. You see people not for what they've done, or even for who they are in the flesh, but who God created them to be. When you choose to align your soul, your mind, will and emotions, line up with the heart of God you begin to hurt for people and their separation from the loving God you know. You learn how to turn the other cheek, how to offer your shirt when your coat is taken, and how to love in the face of someone spitting in your eye.

Grace keeps you acutely aware of your own failings before a holy God and reminds you of your need for a Savior. The ground is level at the foot of the cross. I may not have ever killed someone in the flesh, but I have murdered my abusers a hundred times in my mind. When compared to the holiness of God, both are sin. They both have consequences. When I'm aware of my own need for Jesus, and how easily and often I fail at the perfection God requires, the more grateful I am for Jesus Christ, and the more compassion I can have on those who fail me.

I can remember one instance in particular that I began to grasp this new concept of grace. I was in the middle of a conflict with someone I once considered a very dear friend. She and I were close enough that her home was as good as my home, and there wasn't much when it came to secrets between us. Without any explanation or understanding, her view of me began to change. She began to show contempt, even hostility, without any explanation as to why. Despite multiple efforts to understand and learn how I could repent of whatever offense I'd caused, she was mute on the subject. She would not confide in me, but her behavior toward me became colder, even hostile.

After several months, we finally were able to sit down and talk about what had happened. I was shocked to realize there truly wasn't anything I'd done to justify her change in behavior toward me. The gossip she spread, the bitterness she felt, was not rooted in any behavior or attitude that I needed to repent of, but in the condition of her own heart.

Unfortunately, this conversation did nothing to restore our relationship.

I was angry. How could someone I loved and served and shared my darkest secrets with suddenly turn on me like this? How could she spread lies about me when I had done nothing to deserve her behavior? My dear friend had become my enemy, and I began to understand David's psalm a little more personally: "For it is not an enemy who taunts me - then I could bear it; it is not an adversary who deals insolently with me - then I could hide from him. But it is you, a man, my equal, my companion, my familiar friend. We used to take sweet counsel together; within God's house we walked in the throng" (Psalm 55:12-14, ESV).

What I was most angry about, however, is I could feel the work I'd been doing to rebuild trust in people slipping between my fingers. How could I trust others when this was the result? How could I love others when the love I sowed resulted in betrayal and hatred?

I didn't do anything wrong!

Regardless of my friend's behavior, I was still called to a higher standard as a child of God, an ambassador for Christ. God was clear - I needed to love her. That didn't mean I continued to share my heart with her, nor did it mean I needed to trust her. I did, however, require that I forgive her and speak in love when I saw her.

Practically this involved not ignoring her when I came into close proximity with her. It meant saying hello in a cheerful tone and asking how she was doing because, as Jesus cares for me, I ought to care for her. It involved praying for her, speaking blessings and life over her.

Ask me how I felt about this.

I much preferred avoiding her and all those who knew her. We shared a lot of friends, and I considered, briefly, simply skipping town and starting over again because this was a mess that had infiltrated just about every pore of my personal life. Her actions had stained the opinions others had of me, it impacted where I could go and who I could communicate with. It was enough of a problem that it even had an impact on my professional life months down the road.

Hearing her name made me ill. Hearing stories of people I loved spending quality time with her made me want to cry. Did they share the same feelings about me that she had? Did this mean they supported her behavior and her attitude toward me? Did this mean they felt the same way toward me? Some did. This situation fueled division in other relationships that also ended not many months later.

Still, God wanted me to represent Jesus. He wanted me to love others as Jesus loved them.

This looked a bit like a pimple-faced teenager asking a girl out for the first time.

There was a lot of stuttering, sweaty palms, foot-in-mouth circumstances and missed opportunities. There were moments I knew I should have said something and didn't, and moments I knew I should have kept my mouth shut and chose not to. There were times I said what I knew God wanted me to say, and I even said it with love, only to feel as if I'd betrayed myself in the process. In time there were moments I was able to do exactly what God asked of me and knew I was doing the right thing, while grieving for her persistent bitterness. As I surrendered my own right to see justice, my own resentment and indignation began to fade. As I persisted in being obedient to God's Word and asking God to have His heart for her, I began to hurt for her rather than be hurt by her.

Grace. The ability, through the power of the Holy Spirit, to do what we cannot do on our own.

Remembrance

Sometimes having a steel trap of a mind can be an excellent benefit. I can remember a lot of things well. However, twenty-odd years of trauma branded into my mind can make it a little difficult to remember the things of Jesus. I praise God for His provision of the Holy Spirit because in moments were my flesh seizes, my heart trembles and I feel my palms begin to sweat, the Holy Spirit tosses me what I need to remember to get through the moment.

"But when the Father sends the Advocate as my representative - that is, the Holy Spirit - he will teach you everything and will remind you of everything I have told you" (John 14:26, NLT). The best part about this is that a good teacher teaches according to the student's ability to learn. Some of us are visual learners. Others need to hear something explained. Still others must walk through it and learn in the moment as they do it.

The Holy Spirit knows this, and He knows what kind of learner you are. So, as He teaches you, He is teaching you according to your ability to learn.

The other day I ran into someone I hadn't seen in almost a year. This person and I had not parted on friendly terms, and there was a lot of painful history attached to our broken relationship. When I saw this person, my mouth went dry as cotton and my hands began to tremble. I wanted to ignore this person and walk away, but even as the thought crossed my mind, I considered all the prayers I had prayed for this person. Immediately the Holy Spirit repeated, "Hot coals, Samantha. Hot coals."

Referring to the Proverb, "If your enemy is hungry, give him food to eat; if he is thirsty, give him water to drink. In doing this, you will heap burning coals on his head, and the Lord will reward you" (Proverbs 25:21-22).

I spoke kindly, I even smiled when I spoke to this person and inquired about how they were doing.

It took the Holy Spirit to remind me of this scripture, because I would not have remembered it on my own in that moment. To walk in obedience, not out of pride or self-righteousness, but because it was the loving thing to do was difficult. As soon as the Holy Spirit brought that scripture to mind, I swallowed my pride and smiled, trusting Him to provide me with the grace I needed to do what He was asking me to do.

Freedom

"Now the Lord is the Spirit, and where the Spirit of the Lord is, there is freedom" (2 Corinthians 3:17, ESV). We're all a slave to something.

Money.

Relationships.

Career.

Children.

Expectations.

Addictions.

Even Jesus. Paul himself said he was a slave to Christ (Romans 1:1). The difference between being a slave to things of this world and a slave to Jesus, is that the things of this world - including self - all lead to death. When you're a slave to Christ, His way leads to life. We were designed to have a specific Master, which is why we chase after things that never seem to fulfill us.

To walk in step with and in obedience to God, making no room for any other gods - including self - it can seem akin to slavery. But when your master is the epitome of good, and everything He does is for your benefit and maturity, it's safe to say that such a Master is one worth following. There's nothing to lose but the identity you were never designed to have in the first place.

We are born into sin. Born into slavery to this world and our own evil desires. Christ set us free from that when He died on the cross on our behalf. He silenced the Accuser forever because He bore the punishment for every sin you or I could ever commit, in thought or deed.

If we remain under the protection of Jesus Christ, clothed in Him, in step with Him, in obedience to Him, surrendering to Him, we're covered from such condemnation. It's when we try to take matters into our own hands, or when we allow the demands of this world to determine the course of our lives, that we find ourselves pressured to do and be what God never intended for us.

Where the Holy Spirit is, there is freedom. Slavery to Jesus Christ doesn't hold the weight of chains and lashes we imagine slavery to entail. When we submit and surrender to Christ, we exchange the weight of this world that holds us back for the wings that allow us to soar above our circumstances in the light of His love (Isaiah 40:31).

The Holy Spirit convicts you of your right standing with God. You may tremble when you get near to sin, but it isn't condemnation. It's encouragement to walk away because *that's not who you are.*

When you walk with the Spirit, you walk in freedom.

Power

When Jesus was crucified, and buried, He was raised to life three days later. Forty days after He rose to life (Acts 1:3), Jesus ascended into heaven. Before His ascension, Jesus said to His disciples, "It is not for you to know times or seasons that the Father has fixed by his own authority. But *you will receive power when the Holy Spirit has come upon you,* and you will be my witnesses in Jerusalem and in all Judea and Samaria, and to the end of the earth" (Acts 1:7-8, ESV, *emphasis mine*).

Perhaps it's because I come from a very religious background that I feel the need to point out that the Holy Spirit is not a weaker part of the trinity. He is not a nice idea, or simply one who reminds us of all that Jesus said. He isn't following us around with the Bible reminding us of all the scriptures we're supposed to fulfill and thumping us over the head when we fail.

He dwells within us. He is Christ in us.

The love and joy, compassion and zeal, that Jesus demonstrated during his walk on the earth resides inside of every one of us who has accepted Jesus as Lord and been baptized in the Holy Spirit. The power that Jesus demonstrated, then resides in us. It's up to us to decide whether we're going to use that power or not.

Thankfully, the Holy Spirit only works in line with God's word and will. You will not find yourself operating in the power of the Holy Spirit and bringing fire down from heaven to consume a school of bullies.

You're more likely to find the power of the Holy Spirit healing the broken arm of a child who was pushed by a bully. Or a student who is listening to the Spirit suddenly have a word of knowledge for that bully about his own brokenness that only the Holy Spirit could know, and encouragement to repent and choose love.

Jesus was clear when he told the disciples that it was a good thing for Him to die, be resurrected and ascend into heaven because it was only then that the Holy Spirit could come. "Truly, truly, I say to you, whoever believes in me will also do the works that I do: and greater works than these will he do because I am going to the Father" (John 14:12).

Greater works.

How can you do greater works than raising someone from the dead? What could be greater than healing hundreds, thousands of people, in one day?

Instead of Jesus being the only one with power, the Holy Spirit takes up residence in *every* person, and that means every person with the Holy Spirit can do what only Jesus could do in His day.

What if, instead of hundreds of people being set free from demonic oppression and possession, hundreds of thousands of people are set free because people in every city are taking hold of the power that resides in them in the Holy Spirit? What if, instead of feeling overwhelmed and burdened by the impossibility of being set free yourself, you take God at His word and walk in step with the Holy Spirit in victory toward a physical manifestation of freedom that you already have in the spiritual?

What if you simply believed in the power you have inside of you because the Holy Spirit has taken up residence in you?

In circumstances where Jesus' miracles were limited it wasn't because Jesus himself was limited.

"'And I begged your disciples to cast it out, but they could not.' Jesus answered, 'O faithless and twisted generation, how long am I to be with you and bear with you? Bring your son here'" (Luke 9:40-41).

"Jesus immediately reached out his hand and took hold of him, saying to him, 'O you of little faith, why did you doubt?'" (Matthew 14:31).

"He said to them, 'Because of your little faith. For truly, I say to you, if you have faith like a grain of mustard seed, you will say to this mountain, 'Move from here to there,' and it will move, and nothing will be impossible for you.'" (Matthew 17:20).

"And Jesus said to them, 'A prophet is not without honor, except in his hometown and among his relatives and in his own household.' And he could do no mighty work there, except that he laid his hands on a few sick people and healed them. And he marveled because of their unbelief" (Mark 6:4-6)

"And these signs will accompany those who believe: in my name they will cast out demons; they will speak in new tongues; they will pick up serpents with their hands; and if they drink any deadly poison, it will not hurt them; they will lay their hands on the sick, and they will recover'" (Mark 16:17-19).

Your belief determines the degree the Holy Spirit's power is at work in you. Do you believe even when there doesn't appear to be any manifestation of the Spirit in the physical? Do you believe even when you don't see it?

"Now faith is the assurance of things hoped for the conviction of things not seen... and without faith it is impossible to please him, for whoever would draw near to God must believe that he exists and that he rewards those who seek him" (Hebrews 11:1, 6).

What do you believe?

Advocacy

If I were to make a list of everything that I deserve, it would amount to one thing and one thing only: I deserve hell.

Even on my best behavior, having done everything the way I'm supposed to, I still deserve hell. So do you. We don't like to acknowledge this, but I will tell you it's one thing that has kept Christ at the forefront of my mind. Isaiah tells us that even our most righteous deeds are like dirty rags to God (Isaiah 64:6).

With ten commandments and 613 laws to fulfill in order to be considered righteous, I fall way short of the mark. Jesus didn't. Jesus managed to do uphold the law and commandments perfectly, and then was killed for it. He paid a price he didn't have to pay, suffered as I should have suffered, died the death I should have died, and then defeated death and sin by coming back to life. It's his sacrifice that makes it possible for me to be free from the condemnation I deserve.

He already bore that suffering and shame, so I no longer have to.

We cannot earn our salvation. We cannot earn God's love. We are incapable of justifying ourselves or tallying up enough points to rank a certain place in heaven.

The truth of the matter is people like Billy Graham, or John Wesley, any Pope in history, or even present-day evangelical masterminds don't deserve heaven any more than you or I do. They're people, and all of us sin and fall short of the glory of God (Romans 3:23). The only thing that saves us is Jesus Christ and the cross.

The Holy Spirit acts as our advocate to the only righteous Judge, our Father in heaven. There must be a punishment for sin otherwise God wouldn't be holy and just. There must be a price to pay for unrighteousness, otherwise God wouldn't be good or righteous. God will bring every word and deed into judgment (Ecclesiastes 12:14) and we will give an account for everything we have said and done on the day of judgment (Matthew 12:36). Good and bad.

The Holy Spirit does exactly as scripture says: He advocates for us. An advocate is one who publicly supports or recommends a particular cause or person. The Bible uses the Greek word *parakletos*. The word is found in John 14:16, 26; 15:26; and 16:7 specifically when Jesus is referring to the Holy Spirit. Jesus promised that the Holy

Spirit would remain with Jesus' disciples always. He'd teach His disciples, testify about Christ and enable his disciples to testify about him.

I don't know about you, but I am acutely aware of how short I fall, and I am so thankful for the Holy Spirit acting as one who convicts me of my right standing with the Father in Christ. Yes, I fall short, but I am still justified because of Jesus. Yes, I miss the mark, but Jesus bridged the gap. Yes, I fell, but Jesus has me by the hand. Yes, I forget, but the Holy Spirit helps me remember.

With the Holy Spirit holding me up and defending me, declaring me righteous in Christ before the Father, I cannot fail.

Even when, according to my circumstances, I have. It's one step back to the covering of Christ when I repent and stand under the justification I have in Christ and not on what I deserve apart from Him.

CHAPTER ELEVEN

THE 5% AND 95%

The Power of Jesus

The more trauma in your history, and the more severe it is, the more it can seem as though there's significantly more work to do in being set free than the average person.

Thankfully, Jesus defeated death. So, no matter how devastating your loss, your suffering, His victory over death includes a victory over your circumstances as well. Nothing can be more dead than... well, death.

The difficult part for us is what Paul calls being transformed by the renewal of your mind, that by testing you may discern what is the will of God, what is good and acceptable and perfect (Romans 12:2). It's what Jesus said was denying oneself, taking up your cross daily and following him (Luke 9:23).

It's enduring the refiners fire, testing and persecution as we grow in Christ.

The simplicity of the gospel is astounding. If Jesus is our deliverer (Psalm 34:17; 1 Thessalonians 1:10), who's death and resurrection frees us from all condemnation - from our sins against others and others' sins against us (Romans 8:1), then the simple act of our belief in Jesus as our personal Lord and savior *is our deliverance from all things.*

It's a moment of belief followed by a consistency of believing.

Sometimes it takes days, weeks, months, or even years, of persistent pursuit from our heavenly Father before we surrender ourselves to Jesus and accept the gift He's given, but that's HIS work for our deliverance. We are washed clean by the blood of Jesus the moment we believe.

Clean. Completely pure.

Because of the work He did. Not anything we might have done in response to Him.

Whatever stronghold we find ourselves in indicates a lack of surrender. It's not that Jesus can't set us free from it - it's that He won't take what we don't give Him. If Jesus is your savior, all things must fall under his lordship. Whatever lack of freedom we experience is not proof of Jesus' inadequacy, but evidence of what has yet to be surrendered to the power and authority of Jesus Christ and His Word.

Every knee will bow to the name of Jesus (Philippians 2:10-11). Whether you decide to surrender yourself to Him today or wait until the end - every knee will bow.

The name of Jesus is above *every name* (Philippians 2:9), which means if something has a name, the name of Jesus is more powerful than that name.

The devastation that erupts from *rape*. The power of Jesus covers and restores that devastation.

The shattering of lives from an *earthquake*. The power of Jesus pieces together and protects those who esteem him.

The hole created by *miscarriage* or *abortion* is filled with Jesus.

Ninety-five percent of our walk is training our flesh and soul to see and act based on what is already a reality in the Spirit. Our flesh reaches for that drug or that toxic person because our flesh still believes we need it - but in Christ we don't. We bear the weight of the cross in that moment when we deny our flesh the thing it wants so badly, and train it to press into Christ instead who has already completed us.

Ten seconds of watching the news will tell us how much pain and suffering there is in the world. How much more do we need the Great Physician? Hopelessness threatens to choke us of our joy. How much more do we need to be living and breathing in the words of the One who says hope in Him does not disappoint?

We heal not by removing our past, but about seeing it through the lens of spiritual poverty. By recognizing that apart from Christ we suffer hopelessly. We get to glorify Him for the power and love He provides that covers all suffering and hopelessness.

Jesus obliterates any attachments we have to our trauma. He purchased us for a price, which means he purchased our past. To revisit the past apart from the redemptive work of Christ is to revisit a lie.

When we share the work of Jesus on the cross, the message we have isn't about how this trauma and that trauma impacted me and now God is helping me through it, but rather that I am already the daughter of a King with an identity in Christ that my trauma cannot touch! As painful as this trauma is and as difficult as it was for my flesh and soul to experience it, it has no impact on who God says I am as His beloved bride, His precious child and His dearest friend.

This doesn't mean that we don't share about what we've been through. It doesn't mean that we say that our trauma never impacted us at all, but we glorify God by sharing how His sacrifice on the cross made the price my abusers and I had to pay null and void. So even though I endured a traumatic thing on this earth, God is so much greater. It has zero influence on who He says I am.

Because who I am in Him is not about what I've done or what's been done to me, but about the value He placed on me when He was willing to pay everything to have me as His own.

How to Be

Beloved, so much of this book began before I ever sat down to write it. It began when a dear friend said to me, "Stop doing. Just *be*."

If I remember right my response was something along the lines of a blank stare, followed by, "I don't even know what that means."

Be.

It's taken almost two years of intense biblical study, meditation, honest personal reflection, confession, repentance and several other things for me to start to grasp what this means.

Be.

To exist in the moment. The only thing that exists, is right now. Five seconds ago is no longer present, except in your mind. Five seconds from now isn't happening at all, except in your mind. Be in the moment.

This one.

This breath.

This space.

The sensation of the seat beneath you, the floor under your feet and the texture of the book in your hands. The sounds, almost like white noise to your right and left as you read. What do you smell? What do you taste?

This is now.

Be.

In this moment, nothing can touch you but what you choose to allow to touch you. Yesterday, or five years ago, cannot touch you today because it is nothing more than a story.

Sometimes the story can feel as if it is happening right now. The way our brains are wired, the magnificent way God created our minds to protect ourselves from trauma, and the timing in which he allows certain memories to surface when we're in a place to be able to process it and let it go is just astounding to me. For some people God extends the grace to never remember what happened, emotionally, physically or spiritually.

For others, the memory is as present as the moment and is as intense as when it happened. The symptoms of post-traumatic stress disorder are very real and can be debilitating as we dwell on it.

I know what it is to be triggered so fiercely the panic and pain is suddenly all-consuming. The feeling of a scream exploding in your chest and a thousand vibrant, fierce memories racing behind your eyes like knives slicing away at your very soul. All the while you look as if you've shut down with your eyes open.

I know what it feels like to believe your dearest friend is well-intentioned, and yet your worst enemy because it was her touch or his touch that spiraled you into the drain of despair.

However, no matter how real it feels, or how real it seems, *it is all in our mind*. It doesn't mean it doesn't matter; it simply means we get to control how much it's going to impact us. We obtain control of it by letting it go and living in the now. The truth is, what's happening in this moment, right now, is not the trauma you remember and seem to be experiencing in the moment.

Be in the *now*. This works different ways for different people. Some snap a rubber band against a wrist. Others verbally name three things they can see, smell and hear. Still others tap various parts of their body. Some even have service animals that keep them in the present.

All of these are good grounding tools to help you be in the moment, but the only thing that will keep you anchored there is the truth.

Who are you?

I'm Samantha Means. Daughter of a King who is all-powerful, who loves me and cannot lie. I am beloved, precious, delighted in, treasured, and whole.

Where are you?

I am in my office at my computer.

What's happening right now?

Nothing. I'm typing. My dog is snoring. My tea is getting cold...

To focus on what is *not happening* and yet *seems* to be happening, is to make what is not happening appear real in your mind. To focus on what is happening in the physical reality of present time, and what is true according to the words of Jesus Christ, draws your mind out of yesterday and into today. Into the truth.

Doors open to the past when we open them. It's not spontaneous. The enemy cannot open what you don't give him permission to open. And while he may attempt to throw lies and fear at you, the only things that work are what you give permission to work by choosing to believe.

When you be in the moment, standing on the truth of what's happening and what is true in that moment, his attempts fail. Of course, this means we must be self-aware. Once a day I do a self-inventory. Too much introspection can lead me to veer off course because I'm not paying attention to the road.

I look at my emotional dashboard to make sure I'm on the right track. Am I irritable? Nervous? Content? How am I doing? If it's not lining up with the truth in scripture, and the facts of the moment, I must choose to reset.

What happens when we don't have the mental capacity to do this? When there is a stronghold that torments us? This is where the five percent comes in.

Five percent of walking out our journey is a matter of spiritual deliverance.

Five and Ninety-Five

The summer prior to my divorce I became aware of the spiritual realm on a much deeper level than I'd ever experienced before. I knew scripture, but I'd never walked out my faith with people who understood the practical application of deliverance. I grew up believing that Jesus casting out demons and miraculous healing was something that took place in the first century and just didn't happen anymore.

I was wrong.

The more I opened my mind up to the possibility that what scripture said was 100% true and was as applicable today as it was two thousand years ago, the more tormented I became. Was it possible for a Christian to be demon oppressed? Did demon's still take up space in the souls of believers as they did in the first century when Jesus walked the earth?

Why not?

As I asked these questions, I became riddled with fits of rage and anger toward my husband. Anger is a normal human emotion, but to have violent images and urges flood my brain and make my hands tingle with the desire to harm him was not. My own rage scared me, especially because it seemed so ill-placed. I wasn't just angry at him; I was angry at everything. It literally made me sick to my stomach. I had intense abdominal pain that didn't make any medical sense.

When I spent time with women in my ministry, I'd feel the urge to weep, and was terrified to look any of them in the eye. I was afraid that if I did look at them, they'd see the black sludge that lurked inside of me. I was so tormented I drove to a friend's house at about ten o'clock at night, shaking with fear and rage, scared I was going to hurt myself. I'd done it years ago and wasn't too proud to admit I was somehow on that path again.

I stood by her door that summer night and said, "There's a battle, right?"

She looked at me sideways. "Yes."

"And we win, right?"

She invited me into her garage where over the next hour I tried to put into words what was going on in my head. I couldn't look her in the eye. My entire body shook, a violent shiver from head to foot that had nothing to do with the temperature, almost as if I were having a seizure. I couldn't control it. I couldn't talk. I would try to speak, and it was as if a hand was squeezing my throat cutting off words and air. I'd clear my throat and try again. Anytime my friend tried to get me to look at her I felt this rolling nausea, as if I wanted to throw up, but couldn't hardly look at her without feeling the corners of my mouth turn up in a twisted smile that didn't make any sense to the context of our conversation. I was enraged, I wanted to scream at her to leave me alone, but I was terrified and knew I needed help.

I didn't understand.

She held my shaking hands, demanding me to look at her, and her touch felt white hot. She told me to repeat after her.

"I am a child of God."

I wanted to *laugh*. And cry. And scream. I opened my mouth to speak and felt as if I would faint.

"Look me in the eye. Say it."

It took a while before the words came out like water from a kinked hose. She prayed over me and encouraged me to claim my identity in Christ. We prayed the spirit of fear off me. When the truth of my identity finally passed through my lips, the shaking stopped. Tears flowed. I could breathe. I could think. The intense conflict of emotions and rage were gone. I was exhausted.

While I don't believe deliverance has to take an hour or two, it can happen in a matter of minutes, this was one of several experiences I had being delivered from spiritual strongholds.

Strongholds develop when we persist in a sin that enables the enemy to build a wall around our hearts. Sexual sin, addiction and bitterness are some of the enemy's favorite ways to sneak in and set up camp. There are others, but I've found those three tend to be his favorite.

Whether you've been sexually abused, or you have been entrenched in sexual sin, the abuse against your own body, which is the temple of the Lord, allows the enemy to take up residence in the body created by and for a holy God. We must repent of the sin, as well as the behavior that results from sin against us - bitterness, resentment, fear, addictive and co-dependent relationships. We must give that space back to God by aligning ourselves with our Creator as He intended us to be. When we persist in sin, we give the enemy permission to reign.

Addiction is dependence on something other than God to give what only God can. It's idolatry.

Bitterness is a refusal to accept the redemptive work of Christ on the cross for yourself as well as your fellow man, persisting in anger or hate toward self or others.

Five percent of your journey is identifying areas you've allowed the enemy to get a foothold in your heart and life, areas he's created a stronghold, and repenting of those sins and being obedient to Christ. Once you've identified the stronghold, it can sometimes take the work of several brothers and sisters in Christ to deliver what can only be delivered by multiple persons in prayer. You can't do this journey on your own. Tearing down strongholds is just one area that we often need our brothers and sisters in the faith to do what we can't do alone.

There's no shame in it.

In fact, such a humbling experience of depending on the faithfulness and relationship of my sisters in Christ with my heavenly Father increased my faith. When I saw half a dozen women rallying around me in prayer, rebuking the enemy, speaking life and identity over me, and guiding me out of the darkness and into the light, it gave me a glimpse of heaven that I will never forget. We're meant to be part of the body, and when the finger hurts, the other parts are quick to give it aid in order for it to heal.

It's important to remember, however, that deliverance is not the goal in this walk with Christ. Deliverance is not the finish line of your journey either. Deliverance is the first five percent of this thing. It's an important piece, but not the only piece of walking in victory with Christ.

If you're allowing the enemy to set up camp in your soul, if you've got a stronghold that you just can't overcome despite months or even years of repenting, prayer and fasting, it's time to get some help. If you have Jesus Christ in you, you're already the majority, but sometimes God likes to use more than one person to build the faith of others. Sometimes He uses the gifts He's given to one person to help bring about restoration and healing in someone else, while spurring on the faith of one who might be weak, and humbling one who might need humbling, and showing evidence of the miraculous to one who might be doubting...

We think God is doing one thing, but in that one thing he's really doing a thousand things. So much of it we can't see.

Deliverance is essential, but it's only the beginning.

The other ninety-five percent of your journey is walking out your deliverance. Sharing your faith, telling your testimony, bringing others to Christ, passing on the freedom and healing to others that's been given to you. The real journey is in the ninety-five percent.

CHAPTER TWELVE

WHEN THE GOING GETS TOUGH - REMEMBER

Remember Why You Began

I've been told I have a steel trap for a mind.

I do ministry with a handful of women, many of them over the age of forty-five, and they like to use me as their little memory bank. I'm fairly certain my ability to remember things is a third of the reason I'm part of this ministry. Aside from administrative and logistical things that pertain to my job and volunteer position in the ministry, I can remember intense details of my trauma I would much rather forget.

I have been healed of many of my symptoms of post-traumatic stress disorder, praise God, and yet I can still remember some portions of my sexual trauma with the kind of vivid detail that has become a sort of thorn in my side. I no longer have panic attacks like I used to. What flashbacks I do have come during ministry, which I've learned is a tool I can use when connecting with and prophesying

307

healing and life over those I'm witnessing to. I can recall the emotion, the time of day, even the clothes I was wearing from a traumatic event more than twenty-five years ago.

The difference between post-traumatic stress disorder ten years ago, and PTSD today, is the Holy Spirit. He filters what I remember, and I can look at the pain of yesterday through a lens of love and compassion, forgiveness and hope for myself as well as my abusers. I can see the violence and pray for the lost one who instigated it. I can feel the tragedy and thank God for the healing He's done to my body and continues to do. I can recall the intensity of every emotion and praise God that I am not lost to it.

When the weight of my memory hangs on my shoulders, when grief threatens to consume me because we live in a fallen world of tragedy - my story is just one very small cup in a very large ocean - I must shift my thinking.

I don't need to conjure the memories of my trauma. They make themselves known quite easily on their own. I do, however, need to draw up the memory of why I began this journey in the first place.

Why did I begin this healing process? Why did God insist I spend the entirety of my twenties - years most people focus on a career and starting a family - on healing from the trauma of my earlier years, and enduring more trauma? Why did I agree?

When I remember the answer to that question, I can continue pressing into the Lord for continual healing and restoration. I can stand in the victory I have in Christ, even when the memories of my abuse appear even in the happiest of moments.

Why didn't I just learn to have amnesia like my family told me to? Why didn't I just "forget it?" Why didn't I just move on and grow up and deal with it and get over it...? Because forgetting wasn't enough. I wanted the truth. I wanted Jesus. I wanted to be healed. I knew I wasn't alone, and I didn't want the years of trauma to be wasted. I wanted the time to be redeemed.

Now, when the memory of that bedroom, or that long walk in the dark streets of a foreign country, or that arm pressed against my throat, or those eyes, comes to my attention, I *run* into Jesus' arms. I hide in the folds of His robe and I cling to Him... and the threat associated with those memories' fades. All that's left is an image, and the comforting arms and smile of my Savior who reminds me of the truth - what happened doesn't define me. What happened doesn't impact how He sees me.

It happened, but it doesn't get to become who I am. And then I cry. A lot.

Remember How Far You've Come

Sometimes we can get so caught up in the mess of where we are, we forget how far we've come.

Better yet, we can forget where we are *not*.

A few months ago, I had a bit of a meltdown - I'm realizing meltdowns are just part of my journey. I think I have one about every three to four months or so, and they involve about two hundred tissues, a snot and tear-drenched pillow, a fluffy blanket and perhaps a phone call to a friend to force myself to connect with the body. Usually these meltdowns are the result of stuffing or ignoring emotions I'd rather not process because they feel so insurmountable. If I simply got better about recognizing them when they surfaced in the bite-sized portions God is trying to give them to me, I wouldn't have such a crippling pile several months into the ordeal.

Anyway.

A few months back I had one of these bone-crushing breakdowns and found myself wondering why God bothered to put up with me. I was *nowhere near* where I thought I should be. I wasn't even remotely in the same ballpark of where I wanted to be. In fact, I was still in bed in my pajamas. I wasn't even dressed, in the car, and on the way to the game.

Between sobs and self-pitying thoughts (just being real) God smiled and seemed to say, "Samantha, you try so hard." (Insert sob here). "Where were you a year ago?"

I had an image of myself drinking far too much, emotionally entangled with a friend I shouldn't have been, severely oppressed by the enemy and clinging to religion like a lifeline rather than a relationship with the Lord. I longed for relationship, but I was lost as to how to obtain it. I was without a job, a place to live, and was being persecuted by people I saw as my friends.

"And where are you today?" He seemed to ask.

I'd quit drinking cold-turkey and had been sober for several months. I was free from the strongholds that had such a grip a year ago. I had left the church that held to its religious belief system and was passionately involved in a relationship with Jesus, involved with a ministry and a church that nurtured Bible-based relationship. I had repented of that emotional tie to my friend. God had delivered me of the persecutions of others, I had a full-time job I was good at and was appreciated in, I had my own place, and I had my health.

I may not be where I wanted to be, but I had taken incredible strides in healing, repentance, deliverance and walking out my faith in the last year. Just because we're not where we want to be doesn't mean God doesn't have us right where He wants us. All we can do is love and be obedient today, in the circumstances and situations we face in each moment. What God does with that in the grand scheme of life is God's plan and responsibility. Our job is to simply be willing, loving, and obedient.

Don't forget how far you've come. If you take an honest look and realize you truly haven't taken much of a step forward in your relationship with Jesus, start today. What can you do today that moves you in a closer alignment with God's will and way? How can you walk out in the physical what you're choosing to believe in the spiritual?

Remember Where You're Going

When we accept Jesus Christ as our Lord and Savior, heaven is just around the corner.

Truly, eternity is only a breath away. No one is promised tomorrow. No one is promised the next moment. The blessing of waking up with breath in our lungs shouldn't be forgotten or taken for granted. Life is short, and when we have Jesus as our Lord and eternity waiting, it's even shorter.

When you know and follow Jesus, you know where you're going. Heaven isn't just an idea, it's a destination.

Our time on this earth is fleeting, and when we get so wrapped up in our pain today it's easy to forget where we're headed. Even more than that, it's easy to forget that not everyone else has the same assurance as you. Not everyone you pass on the street - I'd argue most people you pass on the street - are not as certain as you are about where they're headed.

When the pain of this journey becomes too great, or when the trials of life press and threaten to crush, remember this life is not all there is. Everything passes. Every season has an end. Every day comes to a close. Whether that's forever, or just for now, is unknown. When you remember the eternity waiting, it reminds you to share the love and truth of Jesus Christ with others. You may know where you're going - but do they?

No matter the suffering we endure in life, it's nothing compared to the glory we'll experience at the return of Jesus Christ. How can we, at peace with our eternity, allow the impact of the story of our trauma, hold us back from helping others be assured of their eternity?

When all we can see is our pain, we lose sight of God and his eternal perspective.

Stop. Remember the eternal. Remember the kingdom. Remember what is promised. Remember this pain isn't forever. Remember to share the hope you have with others. This hope isn't common. People need what you have - especially those who know your pain, but don't know the One who has a purpose for their pain.

Remember You're Not Alone

I've mentored hundreds of teenagers in recovery. Every one of them felt alone. It's no secret of the enemy to isolate us, because if he can isolate us, he can influence us. Even just *feeling* alone when we're not alone is enough room for him to get to work.

Beloved, when you are in Christ you are *never* alone.

One of the greatest parts of my journey in victory this last year has been learning how to rest in the comfort and company of the Holy Spirit when I have felt utterly and hopelessly alone in my circumstances. When friends who were there for me in my greatest time of need are suddenly not available. When even my counselor can't get to her phone. When the silence of an empty house feels like a consuming black hole and my heart starts to beat like a drum, my mouth turns to cotton and my mind whirls with fear and anxiety. Those moments I send out six text messages, all questions, none of them revealing the reality of my circumstances, just hoping and praying someone will connect with me and let me know I'm not alone... only to face silence.

In those moments, learning how to simply rest in the peace and light of the Holy Spirit is incredibly difficult, but it is incredibly important.

When we have the Holy Spirit, we are never alone.

We might know this intellectually, but when our hearts cry out for validation, our minds for intellectual stimulation to distract us from our own *being,* and our present reality is just too quiet and lonely... the knowledge of the Holy Spirit's presence just isn't enough. We need to experience Him.

He is the comforter. When I'm in need of comfort, I just want to be held. So, I imagine the Holy Spirit has strong arms, a broad chest and a soft lap and I crawl into that space and lay my head where I imagine there might be a beating heart and I let myself fall apart. I ask Him to show me what it means to be comforted like He wants to comfort me, and I filter what happens through scripture. He covers us with His wings, comforts us, touches us in our pain, holds us and sings over us.

I imagine a mother rocking her child when she's had a nightmare. I remember what it was like to hold my little brother after a night terror, his sweating brow against my neck as his breath came out in tiny gasps, his little fingers gripping my shirt as I rocked and sang and rubbed his back. I was seventeen.

If a teenager could think to do such a thing, it wasn't hard to imagine God would do something similar.

You're not alone. Even when you feel alone.

CHAPTER THIRTEEN

THE IMPORTANCE OF REST ALONG THE WAY

What Rest is Not and Why We Need a Sabbath

Rest is an interesting thing. It's possible to rest without sleep, but it's also possible to sleep without getting any rest.

God, who never sleeps, made the entire planet and all it encompasses in six days, and on the seventh day He rested from all the work He'd done (Genesis 2:2). It was this day, the day He rested, that God deemed a holy day. Not the day He made man. Not the day when the earth came into orbit with all the other planets. The day for blessing and sanctification, the day set apart from all the others, was the day of rest.

The actual legal observance of the sabbath didn't begin until the days of Moses (Exodus 31:13; 35:2). Prior to any covenant made with man, God made the day of rest a holy day, a day of blessing, permanent and independent of the 613 laws and ten commandments of Moses' day.

Jesus himself said the Sabbath was made *for man* (Mark 2:27) and that he was Lord of the Sabbath (Matthew 12:8).

I think it's safe to say that a day of rest is high on God's priority list for His people.

Why?

There's something that happens when we stop trying so hard and just let God do what only God can do. When we surrender from all work and entrust the day into God's hands. This doesn't mean we stare at a wall, but that we rest with intentionality.

If we're called to follow Jesus, the most intentional man who ever existed, then what did he do on the sabbath?

"Now (Jesus) was teaching on one of the synagogues on the Sabbath. And there was a woman who had had a disabling spirit for eighteen years. She was bent over and could not fully straighten herself. When Jesus saw her, he called her over and said to her, 'Woman, you are freed from your disability.' And he laid his hands on her, and immediately she was made straight, and she glorified God. But the ruler of the synagogue, indignant because Jesus had healed on the Sabbath, said to the people, 'There are six days in which work ought to be done. Come on those days and be healed, and not on the Sabbath day.' Then the Lord answered him, 'You hypocrites! Does not each of you on the Sabbath untie his ox or his donkey from the manger and lead it away to water it? And ought not this woman, a daughter of Abraham whom Satan bound for eighteen years, be loosed from this bond on the Sabbath day?' As he said these things, all his adversaries were put to shame, and all the people rejoiced at all the glorious things that were done by him" (Luke 13:10-17).

This is just one example of many times Jesus healed on the Sabbath day. One of many examples in which He taught on the Sabbath.

God made the Sabbath as a day to cease work, not a day to cease love. A day to trust in and steward the provision God has already given, knowing He'll provide tomorrow, too. It's a day to remember is chosen and set apart, just as we are a people chosen by God and set apart for good works (1 Peter 2:9; Ephesians 2:10).

The Sabbath wasn't just holy to the people, it was holy *for* the people.

"And the Lord said to Moses, 'You are to speak to the people of Israel and say 'Above all you shall keep my Sabbaths, for this is a sign between me and you throughout your generations, that you may know that I, the Lord, sanctify you. You shall keep the Sabbath, because it is holy for you... Six days shall work be done, but the seventh day is a Sabbath of solemn rest, holy to the Lord... Therefore, the people of Israel shall keep the Sabbath, observing the Sabbath throughout their generations, as a covenant forever. It is a sign forever between me and the people of Israel that in is days the Lord made heaven and earth, and on the seventh day he rested and was refreshed" (Exodus 31:12-17).

The Sabbath day, a day of rest, was set apart *for* us.

We need rest. If you've ever worked seven days a week you know just how true this statement is. But having a day of rest isn't just about having a day of doing nothing, but a day of enjoying and thanking God for what you have.

One of my favorite things to do in the summer on my Sabbath is to sit on my front porch in the sun and listen to the birds and squirrels that make their way from tree to tree in my front yard. I sit still and marvel at the provision God has for the smallest of animals that can do nothing for Him and thank Him for providing even more for me. I pull out a good book and read, because He's given me a joy for reading and an appreciation for the written word. I nurture that joy by reading a novel that entertains and speaks life. I often go for hikes with my dog, rain or shine. I praise Him for the health He's given me to be able to be active and spend time in His creation. It's there among the ancient pine trees and well-worn dirt paths, the damp earth and sunshine that He reminds me He is sovereign. Not a pine needle falls without His intimate knowledge, which means there is not a breath I take that He doesn't feel on His cheek. Just as He is intimately aware of all that this small piece of the woods needs to flourish, He's aware of me and my life and He cares infinitely more about me and my relationship with Him than about what happens in that part of the forest.

I might take a nap, imagining myself wrapped in his arms, completely safe and secure. So secure, in fact, that I can take time out of my day to ignore all that's going on in the middle of it and trust God has it without my help.

I worship, often singing at the top of my lungs in the woods where I'm sure no one can hear me but Him. Because He is God and deserves my highest praise. I nurture my soul with His written word, and I spend much of the day in prayer over every little thing with Him. I listen and I just sit in awe with Him.

There are many ways to rest, but the intention of the Sabbath is to restore.

Spending the entire day playing video games isn't what God had in mind. Spending the entire day reading a fantasy novel isn't what God intended either. Nor was the Sabbath meant to be a day of catching up on all that laundry, or cleaning house, or managing your bank account, or...

None of these things are bad or wrong, but they're not high on a list of things that will help you to feel rested and connected to the God who provides you the hours you live each day. How we spend our time impacts our physical bodies as well as our emotional, mental and spiritual well-being.

Your Body is a Temple - Take Care of It

Before Jesus gave us the Holy Spirit, God resided in a temple in Jerusalem. There's a whole lot of history to this temple and those that were before it but suffice it to say that the temple in Jerusalem was as close as you could get to the presence of God and still live.

"Now even the first covenant had regulations for worship and an earthly place of holiness. For a tent was prepared, the first section, in which were the lamp stand and the table and the bread of the Presence. It is called the Holy Place. Behind the second curtain was a second section called the Most Holy Place, having the golden altar of incense and the ark of the covenant covered on all sides with gold, in which was a golden urn holding the manna, and Aaron's staff that budded, and the tablets of the covenant. Above it were the cherubim of glory overshadowing the mercy seat. Of these things we cannot now speak in detail" (Hebrews 9:1-5).

Once a year someone could enter the second place, the Most Holy Place, but it was only one man, the high priest, and only if he went in with blood as a sacrifice for himself and the unintentional sins of the people. The others would tie a rope around the high priest's ankle. They did this because if the high priest did anything wrong in the Most Holy Place, he would be struck dead. If anyone other than the high priest went into the Most Holy Place, he would be struck dead, too. So, if the high priest died while inside, the people would drag him out by the ankle to prevent anyone else from having to die to bring him out.

The temple was a holy place!

When Jesus ascended into heaven, he sent the Holy Spirit to dwell within those who surrendered their lives to Christ to follow him and became what we know to be Christians. Just as the temple before Christ was the place in which the ark of the covenant was held, the place in which the Spirit of God resided, because of Jesus our body becomes the dwelling place for the Spirit of God. We become the temple of the living God because of the Holy Spirit taking up residence in us.

The miracle of this cannot be overstated.

This also means, however, that anything we do to our body is either building up or tearing down the temple in which the Holy Spirit resides. "Or do you not know that your body is a temple of the Holy Spirit within you, whom you have from God? You are not your own, for you were bought with a price. So, glorify God in your body" (1 Corinthians 6:19-20).

The body God gave us is a gift. It's a vessel. A costume. A thing to carry our spirit. The thing that enables us to navigate from home to work, work to the gym, to dinner and to school and all the places in between.

God paid a very high price for your spirit, and the body that holds it.

If you spend eighty thousand dollars on a brand-new truck, you're going to do everything you can to take care of it, right? You'll take it through the car wash, vacuum the floors and seats and kick the mud off your shoes before getting in. You'll take it off road all right, but you'll think twice before driving it in an area that will lead to damaging to the undercarriage.

God paid far more than eighty thousand dollars for the body you wake up in every day. You are valuable. Far more valuable than you realize.

I smoked cigarettes for years after I joined the Marine Corps. I enjoyed it. The habit, the smoke breaks, the oral fixation, the social aspect, not to mention having something to do with my hands when I got nervous in public. I didn't want to quit. It was the financial strain that got me thinking I probably should stop smoking. I'd save quite a bit of money.

Then it was a religious thing. Christians shouldn't smoke. That's what I was taught. Well, I was a Christian and I smoked. It was getting me some pretty ugly looks from people in my church and I didn't like feeling ostracized. The church I attended made up my entire social circle. Between finances and social acceptance, I finally decided to start trying to quit.

I learned, very quickly, my will was not strong enough to overcome the pull of nicotine.

I think I quit thirty times over the course of eighteen months, and I hated myself every time I lit up again.

It wasn't until I realized my smoking was violating the body God had entrusted me with, that I was able to set aside cigarettes for good. I asked for His help, reminding Him of His own words: "Lord, you tell me this body of mine is a temple and I'm supposed to glorify you with it. I know smoking is not glorifying it, I know it's physically destroying it, but I can't stop on my own. I want to be obedient, but I need your help."

I think I had one or two "relapses" after praying that prayer, but I didn't quit asking for His help. Every day I woke up asking Him to help me through it. Every day He did.

I haven't had a cigarette in years. Sometimes it feels like longer, other times I still crave that menthol taste in my mouth and have to turn away from it and ask the Holy Spirit to meet whatever need I have that's reaching out for that unhealthy habit.

What habits do you have? In what ways are you unnecessarily harming your body? How can you be helping it instead?

This doesn't mean you necessarily need to start working out five days a week, because even obsessive exercising can be harmful. This doesn't mean you start counting calories or jumping on the next fad diet. It just means we need to take an honest look at our lives and see where we can be making some lifestyle changes that help and protect the temple God has given us to steward.

Even now, as I write this at a coffee shop in town, I realized I've had five cups of coffee today and two of them were lattes. My body does not need that much caffeine! It doesn't need that much sugar! I can certainly make a slight adjustment to substitute water or tea after a certain hour in the day. Otherwise a habit of that kind of caffeine and sugar consumption will lead to weight gain and heart palpitations.

No, thank you.

I was in a car accident a few months ago and was unable to exercise for the first month or so. Broken bones are a reasonable reason for not lifting weights or running through the woods. However, I'm certainly capable of getting back on the treadmill and doing a little yoga and band exercises now. Lack of exercise, especially when my primary job involves sitting behind a desk and my primary hobby is spent writing behind a computer, is not good for my body either.

We don't need to make drastic changes, nor do we need to become health fanatics. We do need to be wise stewards of the body God has given us.

When we're wise about getting enough sleep, eating healthy, and exercising - even if it's just a walk during our lunch hour - it can go a long way to helping us do everything mentioned earlier in this book. The physical cannot be neglected. There are enough books out there with specific exercise plans, eating plans and guidelines about physical health.

My advice is simple: eat all the food groups in moderation every day, heavier on certain groups depending on what you're doing that day and exercise every day. If I'm going for an intense run, I make sure I eat the carbohydrates and protein my body needs the meal before the run. If I'm taking it easy and not able to go on a hike or a walk at all because my schedule is too full, I make sure I'm leaning more toward fruits and vegetables throughout the day, but all of this is in moderation.

Make no mistake - I have my cake and eat it, too.

But even this I do in moderation.

Healing Wounds

There's nothing quite like the swell of shame that rolls over you when you confess the angry red mark on your body was self-inflicted.

On purpose.

Self-harm doesn't make any sense to people who haven't done it, but it makes perfect sense to the one doing it. It's not logical, but it works... until it suddenly doesn't.

The pain on the inside can be so all-consuming, so far out of our control, the only thing that makes sense is to create pain that's within our control. I was a Marine going through training in New England, mere months out of boot camp and in the throes of sexual harassment that simply came with the territory of being a woman among Marines. It triggered years of sexual abuse and rape. The torment I endured during those months stole my sleep, my appetite, my sanity and my ability to fake-it-till-you-make-it. I would go into the basement of the barracks and start punching that leather bag bare fisted until my knuckles bled. Then I'd keep punching until the pain in my hands was big enough to distract me from the pain in my head and heart. I'd punch until I was too exhausted to stand. Then I'd wipe the blood from the bag, wrap my hands and fall exhausted into bed.

Then the morning came, and with a new day came new pain. To my fellow Marines, it looked as though I was simply a beast. There wasn't much cause for concern.

It was a few years later I sat in my office with the door closed and learned I was about to be kicked out of the service for not meeting height and weight standards. By then I'd been raped more times than I cared to count, and I'd put myself on an intensive exercise routine and diet plan so rigorous that no Marine I knew would do it with me. My best wasn't enough, and I was a disgrace to the Marine Corps; my last chance at belonging and acceptance.

I scratched the back of my hand down to the tissue. I still have the scar today.

A new day came, and with the wound still fresh, the pain in my head and heart remained. No matter how much I tried to punish myself for being bad, or not being good enough, it was never punishment enough. In fact, each time I inflicted myself with pain I was then filled with such shame for doing this terrible thing. It had the opposite effect it was supposed to! And yet I couldn't seem to stop.

Perhaps your self-harm isn't as obvious as a cut or scratching. Self-harm doesn't have to draw blood. It can be as subtle as working eighty hours a week, driving yourself into exhaustion because you can't imagine sitting still long enough to sit with your pain. It can involve putting yourself in dangerous circumstances in which the threat of harm is high, if not certain, and doing it hoping to have an accident, or hoping to be hurt in the process. Going into the cold in shorts and a tank-top because you want to feel the burn of the cold. Walking on hot asphalt without sandals because you want to feel the scald on your feet. Even taking a shower so hot you scald your skin.

You think no one sees but, Beloved, God does. He not only witnesses every act of self-harm you put yourself through but is in your mind understanding exactly what you're thinking and yearning for you to turn to Him for the salve to heal those wounds.

My dear friend, self-harm doesn't work. Trust me.

You'll end up with nothing but scars, your skin holding onto the memory of the trauma you inflicted on yourself, and it does nothing to alleviate the deeper wound. It simply creates another wound while the deeper one continues to fester. It's not our own blood that heals, but the blood Jesus shed on the cross.

We don't need to punish ourselves because He was already punished for our sins.

We don't need to bleed because His blood was already shed, and His blood heals.

We don't need to distract ourselves from the pain by creating more pain, but by turning to the One who has already felt *all your pain,* has overcome it and can lead you through it to the other side.

How?

When we surrender to Him and tell Him to take what's left and make it into whatever He deems right. Even when all that's left is dust, we can surrender the dust to the Potter.

What could God possibly want with our dust?

Beloved He took dust and created Adam. There's an excerpt from Lysa Terkeurst's book "It's Not Supposed to be This Way" that illustrates this just beautifully:

"Wise potters not only know how to form beautiful things from clay, but they also know how important it is to add some of the dust from previously broken pieces of pottery to the new clay. This type of dust is called "grog." To get this grog, the broken pieces must be shattered to dust just right. If the dust is shattered too finely, then it won't add any structure to the new clay. And if it's not shattered enough, the grog will be too coarse and make the potter's hands bleed.

"But when shattered just right, the grog dust added to the new clay will enable the potter to form the clay into a larger and stronger vessel than ever before. And it can go through fires much hotter as well. Plus, when glazed, these pieces end up having a much more beautiful, artistic look to them than they would have otherwise."

Let God use your dust. Otherwise, if we're simply holding onto it, it will forever remain dust.

God isn't Waiting at the Destination

It was autumn 2017, mere weeks before my husband and I separated and just months prior to our divorce. I didn't know any of this at the time of course, I was just going on a hike with my dog, eager to step into the brisk air and feel the crunch of dead leaves beneath my feet. It was an ordinary hike on an ordinary day.

As usual, I moved with the speed of someone with a destination in mind. I shoved my hands deep in my pockets as I trekked across the forest floor, my dog loping ahead of me on the path and disappearing into the early morning fog. My eyes were fixed on the ground, avoiding ruts and rocks and whatever else might be in my way. Frustrated, hurt, and determined to end the 3-mile hike feeling better, I was almost two thirds of the way through it when God interrupted my process.

"Samantha, stop. You're moving as if you're hurrying to meet me somewhere. I'm right here."

My heart seized and my knees weakened as I stopped at the crest of the trail. I stared at the ground, my breathing labored and tears threatening to spill out of the corner of my eyes.

"Where then? Where are you?" I asked almost accusingly. "Where are you?"

"I'm right here," the Voice seemed to whisper.

Something drew my attention to the tree line on the right. The clammy fog cleared ever so slightly, just enough to let the radiant sunlight burst through the ground clouds in thick, glistening beams. I almost expected to hear a chorus of angels break out in holy song. Instead, the silence was deafening.

Too often we get so focused on getting to where we want to go, we miss out on the preciousness of God being right there with us on the journey. We think we have to get to a certain level of spiritual maturity, or a certain degree of healing, before we'll get to experience the relationship that we so long to have with our Creator. Meanwhile, He's perfectly in step with us in the process waiting for us to slow down enough to notice Him. Waiting, with the patience only God can have, for us to let Him love us.

Consider that for a moment. Our heavenly Father walks with us, even into the darkest of places, offers gifts of love and encouragement and blessings, just waiting for us to notice Him. Sometimes we think we're the ones crying out for His attention, and all the while tears fill His eyes at our misunderstanding. He never took His eyes off us.

It's you and I who took our eyes and our desires off Him.

When all we can see is our pain, when the scream of our inner agony erupts with a force that could shatter mountains, we lose sight of Him. Meanwhile, God offers us rest. He invites us to be still, to cease striving, and wait for the Lord with confidence in who He is as God (Psalm 37:7).

God isn't waiting for us to figure it out. He's waiting for us to give up trying and fall into His arms who know all.

This is one reason the Fall was so devastating. Man was never meant to carry the weight of the knowledge of good and evil. Our perpetual need to know, to understand, to have things *right* is because of the Fall. God's original design was for us to carry none of that weight, but to simply trust that our heavenly Father has it all figured out and will take care of us.

That's why Jesus tells his disciples, "Truly, I say to you, whoever does not receive the kingdom of God like a child shall not enter it" (Mark 10:15, ESV). God invites us to have a child-like faith of absolute trust in our Abba-Father to make all things right - somehow - and turn everything around again - in some way.

We don't need to know how; we just need to trust He'll do what He said He'll do.

Don't miss out on experiencing the life, joy, peace, freedom, love and victory of Christ today because you're too busy trying to get it all together for Him to meet you on the other side. Today is the other side. Right now, is the other side. Turn to Him - He's never left you, and He never will.

CHAPTER FOURTEEN
THE END IS JUST THE BEGINNING

The Process Is Yours Alone

The counselor looked at me with the intensity of a lightning bolt. Her red pixie hair stuck up in odd places and she wore an oversized sweater that seemed like an attempt to hide her natural skin-and-bone frame. She was somewhere north of forty, but the depth of those deep brown eyes and the lines that framed them told me they were carved by stories. Not all of them her own.

It was day three of my stay in the psych-ward of the VA Hospital in Spokane. I'd just gotten my clothes back, and they felt strange after wearing scrubs and shoes without laces for the last three wakeups. My back pressed against the hard metal chair, my legs and arms crossed against the harshness of living in reality.

I admitted myself to the hospital after three days of no sleep, days and nights wrecked by an onslaught of suicidal thoughts. I couldn't function. So, I checked in. The staff was kind and they helped me get some medication figured out. Somehow the locked doors, shatter-proof glass and constant eyes of the nurses made me feel a little safer with myself. The world out there couldn't touch me in here. The counselor who sat across from me that day, however, was inviting me to consider the day I would be released.

"I'm not ready."

"Of course you're not."

"I can't do life."

"Sure you can."

"No, I can't," I insisted. "I should be able to go to work and breathe in and out without thinking about offing myself, but I can't."

"Then maybe you'll have to change jobs."

"What am I going to do?"

"Something different. Something quieter. Less triggering."

"I can't."

She smiled and reached into the breast pocket of her sweater. She dug out what looked like a piece of lint and held it out to me. I frowned at what she showed me. It was a seed.

My eyes went from the seed to her smile, amused as if she were playing a trick on me or holding a secret.

"What is this?" she asked me.

"A seed."

"Right. Is it wrong?"

I frowned. Was this a trick question? "No."

"Why not?"

My brow shot to the ceiling; certain she was playing some kind of joke on me. "It's just a seed."

"Right," she confirmed. "It's doing exactly what it's supposed to do as a seed."

She closed her fist and dropped the seed back in her pocket.

"Okay," I conceded.

"What about when the seed sprouts a couple of leaves? When it's, I don't know, a couple of inches tall. When it's roots are barely deep enough to make a difference."

"What about it?"

"Is it wrong then?"

"No."

"Why not?"

I felt like an idiot, but I wasn't sure why. "Because."

She smiled, silently encouraging me to continue.

"It's just a tiny little plant," I added.

"Right. It's doing what only it can do as a tiny plant. How about when it grows to a foot or so tall? When you're starting to notice that it's actually a tree, but it's hardly much of a tree. The wind comes, threatening to rip it out of the ground. The snow falls, burying it in powder heavy enough to suffocate it, but not quite. Someone on horseback comes trampling through and nearly snaps it's little trunk without a thought."

I felt my insides twist as I realized what she was saying.

"Is it wrong then?" she finally asked.

"No," I whispered.

"You see, Samantha, you're certain that until you're a towering pine tree, you're wrong. You need to realize that no matter what stage of life you're in, no matter what's happened to you in that stage of life, you're not *wrong*. You've made some choices that had consequences

333

you didn't like, but that doesn't make you wrong. You've endured some horrific trauma in your life, people have done terrible things to you, but that doesn't make you wrong."

Life is a process.

Healing is a process.

Jesus healed tens of thousands, if not hundreds of thousands, of people in the three years he did ministry. Many of those were immediate physical manifestations of recovery. Some happened over the course of several minutes, others several days. Whoever wasn't healed was because of one reason: lack of faith. I wonder how many woke up healed days, weeks or months after their encounters with Him?

Jesus set free thousands of people who were oppressed and possessed by demons. These were often demonstrated by people who were mentally tormented, being set free and then in their "right mind" (Mark 5;15; Luke 8:35). Once again, the only thing that prevented freedom for anyone, was lack of faith.

Faith was demanded for immediate healing and transformation. And faith is demanded in order to walk out that healing and freedom. "Now faith is the assurance of things hoped for, the conviction of things *not seen*" (Hebrews 11:1). We must persist even, if not especially when, we don't see the results we think we're supposed to see.

Believing is seeing.

I spent almost a year inundating my mind with the preaching of people like Todd White and other Lifestyle Christianity teachers, Bill Johnson and other Bethel ministry leaders, as well as Beth Moore, Graham Cooke, Joseph Prince and other charismatics who simply put action to their faith and saw results. Every spare moment I had was spent listening to their messages, studying the scriptures they brought to light, spending hours in my Bible and begging God on my knees and my face, to make this my new reality. I even put worship music on repeat when I went to sleep at night. I wanted the enemy to be afraid to attempt to access my mind. He'd simply be drenched in worship and teachings of Jesus if he tried.

I knew that if I was going to retrain my mind, I needed the word and love of Jesus Christ to consume me. If I was going to have a chance at combating more than twenty-five years of lies, I couldn't make any room for more. I didn't need another twenty-five years of truth to be renewed - I just needed Jesus. I knew that if I inundated myself with truth, if I could speak it out loud to myself and everyone I met - with the confidence of it being true whether I saw it or not in my own life, then it would not only be true, but it would become my reality.

When we choose Christ and are made new, standing in victory, we must be persistent in filling our minds with what feeds truth. We must be patient as our fallen human brains learn to rewire the synapses God designed us to have. We're not computers. There is no giant "reset" button. There is no option of going back to our factory settings.

God wants us to remember, but He wants us to remember through the lens of His goodness, redemption and restoration. He wants us to be able to say, "This is who I was before Christ. This is who I am because of, and in, Christ."

Or to be able to say, "This happened to me while I was in Christ, and because I'm in Christ that thing cannot take away who I am as His beloved daughter. While I grieve and experience the loss and pain, I have an incredible loving Father who invites me to come boldly to the throne of grace because I'm His child. I grieve not only for what was lost, but for the one who is lost who hurt me. Because I have the Holy Spirit, I have a comforter with me always, so I'm not dependent on the goodness and provision and wisdom of people to be okay. To be whole and healed. I have Jesus."

The process is a matter of being consistently in the Word of God, in the secret place with Him where there's nothing but you in all your nakedness before the perfect, tender, loving Father who made you. The process of renewing your mind, of healing, will not look the same for you as it does for me. It will not be an identical journey as that of those who have gone before you, or even those who will go after you.

The journey is yours and happens one day at a time. The victory is yours and is today. Right now.

There Isn't Really a Finish Line

If you've been on this journey for a while and are waiting for the finish line, the day when things are suddenly "all better" I'm here to tell you, I don't know if that day will come.

Being "all better" is really a matter of how much we are believing and trusting in God's word to be as true as He says it is.

When I find myself going through my day under the weight of sorrow, I realize it's because I'm walking on a habitual highway of lies and self-reliance and somehow veered off the hiking trail I've been working on for years. The trail that says, "the joy of the Lord is my strength."

If I would just believe that and do something in the physical to represent my belief in that, my mindset will change. I'll never forget the first day I chose to dance to a worship song in response to a very difficult phone call. Someone I loved and did ministry with had an offense against me for something she perceived I had done. After nearly an hour on the phone listening to her yell and scream, say some pretty harsh things and make some hurtful accusations, we managed to end the call with my apologizing for any harm I had unintentionally caused, and validating her emotions.

When I hung up, I felt as if someone had popped my balloon.

I wanted to cry, and I wanted to yell. I wanted to justify myself and yell back - even if it wouldn't have done any good it would have at least made me feel better!

Instead I stood up from the couch, turned on an upbeat worship song and, for reasons I can't explain, I began to dance in my tiny kitchen.

Like a fool.

I was determined to experience joy in the Lord and who He is, rather than allow the circumstances of that phone call drag me into the mud and pin me there. I began to laugh as I danced, because I could almost *feel* my brain struggle to make sense of what it was I was doing! I wanted a glass of wine, but I chose to make tea. I wanted to cry, but I chose to dance. I wanted to yell, but I chose to worship. I wanted to justify myself, but I chose to praise Jesus.

I chose.

This doesn't mean I haven't had a bad day since that day I danced in my kitchen. Hardly! This doesn't mean I dance every time I want to cry or scream. It does mean it knocked down a giant lie that I'd been believing for years. The truth shined like a radiant beacon on a hill - I can dance, laugh, sing and worship and experience joy because my joy is in Jesus, nothing else. No matter what persecution I face, what fear encroaches on my life, or what circumstances threaten to knock me sideways, they can never take away my victory, or my choice to rejoice in that victory.

My voice may be silenced, but you'll see the joy in my eyes, even if they're flooding with tears.

It's a journey. One in which we get stronger every day, if we're intentional about spending time with the Lord and growing in our relationship with Him. The finish line is the day we take our last breath. Pretend that day is today.

How would you live differently?

How would you love differently?

What excuses would you give up?

What would you finally decide to do?

None of us is promised tomorrow. Choose Jesus today.

Your Healing is Far Bigger Than Your Own Little World

This entire journey is about you and Jesus. Regardless of what happens in the end, when your breath is gone and you stand before the Creator of the world, the one who died for you, the one who was living inside of you this whole time, all that will matter is you and Him.

And yet.

The healing God is doing in you, the victory He's given you, isn't just for you.

"And Jesus came and said to them, 'All authority in heaven and on earth has been given to me. Go therefore and make disciples of all nations, baptizing them in the name of the Father and of the Son and of the Holy Spirit, teaching them to observe all that I have commanded you. And behold, I am with you always to the end of the age" (Matthew 28:18-20, ESV).

"He said to him the third time, 'Simon, son of John do you love me?' Peter was grieved because he said to him the third time, 'Do you love me?' and he said to him, 'Lord, you know everything; you know that I love you.' Jesus said to him, 'Feed my sheep'" (John 21:17).

"Whoever believes and is baptized will be saved, but whoever does not believe will be condemned. And these signs will accompany those who believe: in my name they will cast out demons; they will speak in new tongues; they will pick up serpents with their hands; and if they drink any deadly poison, it will not hurt them; they will lay their hands on the sick, and they will recover" (Mark 16:16-18).

"But you will receive power when the Holy Spirit has come upon you, and you will be my witnesses in Jerusalem and in all Judea and Samaria, and to the end of the earth" (Acts 1:8).

All that Jesus does for us is to be shared with others so that they, too, might know Him. We conquer the enemy with the blood of Jesus and the very word of our testimony (Revelation 12:11). Why do you think the enemy tries so hard to keep you silent? Why do you think shame is one of his favorite ways of keeping God's people shut up inside?

Paul asked this question in his letter to the Romans, "How then will they call on him in whom they have not believed? And how are they to believe in him of whom they have never heard? And how are they to hear without someone preaching?" (Romans 10:14).

Your healing and your journey from a place of victory is not just about you, Beloved.

God has blessed you with the weight of glory. The weight of truth that can only be known through the refiner's fire of suffering. He's entrusted a message to you that only you can share, because no one has journeyed through your fire the way you have. No one has been equipped, loved, held and empowered the way you have. What only you possess will be the hand held out to others desperate for someone to say what only you can say.

We can't speak truth until we know truth, and truth has a name.

We can't share the gospel until we have a personal encounter with the cross.

We can't walk in victory until we realize we're already there.

You are not insignificant. Quite the contrary. God has such an incredible plan for your life that neither you nor I can even begin to comprehend. It literally surpasses anything we could think, ask or imagine (Ephesians 3:20). What if your impact had the kind of ripple effect that crushed deceitful governments? What if the victory you have to share could devastate the foundations of organizations built on deceit and corruption?

People like Nelson Mandela, Martin Luther King, Jr and Abraham Lincoln weren't simply born the way they're remembered. They had shaky beginnings. They had their own trauma. They had their own fear and insecurities. They chose truth. Then they did it again. And again. And they took a step in the real world that demonstrated the truth they stood on.

Again.

And again.

One step at a time. One day at a time.

And changed the world.

In one of my moments of going into the Secret Place with my Father, He continually reminds me that he is a gentleman and will never force me to choose Him. He'll allow me to get uncomfortable, but the choice always remains mine. He asked me something that I ask myself almost every day. A question I'll ask you:

What if when you get to heaven God says, "Would you like to see who you would have been if you'd said yes to me?"

Or would you rather get to heaven, exhausted and with calloused hands and a heart broken and healed and broken a thousand times over with God having nothing to say to you but, "Well done, good and faithful servant. Enter into the rest of your Master."

We always get to choose. The pain of regret, or the pain of growth.

It's not just about you.

It's about everyone God is hoping to reach through and because of you. This journey isn't just about your victory, but about the victory waiting for every person you meet.

You choose. Will you be a victim, or will you stand in the victory you already have with Jesus?

The journey is a marathon, not a sprint, and it will take the rest of your life. But oh, what a life it will be when it's drenched in the glory of Jesus Christ.

Victim to Victorious

About the Author

Samantha Means was born and raised in eastern Washington. After years of trauma, she joined the Marine Corps in 2007. In 2008 she was stationed in Okinawa, Japan as a combat correspondent working primarily with American Forces Network as a radio DJ. Her fans knew her as DJ Sam-I-Am. It became her mission to make every listener smile. She was voted Best DJ in the Pacific in *Stars and Stripes Best of the Pacific 2010* magazine.

Unfortunately, at the same time she endured several experiences with military sexual trauma and began counseling. It was there she was diagnosed with complex-PTSD and began the journey toward healing from all her past trauma.

Samantha left the Marine Corps with an honorable discharge in 2011 and returned to eastern Washington. Her healing journey continued as she began working with troubled youth in middle and high school and in a drug rehabilitation facility. At 23-years-old she published her first novel, *A Winter Storm,* and, despite continued counseling, she simultaneously self-committed to a veteran's hospital for suicidal ideation. It would be another few years of intensive therapy, a strong supportive community, and the grace of God before the worst of her post-traumatic symptoms were under control.

From 2011 to 2015 Samantha began traveling abroad for mission work. She discovered a love for people who didn't know Jesus, and she made it her mission to share His love with people of all cultural backgrounds. Between mission trips she worked with youth in recovery and the elderly doing home care. She continued writing and found a love for the outdoors. A favorite hobby involved road trips to national rainforests and state parks to hike with her rescue dog, Meg.

After obtaining her bachelor's degree in 2015 in human development, Samantha lived abroad in the Middle East. She married in 2016 and returned to eastern Washington where she resumed work with troubled youth and continued writing novels. It was also during this season she got involved with an equine ministry in north Idaho serving women and adolescent girls in recovery. It was here she began writing *Victim to Victorious*.

Unfortunately, her marriage came to an end in December 2017. She continued her work with the equine ministry, serving abroad on mission trips, and disappearing into nature to hike with Meg. She ran her first half-marathon and her involvement with the equine ministry developed a new passion: horses.

At the time of the publication of this book, Samantha is happy to call north Idaho home. She's pursuing her master's degree in divinity and planning another mission trip to Germany to work with Syrian and Afghani refugees. She continues to work closely with the equine ministry and plans to start a business in horse therapy.

When she's not writing, traveling, or doing ministry, Samantha can most often be found in nature on foot or horseback. Meg is never far from her side.

Samantha and Meg (2018)

North Idaho (2018)

Made in the USA
Lexington, KY
24 August 2019